JAPAN'S
WASTED WORKERS

by Jon Woronoff

LOTUS PRESS
Tokyo, Japan

Published in Japanese by Kodansha Ltd.
under the title of *Maboroshi no Han'ei, Nippon*.

Fourth Edition 1983

Published by Lotus Press Ltd.
Chofu P.O. Box 15, Chofu-shi, Tokyo, 182-91 Japan
© 1981 by Jon Woronoff
ISBN: 0-87040-509-8
LCC: 82-100939

Cover design by Akira Tsuchiya

Printed in Japan by Komiyama Printing Co.

Contents

Contents

Foreword

It is one of those numerous ironies of history that the world has become keenly interested in Japan's famed management system and is seriously talking of using it as a model just at the very time when the Japanese have become disenchanted with it and are talking of a need for radical change and perhaps its demise.

In some ways, this is not surprising. For the foreigners don't really know much about how the Japanese system works. All they get are bits and snatches carefully selected by admirers of things Japanese and self-appointed management "experts" who wish to sell what little knowledge they possess on an increasingly lively market. What they present are the best aspects garnered from the finest companies. They scrupulously avoid reference to the unpleasant side-effects or any mention of the vast majority of average to mediocre companies.

The Japanese, on the other hand, have the privilege of living with their renowned management system nearly every day in the week and usually longer than the standard eight-hour day. The main subject of conversation, when salarymen get together after hours, is the office they have just left. The contents are usually some form of griping about the company and especially their superiors. This dislike, for some, has reached the breaking point and there is increasing news of *tenshoku* or job hopping even among older employees. Some young people simply refuse to enter major companies.

The companies are none too happy with the situation either. Lifetime employment was fine when they were growing and needed every employee they could lay their hands on. Now, with the recession still here, they would gladly get rid of some and would also like to make the others a bit more conscientious. The most serious complaints about the "system" and the most striking initiatives for reform are coming from top management and often the very firms presented as the epitome of the Japanese company.

Thus, *Japan's Wasted Workers* tries to do two things. First, it takes a look at the less-than-model companies that make up the vast mass of corporate entities and reveals some of their weaknesses. Particular attention is focused on the white-collar workers who have been allowed to perpetuate time-honored methods with little regard to efficiency as well as some categories that are poorly used, if not abused. Reference is also made to a number of sectors that are a serious drag on the economy. When all this is done, some readers will doubtlessly be surprised to find that a majority of Japan's workers are being wasted in one way or another.

The second concern is to show the points where there is already enough dissatisfaction in management or labor circles to begin thinking of improvement or actually implementing reforms. To this is added areas where change is taking place by default, as the old ways crumble before anything is done to trace new paths. Although it is too early to tell just how the system will appear in the future, it is already clear that major transformations can be expected . . . if Japan is to continue advancing smoothly.

The Japanese public, for whom this book was written,

will have no trouble understanding the problems. Nor will foreign businessmen. But it will create confusion among those who view Japan as a well nigh perfect nation peopled by happy salarymen and diligent workers striving to promote their company under the enlightened leadership of totally selfless bosses. They might do better not to read what is here. Let them continue to live in dreamland, read popular books on the Japanese miracle, and try to reproduce a model that doesn't exist to begin with!

The insight provided here is not always a result of the author's flair or genius. After all, a very lively debate is going on now about the Japanese management system and dozens of books delve into the problems. The popular salarymen's magazines are full of polls and case histories, and letters to the editor, which show the feelings of the working population. And there are more than enough solid statistics compiled by a multitude of sources to supply the necessary back-up.

What has been done is largely to take the many elements that usually appear in a dispersed form and bring them together. Japan has plenty of capable writers and scholars. But they rarely pool their efforts. So, I have taken the liberty of collecting the ideas floated in separate but related sectors. The only points on which I have offered an original contribution, or so I believe, is with regard to female labor, the depths of inefficiency of white-collar staff and the potential threats of unemployment, visible or disguised. That is not because people are not aware of what is happening but that they do not like to admit it.

This book was written at the suggestion of one of Japan's leading publishing companies, Kodansha Ltd., and was first published in Japanese. I am grateful to Kodansha for allowing me to print the original English version here. I should also like to thank *The Japan Economic Journal, The Oriental Economist* and *Asian*

Business magazine for permission to reprint certain sections that originally appeared with them.

Among those who helped me gather this information and evaluate it a few deserve special mention. First is Mr. Mitsuru Tomita of Kodansha who guided my steps in deciding on the basic content and approach. Crucial assistance on specific items came from Mr. Mikio Aoki, director of research at the Japan Productivity Center, Mr. Yasuo Kuwahara of the Japan Institute of Labor, and Professor Kazukiyo Kurosawa of the Tokyo Institute of Technology. Thanks must also go to my wife, Maki Hamada-Woronoff, who served as interpreter, translator, and prompter in these activities.

JON WORONOFF

1
No Longer "Cheap Labor"

Japan's Most Precious Resource

For many decades already, everyone living in or writing about Japan has been saying the same thing. The country is very small geographically, it is extremely poor in natural resources, and yet it has a huge population. The only resource it has of real value is the people who inhabit the islands. Thus, the key to Japan's success must be the wisest possible use of its precious human resources.

However, just like everything else, Japan's primary resource, its people, has been getting more expensive all the time. One reason for this is the slowdown in population growth. During most of its development period, there was a teeming population of young, hardworking, and modestly paid employees who were able to boost the economy. Now, however, population growth has slackened and the total population may stabilize in the 21st century, by which time rather than masses of young people there will be vast numbers of old and aging. Those who work will be fewer than ever proportionately and they will have to earn enough to carry the rest.

Higher labor costs also result from the successful economic growth of the past. For, as the economy developed, it increased both production and income. Once upon a time, you could get a Japanese to work for you very cheaply. That was a long time ago, shortly after the war and before the period of rapid growth began. There were millions of Japanese returning from overseas and millions more flocking back to the cities. But the economy had been devastated and there was not enough work to go around. The prevailing situation was one of hunger and hardship. Under such conditions, people had to accept any job that was offered and they didn't quibble about what they were paid.

The wages were low as far as the Japanese were concerned. It may be hard to remember, but not until the late 1950s, a decade after the war, did wages reach ¥10,000 to ¥20,000 per month. This was hardly adequate to buy the necessary food, clothing, and housing. It meant that many Japanese had to suffer even if they got a job. But it also meant that Japanese labor was a real bargain as compared to the cost of labor in richer countries. It was particularly cheap for Americans to have goods produced here and import the products of local factories. Throughout the world, Japanese goods became known for their cheapness, not their quality.

Nevertheless, over the years, the Japanese economy has been catching up. And so have the earnings of its labor force. By the 1950s, the prewar level had been passed and most other Asian countries were left far behind. By the 1960s, wages were approaching those in southern and eastern Europe. By the 1970s, they were higher than pay in most of Europe and nearly as high as countries like the United States, West Germany or Sweden. During the 1980s, Japan may actually become the country with the best paid workers in the world.

This progression can be shown by using the United States as a yardstick. In the 1950s, a Japanese only earned about a tenth as much as an American worker, still in the 1960s barely a fifth, and as late as 1970 just a quarter. However, according to the Ministry of Labor, by now hourly wages are nearly as high as in the United States and West Germany and some 40% higher than in France or Great Britain.[1] Continuing the comparison, one might add that Japanese workers are earning about five times as much as Koreans and ten times as much as Indonesians.

This is excellent in one sense. But, if you look at the other side of the coin, it must be admitted that Japanese labor is anything but cheap. In fact, in some ways, it is outrageously expensive. For example, just a salesgirl or waitress here costs more than a factory worker in southern Europe or a manager in Southeast Asia. A day laborer in Japan earns more than an accountant or technician would in India or China. Wages are so high that many Japanese companies simply cannot afford to pay them and have to move their business abroad, to the "cheap labor" countries, if they wish to survive.

At the same time, one increasingly gets only what one pays for. In the old days, you could often talk the workers into making extraordinary efforts or putting in considerable overtime without much difficulty. That was their duty to the company. If overtime had to be paid, it was at rather low rates. And bonuses were only given when things really went well. Nowadays, most of the overtime has to be paid for, and well paid at that. Bonuses have become a right. Indeed, Japanese workers ask for bonuses even when the company has done poorly. And some of them go slow during the day to find excuses for doing overtime although the company can ill afford it.

Rather than make exceptional efforts for the company, there is a growing category of people who do not even make a proper effort. They have found that they can get by with a minimum of work without being unduly harassed by their fellow employees or threatened with dismissal by the company. Some are so lazy that they clearly stand out, relaxing in a corner and reading a newspaper, chatting with their colleagues while having tea, or disappearing for appointments that do not exist. Others simply join in a generalized decline into slow motion work paces.

But that is not even the worst problem. Many employees in Japan are engaged in tasks which bring them acceptable wages but make a very insignificant contribution to overall economic progress or welfare. Too many are involved in services, in distribution, in clerical work. And an increasing number of people have opted out of the working population as such. Things are no longer so hard, and young people can fall back on their parents or, more rarely, older people can live off their children.

This has brought about a radical change in the situation over the past three decades. Japan used to be able to grow through a combination of cheap raw materials, cheap technology, and cheap labor. This is no longer possible. Raw materials are increasingly hard to find at any price and known technologies have been largely absorbed. Any further progress in better use of raw materials or introduction of technologies will require more inventive action by the Japanese themselves. Human resources are consequently more decisive than ever, both in their own right and to make up for raw materials and technology by developing a knowledge-intensive industrial base and using more know-how in all branches of the economy.

However, Japan is forced to do this at a time when manpower itself is terribly expensive. This means that it must be used more carefully and more frugally than ever. Yet, it could not be claimed that this costly resource is being used with particular care or intelligence. In fact, the Japanese are often engaging in the wasteful and inefficient practices of earlier days when labor was cheap and some of the present phenomena can be traced back much further to Meiji or even Tokugawa times.

Thus, it must be clearly recognized that Japan's sole

QC is all right for the shop floor, but when will the salarymen get together to improve their routine?

Photo credit: Toyota Motor Co.

resource—human beings—has also suddenly become a very costly resource. That makes it precious in a second sense as well. So, the present challenge is to use it more wisely. Japan's success in the future will depend essentially on how it meets this challenge.

Labor Productivity And Unproductivity

The Japanese have become inordinately proud of their high level of productivity in recent years, while foreigners have become almost servile in admiring it. According to the 1980 White Paper on International Trade, the increase in labor productivity—output per working hour—in the manufacturing sector rose an average 8.2% a year during 1960–78. This compared quite favorably with 5.8% in

Italy, 5.5% in France, 5.5% in West Germany, 3.4% in the United States, and 3.2% in Great Britain.[2]

Part of this was due to the fact that Japan as a latecomer was able to benefit from highly advanced technologies developed in the West. And it is quite normal that the rise in productivity should be impressive from a low base such as existed after the war. But it is most striking that the rate of productivity increase has only fallen off a bit recently and is still much higher than in other developed countries. This is because Japan's manufacturers have not ceased introducing new methods and new technologies whenever they become available. They have also repeatedly modernized the facilities, machinery, and processes. This was done not only in the brand new factories built even while the old ones were in good working condition but by making improvements continually in all production units.

When one looks at some of the details of the performance and how it was achieved it becomes easier to understand Japan's pride, for the main thrust has been not mere output but quality. Quality control activities have penetrated Japan's industry increasingly and have worked their way down from the top to the grass roots level. In thousands of factories, workers are encouraged to form QC circles in order to make improvements or solve problems arising in their own daily work. Meanwhile, the foremen are kept well trained and alert. Specialists in plant layout, industrial design and systems management are called in to see that every machine is in its place, that the workers are properly related to them, and that the flow of work is as efficient as possible.

Even today, factory management scouts the world for the most modern and efficient technologies. Many of them are imported under license although admittedly some are just copied. But the factories do not stop there. They systematically try to improve on what they borrow and have shown tremendous skill at innovation. Now, with expanded R&D facilities, they are also showing considerable ability at invention. Since top priority has been allotted to increasing productivity and perfecting technology, those in charge are given a relatively free hand in reshaping not only the work place but the work methods and they frequently have a say on basic company policy.

Lest the Japanese become too proud, however, it must be stressed that the high productivity era has only come to manufacturing. Even there, it is to be found predominantly in big business. Medium-sized companies (500–999 workers) only attained 89.7% of the productivity level of big companies and the smaller companies (less than 500 workers) a mere 52.4%.[3] Moreover, much of the increase in productivity of the big companies is not a result of their own efforts but because they have systematically hived off the backward, complicated, labor-intensive processes which are left to their suppliers and subcontractors, while they have become largely automated assembly operations.

It is also necessary to recall that the greatest successes have been in the actual production work. Yet, over the past years, there has been a gradual shift in personnel away from the direct workers, those physically engaged in production and maintenance, and toward those dealing with engineering, sales, clerical and managerial tasks. These indirect workers have already increased their share from 21.0% in 1965 to 25.4% in 1975 and, according to MITI, are expected to reach 27.4% by 1990.[4] At the same time, there is a broader shift in the economy from "blue-collar" workers (production) to "white-collar" workers (clerical and management) and "gray-collar" workers (sales, transport, etc.). Of the three, only the share of the blue-collar workers has decreased recently, down to 43.1% in 1979. White-collar workers have risen to 29.8% and gray-collar workers to 27.0%.[5]

These trends must be considered seriously for the very pertinent reason that so far quality control and productivity have been mainly a blue-collar concern and then largely in the direct production departments of the factories. Elsewhere, within the very same companies, the progress has been much slower among clerical and sales personnel. And it has been slowest in management. In fact, the productivity worship on the factory floor is often replaced by a veneration of the old methods and traditional techniques in the offices. Even in the administration of major companies, whether in manufacturing, trading, or finance, whether in the private sector or in government agencies and corporations, things have hardly changed over the years. Thus, the archetypical Japanese management system has become almost sacrosanct (although everyone knows its weaknesses and flaws and parts are already eroding).

Moreover, what has been accomplished in manufacturing has not been reproduced, or even attempted, in other sectors. The multi-stage distribution network is recognized as inefficient and long in need of an overhaul. But any advances have been somewhat less than decisive. The service sector is patently frivolous in many cases. But it keeps on expanding pointlessly. And even agriculture, which showed substantial progress toward modernization during the 1950s and 1960s, has not gotten much beyond that stage.

When these sectors are added to the picture, the whole productivity situation looks completely different. On the basis of statistics from MITI and the Economic Planning Agency, it clearly appears that some few branches are keeping well ahead of the average increase in productivity of the economy as a whole. They include manufacturing and mining as well as finance. But, even in the secondary

High productivity versus low productivity. The tertiary sector keeps pulling the average down.

Sector	Annual Increase (%)		
	1970–1975	1975–1978	1970–1978
Primary Sector			
Agriculture, forestry and fishing	7.8	−1.8	4.1
Secondary Sector			
Mining	9.0	6.6	8.1
Manufacturing	5.0	9.4	6.6
Construction	0.8	−3.3	−0.7
Utilities	2.5	−0.4	1.4
Tertiary Sector	(4.1)	(1.2)	(3.0)
Wholesale and retail	6.5	2.2	4.9
Finance	7.1	8.0	7.4
Real estate	0.6	0.3	0.5
Transport, communications	4.0	−0.4	2.3
Services	0.8	−2.7	−0.5
All Sectors	5.2	4.2	4.8

Source: *Outlook and Issues of Industrial Structure in the 1980s.* MITI. derived from statistics of the Economic Planning Agency.

sector, utilities and especially construction have done very poorly, showing a minimal or negative growth. In the tertiary sector, most branches are relatively low, the weakest being services. Distribution has only shown as much growth as it did because wholesale could be rationalized sharply while retail has remained costly and inefficient.[6]

This also shows Japan in a much less flattering light as compared to other countries. True, manufacturing productivity has risen strikingly. But not the rest. Thus, Professor Kazukiyo Kurosawa of the Tokyo Institute of Technology, one of the very few experts on non-industrial productivity, still rated America's overall performance as considerably better for 1978, a good 160 to Japan's 100. That was because, although manufacturing productivity was only 115, agriculture and distribution plus services were much higher in the United States at 277 and 156 to Japan's 100. He recently evaluated the productivity of American white-collar workers at 130–150 against Japan's 100.[7]

Basically, this means that in the productivity race, Japan has only won the first lap. Manufacturing appears more as an exception and other branches are a serious drag. So far, this has just been unfortunate. In the future, it can be more perilous. For, the dynamic manufacturing sector is growing smaller as compared with the unproductive parts of the economy. Its share of net national product peaked at 37% in the 1960s and has fallen slowly since. Meanwhile, the far less efficient tertiary sector has increased its share from 48% to 58%.[8] If Japan is to progress further it cannot afford to allow its most rapidly expanding branches to wallow in poor productivity.

The time has obviously come to deal with these backward areas a bit more vigorously than in the past. This has been recognized by some businessmen, bureaucrats and academics, but not all by any means. It has also been taken up by the prime mover in such matters, the Japan Productivity Center. In its platform for the 1980s, it includes as a major task: "to find a way to develop tertiary industry, especially knowledge, information, distribution, and service industries."[9] Despite this, it will not be easy to make progress either in the tertiary sector or among white-collar and gray-collar employees in general.

Catching Up With The Times

Improving productivity is a very important matter. But it is a relatively mechanical one that can be accomplished in a multitude of small ways without seriously questioning the underlying system. It is possible to change a bit of layout, introduce new machines, or teach workers different techniques. That sort of thing has been done in the past and can be done again in the future. After all, it basically involves cold and objective processes more than people.

Where Japan is going to have the greatest difficulties is in modifying the attitudes of the population, something that is becoming increasingly essential. One could hardly claim that interpersonal relations in Japan's economy have been keeping up with the times anywhere near as well as its research and technology. This applies to the way people are organized, directed, and motivated in different sectors, like services, distribution, agriculture, and even industry. It applies to the relations within companies, between superiors and subordinates, and between companies, namely how firms deal with their suppliers and clients. It also applies to the very meaning of *work*.

Despite the rapid growth of the economy and its "modernization," the human foundation supporting it has changed very little since the war. The Japanese management system, which is so highly praised by Japanese and foreigners alike, has not been seriously revised in decades. More ominously, it claims roots that go all the way back into Japan's history, sinking down into Meiji days and clinging to what were virtues under the Tokugawa. This has made the system almost sacrosanct, hard to criticize when the failings are evident, harder yet to reform. It is about time for Japan to catch up here as well, not necessarily to adopt a system similar to western countries but to keep pace with its own society.

While the management system has been standing still, many aspects of the economy it is supposed to dominate have been racing ahead or changing drastically. Factories, for one, have been turned into something completely different from what they used to be, not only as concerns the machinery but also the way personnel must be used. Computers will bring a similar revolution in the offices. This revolution will be lost, or much fewer of its fruits gathered, unless the personnel systems there are also updated. To a lesser degree, but still quite significantly, there will be major changes in merchandising techniques, affecting wholesale and retail, as well as new types of service trades. If the people in those branches are not used differently, many of them will be wasted or get in the way of progress.

The biggest concern is probably not even with lower level staff but those at the top. The whole business philosophy of the people who have brought about the Japanese economic miracle, many of whom are still in charge, will have to change as the miracle peters out. It is impossible to run a company in the same way during a period of rapid or slow growth. The time for expansion (aside from some few fields) has been replaced by a time for rationalization and sometimes retrenchment. The day when one could conquer market share and regard profit figures as secondary is gone. Even if the banks are more than willing to offer loans, many companies may not be able to afford the cost. Yet, despite all the talk, how many managers have really adapted to these harder times? Equally important, how many know how to take advantage of the new opportunities that have arisen and make them work for the company?

The management system, praised as "unique to Japan" and considered a success because the Japanese are "different" and react well to its demands, is in need of a thorough review not only because the times have changed. The people have changed as well. The values that guided workers just after the war, which had been inculcated in them before or during the war, are completely different from the values their children and grandchildren cling to. Self-sacrifice and dedication are no longer among them. Willingness to follow orders blindly is less noticeable. Instead, there has been an upsurge of individualism, a preference to work for the palpable (rather than moral) rewards, and no desire whatsoever to sacrifice one's life for work. Using the old methods to get the most out of personnel could backfire today.

Women, although they are hardly thought of in corporate planning, have come to play a significant role in the modern economy. Nevertheless, it is still a rather subalternate and secondary role. But it cannot be ignored because many women will no longer accept that kind of treatment. And even those who do can be used much more successfully if improvements are made.

If the management system has become a bit obsolete, the educational system is in many ways archaic. Supposedly geared to training salarymen at the highest level, and clerks or technicians further down, it has not kept up with the times. It still produces generalists when everyone knows the biggest need is for specialists. On the other hand, it does not inspire the sort of curiosity and initiative that will be needed in the future. Japan must cease being a copier, since there is nothing much left to copy, and become an innovator. It must produce some of the most highly trained personnel to open up the knowledge-intensive industries. Yet, its graduates are widely criticized by educators as substandard and by employers as inadequate.

Modernization has taken an unusual form in Japan. It is sometimes referred to as blending East and West or borrowing techniques from outside while maintaining the Japanese "spirit." But one can hardly speak of a blend as much as a separation, keeping the traditional values, the human relations, and many old-fashioned mental sets in one compartment reserved for what is authentically Japanese while accepting other things which can be useful. These other things are hard, impersonal and material. Such a division, whatever its advantages, has created a dichotomy or even a split personality. Everything to do with the factory, science, technology, to some extent business in the crude commercial sense, can be approached rationally and by using cold logic. The rest, everything concerning people, becomes soft, emotional, often irrational. This is bound to make the process of change a difficult one because now the time has come to tamper with what many Japanese hold sacred.

The oil crisis, which is now used by Japanese businessmen as the starting point for a new era, has ushered in a period of challenge. It has already resulted in more changes than one would have expected a short time before. Many have been purely technical, a better use of equipment or energy. Some have affected basic characteristics like lifetime employment and seniority. But only the first steps have been taken. The process of change has begun but no one really knows in which direction it is moving, how far it will go, and what the final outcome will be.

Change can be positive or negative. The Japanese themselves are not quite certain how this transition will work out. Some tend to be blindly optimistic. Those whose eyes are open realize that many of the trends are less promising. Much that the future holds is frightening. Yet, resisting change or putting reforms off for later is more likely to hurt than to help. It is better to move ahead and improve what can be improved while at least reducing the impact of any evils. Japan did this in Meiji days and again after the war. Can it succeed this time as well?

NOTES

1. *Japan Economic Journal*, August 28, 1979.
2. *1980 White Paper on International Trade*, MITI.
3. *Industrial Census*, MITI.
4. *Asahi Shimbun*, August 31, 1980.
5. *Asahi Shimbun*, July 6, 1980.
6. *Outlook and Issues of Industrial Structure in the 1980s*, MITI.
7. See *International Comparison of Labor Productivity*.
8. Economic Planning Agency.
9. *Platform of the Productivity Movement in the 1980s*, Japan Productivity Center.

2
Modern Factories, Backward Offices

Low-Productivity Administration

When a foreign visitor enters a modern Japanese factory, he is likely to gasp at what he sees. The factory itself is carefully designed, well arranged, and often attractive. The machinery is laid out in just the right place so that the flow of work will be smooth and continuous. The workers are stationed in the best positon to use the machinery and to cooperate with one another.Their uniforms are spick and span and they are thoroughly absorbed in their work. Also in uniform, the foremen and supervisors, who know every aspect of operations, move about seeing that the work is done right and occasionally giving instructions. Then, after a long day's work, both senior operators and younger employees may stay on for a QC circle meeting to get their job done even better tomorrow.

When a foreign visitor enters a Japanese office, he is likely to gasp as well. This time it will be due to surprise and disappointment. In broad open spaces, with few partitions to provide the slightest privacy or even the possibility of concentration, there are masses of desks arranged seemingly every which way. Each cluster may represent a group or section with the respective supervisor at a desk on the end or a slight distance away. The desks of the employees will be facing one another and right next to each other so that they can consult . . . and also chat, it being rather hard to tell which is occurring. In a corner, there may be a partition with a table and some chairs where official guests can be received and served tea before the meeting. These places are usually full. And the atmosphere is so drab that often the employee takes his visitor out to a nearby coffee shop instead.

The desks are not tidy with everything in its place. Rather, papers and books are piled up helter skelter. If someone needs something he will go searching through the mass and perhaps end up not finding it there. These piles grow from day to day but rarely is an effort made to systematize them. And the standard office furnishings, including such common items as shelves and filing cabinets, are notably lacking. Forms are not much in use and messages are just jotted down on a handy scrap of paper. It frequently happens that someone has to leave his desk. But there may be no one in the room who knows just where he's gone or when he'll be back.

Working in this atmosphere are a variegated lot of employees. Some of the salarymen are impeccably dressed, others turn the office into a substitute living room or worse, dropping their jackets and getting into their slippers. Off to the side someone is making tea or perhaps even shaving. Only the young ladies are meticulous about their appearance, coming in the latest fashions and exquisitely made up for what, after all, is just a job. But, what is inside their heads is much more important than what they wear. And it could hardly be claimed that they are anywhere near as careful and meticulous about what they do and how they do it as the factory workers. Time is spent on essentials and inessentials indifferently, as things crop up. What cannot be done today will be continued after hours, or put off until the next day, or the day after.

That productivity is not a pressing matter is shown by

Office layout still isn't quite the same art as plant layout.

the clear lack of the very things that symbolize it in the factory.[1] There are very few graphs of anything, aside perhaps from sales. Memos are rarely circulated to remind people of deadlines that must be met . . . and are sometimes missed. Basic records are scant. An employee will go about his daily work, meeting with suppliers or clients, discussing matters like prices and specifications, and finally reaching decisions that will bind the company and involve others in the implementation. Yet, he may just mention it to them in passing or bring it up in a meeting. Making him write it down would be an imposition. Thus, when a crucial person is absent or has been replaced, his successor may not know what to do.

When we consider the use of people, the contrast with the factory becomes particularly noticeable. Whereas every blue-collar worker is in his place, doing a specific job and one carefully designed to make the best use of him, it is often hard to know just what a white-collar employee is doing or supposed to do. Unlike Western companies, where the jobs are determined first and the employees hired to fill them, in Japan one recruits fresh batches of employees annually. They are differentiated by background, things like education and age, but rarely by specific job skills. Then they are sorted into categories, such as operational or clerical, also according to background. Finally, they are allocated to the sections and divisions that say they need more staff (or just want to grow) and any surplus seems to be dumped with sales, for the more sales personnel the better.

But there is no clearly defined job for them. "Job descriptions" do not exist in Japanese offices nor does the concept really exist in the Japanese mind.[2] Attempts at introducing job classifications have been strongly resisted so those assigned to a unit are usually left to sort out how the tasks they encounter will be shared. In some cases, each person may handle a given aspect. More often, the group will take it on as a group project. Obviously, many assignments can be accomplished either by individuals or a group. With a group, however, there is a greater probability that there will be either too few members, straining their capacity, or more likely yet, too many group members, meaning that some have little to do or all accomplish less than otherwise. How they tackle a given task is also left up to them more than in a Western enterprise—or a Japanese factory—where there are clear instructions as to how things are to be done. They will receive advice from older employees and can check with their supervisor. In cases where there are no guidelines or precedents, they can initiate a *ringisho*. But it would be much simpler and more sensible if jobs were regarded as a valid concept.

The whole situation becomes even more fluid due to the considerable degree of rotation that occurs in any administration. Admittedly, in the factory, a lathe operator can be turned into a welder if the company needs that. But, by and large, a person has a specific job which he keeps, in which he accumulates experience, and which he ends up knowing through and through. In offices, clerical staff, and especially potential managers, are kept on the move. They are sent from one section to the next every two or three years, sometimes they move after a single year. This makes it hard for them to gain more than a passing familiarity with the job and they are never as competent as Westerners trained and hired to do a specific job.

Supervisors, whether at section, division, or department level, also lack specific competences. Unlike Western managers, they are not there to give orders and see that they are carried out. Unlike a Japanese foreman, they are not supposed to keep a constant check on how well subordinate staff is performing. In the office, they tend more to create an atmosphere in which everyone will do his best.

Such an atmosphere involves leaving subordinates a considerable amount of leeway, guiding them on occasion, but never bearing down on them or making unpleasant criticism. The major tasks seem to be maintaining morale and arousing enthusiasm. Thus, the Japanese often compare this kind of manager to the leader of a group carrying the portable shrine (*mikoshi*) during festivals, giving directions and urging them on. Westerners might regard the manager as a mixture of coach and cheerleader.[3]

In such a situation, one cannot expect very high efficiency in the office or any degree of regularity in the way the company's affairs are handled. Too much is left to chance and to the personality of those involved. There is a saving grace in the sense that, once given their head and aroused to a high enough pitch, the Japanese will make every effort to fulfill the trust placed in them. But it is extremely hard to keep the level of enthusiasm up and perhaps dangerous to take decisions and act in such an exalted state. Companies are rather humdrum affairs once they have been run in. The brilliant campaigns and actions that were appropriate while Japan's economy was growing rapidly could be counterproductive today.

The disadvantages of the Japanese approach should also not be obscured by the well-known fact that the Japanese work very long hours and are willing to put in overtime (which leads some foreigners to assume that they work "hard"). Much of this is pointless since, in all too many cases, the Japanese employees accomplish no more than they could have, or many Western employees do, in much fewer hours by working in a more concentrated and rational fashion.[4] Their efficiency could be increased vastly by a few appropriate measures and probably doubled by a systematic revision. Whereas this sort of savings could be ignored in earlier days, now that increasingly "time means money" even in Japan it cannot be tolerated.

Nor will those late hours be accepted so readily by the growing categories of salarymen who do not want to sacrifice their personal life to the company.

More important than method is substance. And it is worrisome that a number of the primary purposes of administrative offices seem to get short shrift. The factory is expected to produce, but it is the office that must keep very careful track of production costs. During much of the period of rapid growth, the main concern was to get enough raw materials from the suppliers at whatever price. Now price has to be scrutinized more minutely. Increasingly the amount of raw materials and energy used is controlled. But the office keeps much poorer records of other costs, especially for functions accomplishd in-house, whether this is sales, transport, advertising, or other. With a staff of a given size, which has to be used one way or the other, it apparently does not make much sense to check whether each staff member is really carrying his weight in financial terms.

If the factory is to produce, then certainly the office must decide how much to produce as a function of potential sales. It is very risky to expand production facilities without having a good idea of who will buy the products. Yet, market forecasting is still backward and many essential decisions, involving tremendous amounts of money that will be immobilized for extended periods of time, result from rather extraneous factors. Expansion will occur if the man in charge is dynamic, or if there are excess funds available, or in order to keep up with the competitors. The urge for market share has encouraged many ill-conceived investments and resulted in overcapacity and overproduction. Japanese managers may deny these flaws. But, how else can one explain the repeated bursts of expansion, followed by price wars, followed by the freezing and finally scrapping of plant in a whole string of industries, from textiles, to shipbuilding, and now basic metals?

The art of proper management, as many Japanese managers have yet to learn, is the art of balance. There is no point to increasing productive capacity unless one is pretty certain of sales. Otherwise, the company will work under capacity or produce too much and have to sell at a low price. This the Japanese try to avoid by turning sales into a campaign just as expanding production had been. Sales, however, is a costly operation since it employs large numbers of personnel. And once it becomes a serious campaign the chance that the salesmen will get good prices for their products are more limited than ever. In companies as highly leveraged as the Japanese, increasing productive capacity usually implies taking out more loans. This, too, is a cost that must be covered and could have been avoided with more balanced growth, one based more on the company's own resources. Finally, no matter how important production or sales may be, nothing exceeds the significance of keeping a healthy balance between receipts and expenditures. No conceivable amount of future benefits (often quite dimly seen) should blind a manager to the dangers of a cash flow squeeze.

These are not minor problems by any means. From top to bottom, measures could be taken that would make better use of personnel or permit a company to use less personnel to accomplish as much. The savings are not just a few yen here and there but very substantial amounts that would accrue over long years. In more serious cases, failing to abide by what is standard managerial practice elsewhere can even place the company in jeopardy. Of course, the Japanese frequently admit the weaknesses of their system and on occasion modest reforms are actually introduced. But so far productivity has made little headway at the administrative and management level. It has run into too solid resistance rooted not in any objective view of the situation but subjective preferences and time-honored traditions.

No Time To Work

Man, we all know, is the most crucial element in any Japanese company, bureaucracy, or social institution of any sort. Without his cooperation nothing can be accomplished and he must be treated properly. The greatest care must be shown in treating staff right and staffers must feel they enjoy respect. Yet, paradoxically, because man is so important in Japan he is often wasted and squandered outrageously. He can end up accomplishing much less than man in other countries where his worth is not realized and he is treated more impersonally.

Nowhere is this clearer than when it comes to Japanese-style decision-making. This involves various methods that are too well known to bother describing in much detail. There is *ringi seido*, a consultation system which theoretically at least starts at the bottom, with a proposal (*ringisho*) working its way upward for approval or sanction (*kessai*). There is *nemawashi*, where informal approaches are made to gain support of a given action and may result in an informal meeting (*kondankai*) or a more formal conference to consider implementation (*kaigi*). But there is not—in theory at least— a situation in which one person or a small group can take basic decisions for the whole company.

There are many advantages to the Japanese form of decision-making.[5] It provides for some degree of democracy and spontaneity in that staff at lower levels can initiate measures, or work out plans, or make proposals, which will be channeled upward to higher levels. This also provides for greater participation, especially when combined with meetings, since all those even remotely related to an issue will be invited to attend and present their views. They will also hear the views of the other parties. This having been done, a decision adopted on the basis of consensus, or so it is claimed, will meet with general acceptance. This reinforces harmony within the company and should encourage all to give their unstinting support to implementation of the measures.

Still, admitting the advantages is no reason to overlook the drawbacks. Some of them are minor and tolerable, others are essential and can cause considerable problems. Most of them are known to the Japanese salarymen, some of whom are quite annoyed by the defects. Those which are of greatest interest here are the ones that encourage a poor use of personnel.

The first demerit is that there are too many people involved. A *ringisho*, which may actually only concern one section and quite a minor matter, may well end up being sent to various other sections and collecting an incredible number of stamps before it gets back to its originator. Meetings tend to expand, as more people are invited, whether or not directly involved. In fact, when in doubt a person is more likely to be invited than left out . . . just in case. There is no desire to slight those who will feel they are being ignored although, once asked to come, they may discover that they are wasting their time. Worse, by coming and raising unnecessary questions or making proposals concerning matters that do not really concern them, they will be wasting everyone else's time as well.

This sort of exercise also occurs too frequently. There are many important and valid reasons for holding meetings. Members of different sections and divisions must cooperate, coordination is necessary between the various members of a group, contacts have to be maintained with suppliers and clients. But meetings are also held for minor things, requesting a favor that is easier to ask in person or, worse, holding meetings or seeing people just because the more personal relations there are the smoother things should run even if there is no specific purpose. And one meeting always seems to call for another. According to a *Japan Economic Journal* survey, not only are 70% to 80% of managerial staff participating in decision-making, they are engaged in nearly every basic planning category, some of which at least they might have been spared.[6]

Too many people attending too many meetings is obviously compounded if the meetings are also too long. This they will certainly be if more, rather than fewer, participants attend. But they will also be longer because of the Japanese approach to decision-making. Rather than come right out with a proposal, debate it, and approve or reject it, one must go through all the proper motions. The participants, to avoid upsetting one another, will only make their proposals slowly and cautiously, waiting for signs of approval, before proceeding further. Any opponents will be just as cautious, not wishing to make enemies unnecessarily. And, if it is impossible for a decision to be reached at the first meeting, there will be a second, and a third, and more.

The Japanese seem to think that the loss of time doesn't really matter as long as one ends up with a good decision. But they are very wrong. First of all, there is the fact that time does mean money. Although frequently ignored by Japanese companies, now that wages are so high, excessive time spent can cost extraordinary sums. Secondly, there is no reason to believe that a decision that has taken a longer time to mature is inherently that much better. But, the biggest problem is that while the decision is being forged there can be no action. Whatever inappropriate methods called for a *ringisho* will continue until it is approved. If a decision is necessary to implement a plan, that plan will have to wait.

Sometimes it may not matter; other times the decision may simply come too late. It is, of course, easy to tell when a hasty decision has led to damage or loss for the company. A tardy decision can have equally bad effects, even if they are hard to see or judge. Thus, for example, if a foreign buyer gets tired of waiting for a decision and lets another Japanese or more likely Korean or Taiwanese company clinch the deal, the loss of earnings will not be visible but it will be real. When, in a particularly decisive case, Sumitomo Shoji was too slow in making up its mind, it lost the remnants of Ataka to its rival, C. Itoh. This is just one case among countless others.

Alongside the quantitative factors, there is also a qualitative one. Since great efforts were made at being cooperative and preserving harmony, one could hardly say that everything was clearly expressed. People who were against a measure, noting they were in a minority, may well have kept their view to themselves. There is usually also an effort at keeping decisions as flexible and open to change as possible. All this combines to make many agreements sufficiently vague that they can be implemented differently by the various parties with each claiming it has followed the consensus. If the decision was never written down, as frequently happens, it would be impossible to prove who really was right.

But the biggest flaw lies elsewhere. To some extent the decision-making process is just for show. It is not a spontaneous coming together in which ideas can proceed from the bottom upward. No matter how diffuse they may seem, there is always an originator, someone who writes the *ringisho* or someone who starts convincing the others of his own view in *nemawashi*. The meetings convened are only ceremonial . . . unless there is strong resistance from another party. The final decision, however, will result from the basic power relationships between the participants. Although lower ranking staff are also invited, they know better than to sponsor proposals without backing from higher up. So the decisions will very rarely, if ever, be imposed by those below. Rather, those above just wait until they get the response they want.

This may explain why the *Japan Economic Journal* survey showed that there has been a considerable shift in the decision-making process in the last decade, at which point it was already quite different from the idealized form. According to Kazuo Noda, 63% of all corporations worked on the basis of proposals made by middle management and sent for approval by top management. Even then, top management had the final say. Now, however, the various plans and proposals are being handled by senior managing directors, which means that decision-making has moved upward to those who are not afraid to take their own decisions.[7] This was found in large, often bureaucratic, corporations. Among the smaller and founder-directed companies, there never was any doubt as to who took decisions.

This seems to indicate that the traditional decision-making process is less important materially than morally and psychologically. It is essential, as Western managers have learned, to get as much of the staff as possible involved in decision-making, to obtain their voluntary participation, and to arouse their enthusiasm. But Western managers are not yet willing to devote as much time to that as the Japanese. And Japanese companies would be wise to consider how the appearances can be saved, after the reality vanishes, without spending more time and money on it than necessary.

The first few steps could be quite simple. They would imply no basic break with the past. One could merely invite a few less people to meetings and call a few less meetings. They might also be kept shorter. If the Japanese were courageous enough, they could be expedited by expressing one's views openly rather than hedging so much. If the Japanese were particularly courageous, they could even vote on the matter rather than let things run on indefinitely until everyone has been convinced or just gotten tired of objecting.

To the extent that the decision-making process is also a learning process, the rest of the staff, those who do not attend a given meeting, could be kept informed through memos, circular letters, company newspapers, notices on the bulletin board and the like. To the extent that a *ringisho* is needed to clarify routine matters, that might be obviated by a clearer definition of the competences of different sections, divisions, and departments as well as by more exact job descriptions.

Finally, for important decisions that cannot be delayed, the company can have a parallel system not too different from the Western manner. Top managers would simply decide on their own and inform their subordinates later. Trading companies, which frequently cannot afford to wait, already have their strategic planning groups and most other companies also have informal units that act first and engage in *nemawashi* later. This kind of body could be reinforced. It would also gain by being praised for its virtues rather than played down as a breach in the traditional decision-making process.

Harmony And Loyalty First!

Japanese companies and government bureaucracies are often more like social organisms than commercial enterprises or administrative operations especially because of the strong emphasis placed on the type of person wanted rather than his abilities. Personality plays an exceptional role in determining who is recruited, how one behaves, and who gets promoted. Among the characteristics most praised, none are evaluated more highly than harmony and loyalty. They are enshrined in the slogans and mottos of the corporation and placed, in delicately formed calligraphy, in prominent locations. They crop up in every speech by executives, from the president on down.

Candidates for recruitment know that, whether this is their true character or not, they have to appear as tame and responsive as possible and emphasize their willingness to serve the company in any way it desires. They should not have any strong attachments or family obligations that could lessen their commitment. Although they can have their own ideas and hobbies, this should not get in the way of serving the company. The company personnel officers meanwhile are looking for likeable young people who can be molded later to fit the company's needs. This is admitted by any number of senior staff who refer to the ideal young recruit as a "blank sheet of paper."

True, Mitsui likes slightly aggressive types, while Mitsubishi is more on the conservative side. And there are fashions when the corporate world claims it is seeking self-confident, dynamic or daring employees. This is duly noted by the university grads who then show up for interviews prepared to go through that act. But the basic fact remains that, to get and keep a job, most Japanese are willing to alter or hide their true feelings and adopt the outer shell their employer wants. One must give up one's "self" on entering the company.

It is not enough just to find people who "fit" the company image. Once within, they must become a different kind of person. This process begins with the initiation ceremony and carries over to a bit of training that places more emphasis than elsewhere on the spiritual side. More extreme cases include "work-begging" or camps that include marathons, self-criticism and zen. Even the Self-Defense Force lends a hand to train tough salarymen. Throughout, the emphasis is on duty, obedience, loyalty and harmony.

Over the following years the salaryman gets to know his colleagues, with some of whom he will spend his whole career. Slowly but surely, he works his way through the company, transferred to this division and that, sent off to distant subsidiaries and overseas offices. Gradually, he becomes part of a growing circle of company people and his style adapts to theirs. He meets his colleagues not only during working hours, but at lunch in the company canteen or a nearby restaurant, after work for a drink, or during a night on the town. He may go on company trips, attend company social activities, and belong to company clubs or sports teams. As if that were not enough, many employees also live in company housing.

Such constant contact with other company people helps create a spirit of teamwork that can hardly be replicated elsewhere. But it is apparently not quite enough for the company. For, any rough edges must be smoothed. It is not good enough to be a team member, one must merge with the team. Standing out and being noticed in teamwork is almost as bad as not participating and is more likely to show wrong attitude than mark one for later promotion as having more initiative or dynamism.

The experience of working together rounds off other rough edges. One will not get very far in the company without a fair number of friends. The easiest way to win, and hold them, is to be as understanding and accepting as possible. Even at meetings which are supposedly called to obtain people's reactions, it would be extremely foolish to say anything that might be taken as criticism or just a slight on someone else. Naturally, one should say and do nothing that might lead people to suspect any self-flattery was intended or that there was an undue sign of ambition. No matter how badly a promotion is desired, the best thing is to wait and be discovered. Drawing attention to oneself only arouses jealousy and antagonism.

Thus, even the most spirited and recalcitrant subject can, over the years, be turned into a model company man. We have all seen freshman employees who undergo a complete conversion. Only a few years before they were insisting they would never join the rat race and now it's everything for the company. It is quite possible that the same process will continue even with the less than ideal material of the present younger generation. But it is bound to be harder to convince them and there will be a growing segment who refuse to give up all their outside interests. There will be more and more who quite simply refuse to enter companies whose demands are too stringent.

The radical students who protested against the war in Vietnam, the Japanese goverment, and also big business, were not coopted as much as their predecessors. When the conversion came, it was likely to be stronger than with anyone else. But some have carried on their anti-business activities from within the company's own trade union. Today's less dynamic youth pose a different sort of problem. The strong tendency toward dependence or *amaé* does not prevent attachment to the company. In some ways, it reinforces the urge since they are seeking something to depend on. But the purpose of harmony, as seen by the company, is not to look after its personnel more than otherwise but for them to make exceptional sacrifices for the company.

Although harmony is an admirable trait, it does have drawbacks and they are particularly serious when the drive for harmony is pushed this far. One problem is the lack of an objective yardstick for evaluating the success of policy. Another is the difficulty in having a sufficiently detached attitude to attempt evaluation. When everyone is on the same team, it is very hard for a member to judge the whole team. When anything resembling criticism of the team or its members is regarded as disturbing harmony, it is quite impossible to admit failings, seek the causes, and make changes.

In fact, the relations are such that the very idea of objectivity is not quite in its place. Like the wartime leaders, Japanese managers make appeals to the spirit of their subordinates. They try to arouse a passionate loyalty, a keen urge to win, a tenaciousness in attaining goals . . . but never an attempt to question the goals or purposes. No appeal is made to the mind to stop, consider attentively, and then systematically judge both what is right and wrong in a given policy. That is why it so often happens that Japanese companies, once having come to a decision, will follow through ruthlessly whatever the results may be. If the decision was wise, harmony is a plus; if the decision was mistaken, harmony can be utterly destructive.

Japanese companies would be much better off if they did provide some means of outside or objective evaluation. And many of them seem to realize it since there is a growing demand for management consultants. It would be even better if the team members were asked to exercise their intelligence as well as their fighting will by scrutinizing any measure not only before it is introduced but while it is being implemented. It should be realized that criticism may be the most positive contribution they can make in certain circumstances and thus welcomed rather than discouraged.

Without wishing to be heretical, it must be admitted that there are some things for which teamwork is not particularly suitable. The group approach is admirable for assembly line work, excellent to keep up morale in the office, and can arouse greater efforts in sales. Teamwork is supposedly an asset in research and development. But making the team a must often means that more people than necessary are assigned to a given project. There are many things that can be done just as well, or almost as well, by individuals or a few persons. This involves a definite savings in personnel expenses that can no longer be ignored. More crucially, there are things of a creative nature which can only be done well by individuals. Most truly great ideas can be traced back to one person who would have performed less well in the stultifying atmosphere of Japanese teams. This might be remembered when dealing with research workers, copywriters, designers, creatives in publicity, translators, and many others.

Teamwork and harmony are not the only path to success. In the West, the degree of cooperation is much lower. Yet, if each person knows his job and does his job, they can often outperform a Japanese team. By putting greater stress on ability than teamwork, it is possible to draw people together from many different companies and bureaucracies to work on a specific "task," for a specific period, and release them later. It is possible to merge companies when needed. The task-orientation makes up for the lack of harmony. Meanwhile, harmony pushed to the extent it is within Japanese companies makes it nearly impossible for anyone to cooperate with others outside the group.

There have also been Japanese companies whose harmony was flawless and whose human relations were ideal. They were led by men who knew how to speak to the hearts of their colleagues. And yet they went bankrupt. Business is not just a social game. It is a cold, calculating operation. Sometimes unpleasant decisions have to be made, like laying off personnel in a recession or simply firing someone whose contribution is negligible or perhaps negative. Brilliant ideas rarely come to those who think and act like others; they occur to those who are different, those who don't fit in. Making a fetish of harmony leads one to forget that harmony is just one virtue in business, and not necessarily the decisive one.

Moreover, the stress on harmony is in its own way disruptive of good relations. There are natural differences between people and it is absurd to assume that all members of any group think alike. Making them conceal the differences, keep in their views, and put up a good show of supporting the consensus can have two negative effects. Either, there is a tendency toward hypocrisy, which flourishes in Japan. Few people really know which of their closer associates actually agree and which just engage in lip-service. Or there is a tendency toward factionalism, another typical hallmark of Japanese companies. Since everyone is locked up within the same group and some can only succeed because others fail, the tension is actually stronger than in more relaxed societies where people come and go.

Loyalty is also a fine virtue. But it has its drawbacks, too. One has already been referred to, the willingness to blindly accept something because it is suggested by one's superior or imposed for the good of the company. This weakens the critical faculty that every businessman (and every human being) should preserve. Another is that such loyalty discourages all of the virtues that are associated with leadership. Throughout a person's early career, his advancement depends on his ability to follow orders whether they appeal to him or not. His opinion is asked but it is the foolhardy salaryman who would contradict his boss or suggest an alternative without great diplomacy. Not until one enters middle management can one act as a leader. For reasons of harmony, however, this type of leadership is to look after one's subordinates or raise their morale. So, only on entering top management, after nearly three decades of taking orders, does one finally give orders and show true leadership.

Loyalty makes the crisis more serious. For, Japanese leaders almost systematically seek out weak and compliant successors. Even founders of great companies, men who showed their personal ability, like Konosuke Matsushita, prefer less dynamic subordinates, men who lack "self."[8] Further on down, each new class of freshman employees is taught about loyalty and expected to follow the path indicated to them. We have now gone through about thirty entry classes since the war. Just about everyone on the spiral staircase has been thoroughly drilled in all matters of harmony and loyalty. Will they still be able to direct their companies and the economy when they reach the top?

Keeping Up Human Relations

Ever since Meiji days, businessmen have compared the company to the family, more exactly, to the tight-knit and strictly disciplined Japanese family. There were periods in which familism became the predominant philosophy of Japanese business leaders and ultimately the official ideology of the state.[9] Of course, those insisting the company was a family were not just being sentimental. They had their own reasons. They wished to foster dedication and hard work, they wanted to hold on to their personnel, and they wished to direct things as freely and unrestrictedly as possible.

Familism collapsed after the war. In fact, the traditonal Japanese family has unergone such drastic changes that it might not really serve very well as the basis for a company structure. But the Japanese have not been able to throw off their attachment to close social relations that often influence, and sometimes even dominate, purely commercial matters. In many ways, the Japanese company is a social unit just as much as an economic unit. And the action of management and labor can never be grasped without taking the social arrangements into account.

In order to hold on to its staff, the company offers many benefits that are not readily available elsewhere. Over and above the wages, the company often provides dormitories or housing, medical care, perhaps its own doctor and clinic. It promises a welcome retirement payment or pension after the career with the company is over and sometimes also a second job. It subsidizes meals in the company canteen and pays for travel expenses to work. It often goes so far as to provide sports grounds, club rooms, and vacation homes. The frills vary with the size and wealth of the company, but there are always special advantages that make the employees depend more heavily on the employer.

Not only are there material facilities of this sort, the company also takes an active interest in the life of its employees. From the very start, the personnel division carefully looks into the family background and personality of prospective staff. It informs them of their duties and sees to it that they accept their responsibilities. On the other hand, it also shows unusual interest in how the employee is doing. Any sign that a person is poorly accepted or discontented will be noted. If there are personal problems that can be solved, assistance will be offered. In short, it pries into the employee's personal life to an extent that would hardly he accepted elsewhere but seems quite normal in Japan.[10]

Going considerably further, the personnel division carefully organizes the original training and initiation sessions when the new staff is welcomed into the company. It follows up by seeing that the new personnel is well integrated in their sections. Outside of work, there may be lessons, classes, parties, trips and the like to allow staff members to meet one another. Some companies even go so far as to have their own clubs to encourage matrimony and many a manager would propose a person in *omiai* and appear at the wedding as the go-between.

The foreman or supervisor also does his bit. He shares most of the work activities with his subordinates and eats in the same canteen. He is encouraged to be as friendly as possible and is evaluated by his ability to get along with, as opposed to directing or ordering about, his men. He may take this a step further and join them periodically in their drinking bouts outside of work. Having created this rapport, he is repaid with trust. His subordinates will work harder and show greater loyalty so that he looks better in the eyes of higher management. In return, he is expected to prevail in their favor if there is trouble.[11]

Among the white-collar workers, the section chief or *kacho* performs much the same tasks. He is not meant to be a supervisor in the sense of keeping a sharp eye out for mistakes. Rather, he offers a presence so that when his subordinates are in need of advice or think they have made a mistake, they can come to him. Even if they make foolish errors, he would tend not to criticize too harshly for fear of destroying the rapport he has striven so hard to create. Instead, he may just chide them or actually assume the responsibility. In addition to this, our poor *kacho* has to spend countless hours drinking with his staff to get to know their innermost feelings.

Finally, the president and top directors, aside from their normal tasks in running the company, have a whole array of ceremonial tasks which keep them busy making speeches, officiating at meetings, attending receptions and so on. They must also appear as peace-makers if there are disputes among the lower level managers or help smooth over differences between sections and divisions. Indeed, at this level the social tasks are often so numerous that there is hardly any time left over for managing.

The web of social relationships, already quite dense by non-Japanese standards, spreads yet further. There are many informal relations that are equally important. Some of them are between employees of the same entry year. The men will tend to go out for a drink after work, the women perhaps for a coffee and cake. Those who studied at the same university, or worked together at the same overseas office, will also meet periodically. Many younger employees enter friendly links with older colleagues which over the years solidify into *oyabun-kobun* type relations. Through these various networks they will occasionally become part of broader cliques.[12]

Those in managerial positions will have further social demands placed on them. Relations with other managers, either on the same level or higher up, must be maintained formally as well as informally. Anyone dealing with either clients or suppliers cannot avoid getting to know them personally, for the greater good of their mutual relations. And this also entails a meal or an evening out for drinks. Just how far this custom goes is shown by repeated polls where many young salarymen entertain or meet colleagues at least once a week while some older ones almost never get home before midnight.

There is no doubt that such activities are extremely fruitful. They contribute to more harmonious relations between staff members at high or low levels. They oil the social relations that make business flow more smoothly. They create an essential rapport among those responsible for getting things done. In the context of lifetime employment, they are even more crucial than otherwise. For, working together a good twenty or thirty years, employees are more seriously in need of good friendly relations than

How to succeed in business. Social skills and connections outweigh commercial ability and know-how.

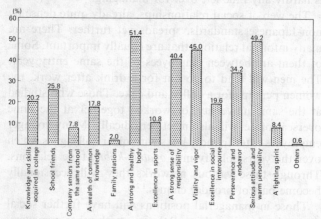

• *What is essential for life in the business world?*

(%)

Knowledge and skills acquired in college	20.2
School friends	25.8
Company seniors from the same school	7.8
A wealth of common knowledge	17.8
Family relations	2.0
A strong and healthy body	51.4
Excellence in sports	10.8
A strong sense of responsibility	40.4
Vitality and vigor	45.0
Excellence in social intercourse	19.6
Perseverance and endeavor	34.2
Serious attitude and warm personality	49.2
A fighting spirit	8.4
Others	0.6

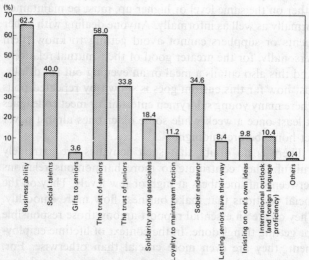

• *What is essential for getting ahead?*

(%)

Business ability	62.2
Social talents	40.0
Gifts to seniors	3.6
The trust of seniors	58.0
The trust of juniors	33.8
Solidarity among associates	18.4
Loyalty to mainstream faction	11.2
Sober endeavor	34.6
Letting seniors have their way	8.4
Insisting on one's own ideas	9.8
International outlook (and foreign language proficiency)	10.4
Others	0.4

Note: Multiple responses permitted.

Source: *Survey on attitudes of new employees toward work and life*, Dai-Ichi Kangyo Bank, March 1979.

if they would only be dealing with one another briefly or less directly.

The most palpable success has been to smooth relations between management and labor, something that could never have been accomplished purely through formal negotiations.[13] Rather than try to reason with the union when a strike action is in the offing, the personnel division and other officers will spend untold hours trying to explain things to the union officials beforehand. The rest of management will keep trying to win understanding from their subordinates. But this can only be done because the relations have been maintained all along and are not just established when there is an emergency. Harmony prevails not because it is demanded but because the company has been promoting it from the start.

Nevertheless, just as for everything else in business, keeping up human relations has a price. There are good reasons to believe that this price is terribly high.

First come the direct costs. The various aspects of welfare are not inexpensive. Most companies offer an impressive array of allowances from commuting, to dangerous work, or postings in remote areas. Some contribute to medical insurance, social security, and old age pensions beyond the legal requirements. Frills like company picnics, company trips, and company parties add up. If they also provide subsidized housing, or just housing loans, the burden becomes heavier. Welfare can run rather high, representing as much as 14% of earnings plus another 5% for retirement payments according to Nikkeiren.[14]

In addition to this, there is the far from minor expense of entertainment offered clients and suppliers. Given the many pretexts for such activities, this also mounts up quite rapidly. In fact, in 1979, total business entertainment costs were estimated at ¥2.9 trillion.[15] This represented about

"Getting to know you," Japanese company style.
A costly, but necessary, operation.

Photo credit: Matsushita Electric Industrial Co.

¥4.6 for each ¥1,000 of sales and amounted to a massive flow of nearly ¥8 billion a day spent on wining and dining at a time when nearly half the companies were making losses rather than profits. The total was about as much as Japan's companies spent for R&D or the government for elementary education.

No less important, these activities are tremendously time-consuming in that any number of people, not only in the personnel and sales divisions but throughout the hierarchy, have to take it upon themselves to create better relations. Since it is harder to pry open the shell of most Japanese, the time consumed is greater than in other societies. Since it takes a long time for business relationships to mature, and it is essential to keep them cordial, the entertainment stints have to be relatively frequent. So it is not only the direct costs but the time spent by staff in keeping up human relations that must be evaluated either in terms of extra wages or what else could have been accomplished by the persons concerned. On this basis, the price may be staggering.

Obviously, since the recession, companies are more concerned about reducing costs and they increasingly wonder whether these particular costs are not too high. An added reason for doubt is that the companies seem to be getting less back for their investment than ever. After all, the purpose of company welfare and entertainment is not just to spread good will but to keep the personnel working diligently and showing loyalty. In the meanwhile, what was once a gift has often turned into a right. Unions now regard welfare facilities as their due and even bonuses, once given out at its option by the company, have become regular payments which are painfully negotiated each year.

Despite everything they give, and although morale is still high by international standards, Japanese companies are certainly not getting the same old dedication. No matter what they do they cannot convince the new classes of salarymen to relinquish all their other concerns and interests. That is because, with a different upbringing and life style, many younger employees feel that they are not getting what they want either. The price for surrendering their "self" to the company is too high when what they want most is to get back home, see their family or engage in sports and leisure.

Thus, the old social contract between management and labor, the contract that has never been written down but is almost as important as the employment contract, may be altered seriously in the future. The company will count what it gives more stingily just as its employees begrudge the time and emotion they have to invest. Increasingly Japan will become a society in which people work for a salary and expect their rewards in material rather than moral form.

The Bureaucracy-Man

Although the term "salaryman" is derived from English, in practice the Japanese salaryman hardly compares with an office worker, middle manager or other employee in the Western world. The model for the Japanese management system, despite any superficial resemblance, does not seem to be that of Western management. Actually, the salaryman barely even resembles a businessman, whether an entrepreneur or less dynamic type. Looking for Japanese parallels is also confusing. The basic inspiration does not appear to be the Edo merchant, nor the rich landowner, nor the *samurai*. If anything, it is the bureaucrat.

The salaryman is recruited much like a bureaucrat.[16] He is not hired for a specific job but membership in a given group. New entrants are taken in once a year at the bottom. What is sought is more the generalist than the specialist and more stress is placed on loyalty than ability. Thus, the test to screen new entrants consists of some generally accessible knowledge and then a much more careful examination of personality to see how one's character fits in with the prevailing mentality. Attention is paid to the schools one attended, one's family background, and increasingly character references from sponsors or other connections.

The process is very similar to the choice of Japanese bureaucrats for the civil service. Many of the same people who end up in a Japanese business concern might just as well have entered a government department. In fact, many of the college graduates, and increasingly high school grads as well, apply both for jobs in government and business, indifferently. The earlier preference for business, with its possibilities of rising to the top, is now succumbing to interest in government, where one's career is calmer and more secure. Thus, a tendency to adopt a bureaucratic mentality is spreading even among young people from whom one might have expected more ambition.

Once within a company, promotion is gradual, one step at a time, just like a bureaucrat. One reaches managerial positions not through clear signs of talent but by slow movement along the spiral staircase. True, more clever or dynamic individuals may arrive a bit earlier, but only a wee bit. And they arouse enmity among those they pass. Ambition is not really rewarded by the system and it is penalized by all those who fear they cannot do as well. Thus, every effort so far to introduce merit rating, evaluation of work, or even job descriptions that would single out individuals and make it possible to see how well they perform, as opposed to others, has been rejected. Seniority, although not fully approved of, is accepted as the safer and "more objective" means of promotion.

Of course, some people do make it to the top and others get stuck further down. Doubtlessly, those who show greater ability will have an advantage. But this is balanced by another bureaucratic trait, namely the role of personal connections. They often arise out of the job rotation system, a method rarely followed by commercial enterprises elsewhere. Over the years, the salaryman is shifted from office to office, job to job, and gets to know the company as a business. He also gets to know the people who make up the company and establish personal relations with them. He creates a network of personal relations that will ultimately help him and in the meanwhile aid those above him, his friends and sponsors, his *sempai* or *oyabun*, to rise. The guiding principle thus becomes not what you know but who you know.

The fact that a person's career occurs within the same company and that one is constantly dealing with the same people means the personal relations and subjective reactions frequently gain precedence over more impersonal and objective concerns. As long as an issue is relatively straightforward, where to place a machine, how to use it, or the like, there is little trouble. But almost all issues also have consequences for the people involved. Thus, for example, it might be harder to decide on investment, expansion, retrenchment, or especially personnel and promotion issues, because any decision is likely to raise or lower the status of those concerned. The hardest point is to admit the failure of past policy and especially to pin the blame for having introduced an unsuccessful measure.

Despite the breathe of democratization after the war, a bureaucratic system like Japan's does not take long to replace the old order with a new ranking. Thus, there are clear distinctions once again between white-collar and blue-collar, between men and women, between those with or without titles. The competition for a title, any title, has become so intense that many companies have to grant titles when employees reach a certain level (or just age) although they are not accompanied by an increase in responsibility and sometimes even salary. Yet, to forget one's position would be very dangerous. It is necessary for subordinates to address superiors correctly, using the proper polite language, and occasionally to make a modest bow. Even the petty distinctions between those who entered a year earlier or a year later, who is called *san* and who *kun*, have not disappeared at the bottom. Meanwhile, at the top, the bowing and scraping is tremendous, a grotesque reminder of the days when the elite bureaucrats were also high ranking *samurai*.

It is not that the basic motive is bad. Every company, factory, or store can do with a degree of institutionalization. For any human organism to run smoothly it is necessary to work out the best ways of doing things and then see to it that these ways are maintained. It is useful to lay down routines and procedures and keep them going. Rules and regulations have to be established and passed down so that one knows how to act in a given situation. But there must always be some flexibility so as to introduce changes when appropriate. And decisions once taken must not continue perpetually without carefully checking that the circumstances have not changed.

Unfortunately, Japan tends to be an unusually conservative society. It is extremely difficult to come to decisions or to create precedents. Once that is done, however, it is well nigh impossible to change them unless there are very compelling reasons. The first thing one does when an issue arises is not even to judge it on its own merits but to check the precedents. The most common reason for rejecting a proposal or request is quite simply ". . . since there are no precedents (*zenrei*)." In the world of business, however, things are always occurring for which there are no precedents although a bureaucracy dislikes such repeated challenges.

Going by the rules is fine. But a rule tends to bind a person even more when he is also encouraged to maintain harmony or follow tradition rather than show imagination or seize initiative. Thus, Japanese companies—like Japanese bureaucracies—tend to get bogged down under a mountain of precedents and rules that may no longer apply. And the method of reversing them is equally slow and bureaucratic: *ringisho* and meetings.

A bureaucratic approach can be very expensive as well. With the need to appear solid or powerful, staffs expand beyond normal needs and office space, let alone facade and decoration, are sometimes excessive. With a clear hierarchy geared not only to production or sales but to keeping up appearances and assuming status, it is too easy to give in to empire building. We all know of companies that have set up subsidiaries locally or opened offices abroad just to keep up with the competitors. What is worse, many have done so just because they had the staff on the payroll and did not know what to do with them. And sometimes a subsidiary was created simply so that those in power would have a place to retire to. For such reasons, Japan falls victim to all of Parkinson's laws with an exceptional facility.

Living within their own closed circle, namely a company whose members have largely been trained there and rarely worked anywhere else, Japanese salarymen tend to have a very limited horizon. They do not really know how things are done in other companies, aside from bits of gossip or short articles in the press. They know even less about how things are really done abroad. Thus, as Gojiro Hata, President of ECI, pointed out, the Japanese not only lack internationality, they also lack "intercompaniality."[17] That means that all they know is what is happening within their own company and their main advantage, as an executive, is to be able to react well there. But the abilities they show there may be worthless elsewhere. And certainly their most important asset, a solid network of intracompany connections, cannot be transferred.

This creates serious problems for their companies. Working together so long, the bureaucracy-men tend to think alike and act alike. Even if they hold radically different views, they hesitate to admit it. This is an excellent breeding ground for stereotyped reactions and group think. It is very dangerous when the range of options is cut down to this extent. A company in trouble would hardly know where to find advice or simply fresh ideas. There is little intake of older staff. Advisors are not really welcome. And business consultants have general solutions while companies are very specific. So, many companies continue struggling with their problems—some do not even realize that any exist—until they solve them by trial and error or the situation becomes so bad that they succumb.

Bureaucracy stifles initiative within the company. But it also spreads throughout the economy. When companies form groups and associations to defend their interests, they may surreptitiously smother competition. Lack of competition can harm the consumer. But it can undermine the economy in an even more decisive manner. It can snuff out the spark that led entrepreneurs not so long ago to launch new ventures that have since proven their validity. Only because the industrial structure was still loose and there was room for new companies could entrepreneurs like Soichiro Honda, Konosuke Matsushita, Akio Morita and many more rise.[18] Only because the distribution system had to be reconstructed could it be altered by people like Isao Nakauchi, Seiji Tsutsumi, and Noboru Goto.

Now, however, things have settled down considerably. Japan once again has its groups and quasi-*zaibatsu*, oligopolistic companies dominate most major fields, and distributors control the market by regulating the outlets. Government bureaucrats join together with company bureaucrats to encourage a more "stable" economy whereby there is an orderly growth or decrease in production and sales among those concerned. But there is no thought to the companies that do not yet exist or are too small to make their interests known. Japan, Inc. has always united the bureaucrats, but it was usually spurned by the most dynamic entrepreneurs. Now there is reason to wonder how many such entrepreneurs will see the light of day.

Thus, the spread of the bureaucratic mentality can be one of the gravest threats to Japan's economy. There is no reason to believe that bureaucratic modes are any good for business. Since one must constantly adapt to the market situation, try to match supply and demand, seek sales wherever they are available, keep up with technology and also introduce innovations, business is—or should be—a very lively field. The businessman's strong point is not solidity or stability but the ability to adapt and change. Crucial talents like business acumen, imagination, or simply competence, should be given far more stress than is possible in a bureaucracy. The field should be left wide open so that new ideas and new people can always enter.

One should not be misled by the views of some business leaders who claim that a time of recession is a time for greater control and conservatism. The opposite may be needed more. True, it is presently necessary to continue the companies that exist and to consolidate them further. With less chance for expansion and growth, stability must be sought. This sort of holding operation may appeal to the bureaucratic mind. But, to succeed, it is essential not just to maintain but to revamp, to restructure, and to reform. It is even more crucial to create. With fewer possibilities than in the past, one needs more imagination than ever to seek them out. This is not really the forte of the bureaucrat!

QC In The Office

For years now, Japan has been fooling the outside world—and more seriously, fooling itself—by presenting the sophisticated factories of its leading companies and making believe that this is the model followed throughout the economy. The sad fact is that these factories are not typical, they are the exception. They are a marvel of rationality and productivity in a general morass of inefficiency and pointless, if comfortable, waste.

These factories manage to combine the best of the West with the best of Japan. The modern machinery is there, the most efficient processes are used and improved upon, layout and engineering are tip top. The people are in the right place and used well. More important, their enthusiasm is aroused to some extent and they care more than their counterparts abroad about how things are done. But little of this can be found in the offices. No one cares much about time and motion studies and quality control is seldom heard of.

One tends to speak of the "Japanese system" as if it were a single integrated phenomenon. As we saw, the factory and the office are both Japanese, but they could be existing in different worlds. The rallying call of *wakon yosai* or "Japanese spirit and Western technology" revolutionized industry with the most modern techniques. In the administration, there is nothing but Japanese spirit, some of it terribly old and stultifying. What was good enough for the assembly line worker was apparently not good enough for the salaryman and manager. What could be accomplished on the shop floor was banned from the office.

This can be seen from the records of a leading manufacturing company, whose name shall not be mentioned because its performance is much better than average. The number of QC circles in its manufacturing plants far exceeds those in the marketing divisions or headquarters. In the offices, not only is the participation rate lower, the solution rate is minimal. Like many others, it holds management seminars at various levels. But this amounts to little more than another opportunity for the president and chairman to make speeches on the need for hard work and harmony. The company philosophy is thoroughly exposed but not the latest in computer technology or management techniques.

The offices have thus fallen far behind the factories in their degree of modernization and this gap has only grown as productivity in the factory kept increasing. Now, however, the improvements that can be sought in manufacturing are less easy to find and proportionately more expensive. The share of the administrative and white-collar staff has become too considerable. Thus, a higher priority must be attached to what can be done to update clerical and managerial functions. In this operation, it may no longer be possible to avoid changes in the sacrosanct Japanese management system.

It will doubtlessly be easier to introduce improvements at the lower level. Many clerical tasks are extremely routine, almost industrial-type tasks, and there is no reason they cannot be analyzed more carefully so that the work is carried out as efficiently as possible. This can involve time and motion studies; it would also gain from QC activities in which the people concerned study their own performance and make suggestions. The logical extension of this line of thinking will obviously be to automate and mechanize the simplest, most routine work. The move has started in the United States with all sorts of word processing equipment, computerized information supply, and recording and retrieving systems.

However, it is not certain how fast this will progress in Japan since lifetime employment makes it impossible to dismiss personnel just because their task has become redundant. American industrial engineers visiting Japanese offices recently were amazed to find that some companies had introduced the latest computers . . . but kept on the staff although it had nothing much to do. Doubtlessly, some of the staff will ultimately be assigned to other tasks. However, during a recession, these other tasks may not be terribly useful either. Consequently, some companies will not bother using the latest gadgets because they do not know what to do with the surplus staff.

Going yet deeper, many companies will not introduce some of this modern equipment because they treasure the human element, or so they claim. It is amazing how the banks in particular can use not one but two rows of pretty but superfluous girls in uniform to handle simple routine tasks. What they can do that a machine cannot is to smile, bow pleasantly, and add that personal touch. But they cannot be done without because their work is the sort of thing no man would accept. Similarly, even when companies introduce minicomputers in the office, assistants will be recruited to handle them since such work is beneath any self-respecting manager.

It is just as hard to understand how Japanese employees can still devote endless hours to holding meetings within the company and yet more time to visiting clients on the other side of the city or consulting suppliers out in the suburbs at every occasion. Other societies have realized that a person's time is too precious to spend in friendly visits or formalities. But Japan continues this exorbitant waste of human resources because of the great stress on personal relations. So, the biggest revolution, and the greatest increase in productivity, would come from a simple and rational use of the telephone and mail.

Efficiency would also be improved substantially if not only computers were used to store data but also simple sheets of paper. The reporting systems are clearly inadequate, meetings which take up tremendous time are left without written records to guarantee that everyone knows the results and even solemn agreements regarding sales and prices are not always given the formal consecration they merit. The Japanese often do not maintain a logical filing system and they detest a contractual society which, they claim, indicates that people do not trust one another. However, it must be obvious that this protects the party in the right more than the party that breaks an agreement and thus should not reflect poorly on mutual relations unless one party is unworthy of trust.

Among the rising salarymen and managers, one should expect more specialization than in the past. Some of the tasks have gotten so complex and sophisticated over the years that they cannot be learnt through quick in-service training and it would be foolish to waste accumulated experience by switching people to other posts. Those tasks which can best be handled by a single individual should increasingly fall outside of group activities. Teamwork is an excellent characteristic of the Japanese system. But, while some things can be done best in groups, others either cannot or are made too costly and inefficient.

As smaller units like sections and divisions are given more specific tasks, and some become profit centers, the role of middle management will shift from a somewhat withdrawn one to more active supervision and direction. If it becomes clear that the *bucho* or *kacho* are responsible for how their subordinates perform and their own hopes of promotion are related to success in direct terms such as sales or profits, they cannot afford to be a gentle father figure or entrust their fate to decisions reached at rambling group meetings. They may also find that the old style *mikoshi*-leadership, arousing staff for a task, then urging it on again when the ardor drops, produces a stop-and-go pace that is not very conducive to their aims during the long haul. Their approach may thus come to resemble that of Western managers a bit more and they are likely to use Western techniques that provide at least a quasi-scientific basis for decision-making and management.

Similar changes may occur at the top. There is a need for much tighter organization than in the past. Too many companies grew in a rather uncoordinated way, adding new branches, subsidiaries, and products as the occasion arose. They are none too well integrated now and obviously some acquisitions were better than others. The time has come to relate them to one another and perhaps weed out those that contribute least to financial success. There is also a need for closer supervision over the lower levels of the hierarchy. Power has been accumulating with the managing directors and they can be expected to use it, especially if they want the well earned reward of president one day.

During the period of rapid growth, ambitious and dynamic leaders were needed, production was the main function, and growth the clearest measure of success. Now that the situation has changed drastically, strong but cautious leaders concerned more with profitability (or at least avoiding losses) should be coming to the fore. Not only will they be different types of men, their expertise is more likely to reside in finance or marketing. Those with skill at directing research will also be sought. Meanwhile, the managers may learn that a company does not grow best in sudden spurts and that balance is more desirable: balance between production and sales, balance between receipts and disbursements, and balance between own resources and dependence on banks.

Changes are obviously coming. As soon as growth slowed down, companies had more time to show an interest in profits (and how to pay back the tremendous sums they had borrowed). And the oil shock made it clear that Japan could not continue as it had in the past. Now most companies are primarily concerned with profits, which puts them on much the same wave length as their Western colleagues whose admonitions and advice they had scorned in the past. There is a vast array of measures developed in the West to deal with just the same problems cropping up in Japan today, but which are older there since the decline began earlier. Japanese companies are already picking among the methods and trying them out.

This is not the first time reforms are attempted. Many methods were adopted in the past. Some, like those introduced by Isuzu Motors at the suggestion of GM, were a success, such as more careful analysis of production costs, consolidated purchasing, and prudent calculation of the rate of return on investment. Others, including everything related to evaluation of personnel, failed. They failed to some extent because they were not implemented well and just became a modified *nenko* (seniority) system. They also failed because they did not fit into the Japanese style of group work. And they failed because they were rejected by those who would be hurt, primarily employees with high seniority who expected to gain least.

In the future, any new techniques will have to be carefully chosen if they are to be integrated. They will obviously also be modified once they are applied by Japanese in Japanese companies. But there will always be some resistance. This time, if Japan is to succeed, the resistance will have to be overcome. If modern methods, upsetting many traditional customs, could be adopted in the factory, they can in the office as well. They may even find considerable approval among younger employees or those who want to show their ability. If they are subverted by those who fear they may lose, the final result is likely to be that everyone will lose in the long run.

NOTES

1. See Kazukiyo Kurosawa, *Productivity Measurement of White-Collar Workers*, Tokyo Institute of Technology, 1980.
2. See Arthur M. Whitehill, *The Other Worker*, pp. 196–205.
3. See Rodney Clark, *The Japanese Company*, and Thomas P. Rohlen, *For Harmony and Strength*.
4. For a comparison of Japanese and American work ethic, see Robert E. Cole, *Work, Mobility & Participation*, pp. 224–50.

5. See Ezra F. Vogel, *Modern Japanese Organization and Decision-Making*.
6. *Japan Economic Journal*, June 10, 1980, pp. 36–9.
7. Ibid.
8. *PHP*, December 1975, pp. 60–1.
9. See Byron K. Marshall, *Capitalism and Nationalism in Prewar Japan*.
10. See Rohlen, op. cit.
11. See Ronald P. Dore, *British Factory-Japanese Factory*, and Robert E. Cole, *Japanese Blue Collar*.
12. See Jon Woronoff, *Japan: The Coming Economic Crisis*, pp. 41–7.
13. See Tadashi Hanami, *Labor Relations in Japan Today*.
14. *Survey of Welfare Costs*, Japanese Federation of Employers' Associations.
15. *Japan Times*, December 15, 1980.
16. See Robert J. Ballon, *The Japanese Employee*.
17. *Jitsugyo-no-Nihon*, December 1, 1978.
18. For example, see Nick Lyons, *The Sony Vision*.

3
Updating The Management System

The Management System Crumbles

Even foreign visitors know all about the typical Japanese management system. It is presented to them as the secret of Japan's economic success. You have lifetime employment, payment by seniority and promotion gradually along the career escalator. Since personnel will remain with the company for their whole career, it is willing to provide in-house training and takes in generalists rather than specialists. The cornerstone of the whole structure is loyalty to the company, whereby not only the management but the enterprise union show unusual dedication and abnegation, accept to work hard, care for the company's reputation, and see to it that it succeeds.

The Japanese know that this idyllic picture is somewhat overdone, that the typical system only applies to the bigger companies and even there only includes regular workers. They know that there are imperfections and drawbacks. What worries them far more now is that the management system itself is undergoing tremendous pressure. This has already wrought substantial changes and the system may not exist in its present form in just another five or ten years. Some of the changes are feared while others are hoped for and desired by some of the salarymen—although not all. But the biggest concern is probably that no one really knows what the future holds in store. If there is anything the Japanese dislike, it is confusion and uncertainty.

Yet, this has been the situation ever since the oil crisis and it is clear to everyone that the most solid pillars of Japanese economic life are being shaken and the old management system has begun to crumble. This creates much more serious problems for most companies than the various concrete concerns such as updating techniques and modernizing office practices and managerial methods. What arises now is a problem of morale that is bound to spread until a new Japanese system is formed.

That there should be changes in this "typical" system is hardly surprising. After all, despite any insistence on its traditional roots, the system only came into existence after the Second World War. It had precedents before. But the present arrangements did not exist in Tokugawa Japan, in Meiji Japan, nor in prewar Japan. In fact, the system as such still does not exist in smaller companies or for the masses of temporary employees. Being less pervasive and systematic than claimed, it is natural that it could be shaken by something major.

The decisive weakness has proven to be that the management system was highly effective in times of rapid growth and economic boom. Since such conditions existed from shortly after the war until the oil crisis, many seemed to think that they would last forever and thus the system could be maintained forever. However, no sooner did the drop in profits, the need to reduce staff, the uncertainty about future business trends appear, than management itself had second thoughts.

Obviously, when the economy was expanding, it was important to bring in as many employees as possible and hold on to them until they might be needed. One could not afford to let them leave and have to train new ones. The switch into new branches and sectors also made it useful to have generalists, who could be trained for many things, and would not have a vested interest in a given job. With a young work force, it was financially advantageous to pay seniority-based wages because most of the employees were on the lower steps of the escalator. And rapid expansion meant that an employee's devotion could be more readily rewarded by promotion and wage hikes.

Now Japan's managers are discovering the disadvantages of the system. One that was bound to come anyway arose out of the aging of the population. All of a sudden, rather than most people being on low wages, more were earning high ones and the companies were pricing themselves out of the market. With the recession, they often quite simply had too much staff and had to oust some . . . loyalty or no loyalty. Here they encountered the resistance of the unions. From often bitter opponents of lifetime employment, which meant a regimentation of labor, they switched to its strongest supporters in the guise of "job security." But they were not enough to block the changes and in some ways were not really interested in doing so.

What then will happen to loyalty? Those who assume that loyalty is an inherent Japanese virtue may assume that it will not change. Those who know Japanese history better will realize that it is equally perishable and that the tremendous fuss made about loyalty results not from its spontaneous presence but the need to nurture it. The whole management system, in very subtle manners, creates a solid material foundation for that spiritual trait. It is encouraged palpably by higher wages for longer years service. It is enhanced by promotion from within the organization. And it is oiled by company entertainment, human relations, and welfare. If that foundation were to become less solid there is no telling what might happen.

A collapse of the present system could be disastrous. There is no reason to suppose that employees who no longer expect lifetime employment nor are guaranteed promotions will not seek what is best for them. If they have greater know-how and specific skills, they will find it much easier to enter the job market alone. With larger personal savings, more state-funded social security, and perhaps unemployment benefits to tide them over for a while, they could take the leap. This does not mean that job hopping would set in immediately. The offer would have to be rather good to make them betray their allegience. But, once started, this kind of action would become more natural and easier to engage in.

However, despite threats like a loss of loyalty and an ultimate collapse of the present system, the future does not necessarily offer a doomsday scenario. There are just as many promising elements. While growing individualism among the younger generations can erode loyalty, it can also increase initiative and imagination. If given a bigger chance than has been offered young people in the past they might respond by making greater efforts. If payment by merit or performance becomes a serious alternative to payment by seniority, there could be a sharp increase in ability and professionalism. Basing company relations more on money than loyalty has the advantage of each side knowing what it is giving and what it can expect in return. And, even if the company becomes a somewhat looser organization, that does not mean that the economy as a whole must suffer since new outlets may be created for those with greater drive or original ideas.

The essential point is not that change is coming. It cannot be avoided. More important is how Japan reacts to the change and how it uses the opportunities. Depending on what is done today, the management system of tomorrow can be better or worse.

From Master Sergeant To Baby-Sitter

Japan's personnel officers have been through a lot in past years. Just after the war, when they had to enroll the masses of returning soldiers to rebuild the economy, they probably felt like master sergeants. Gradually, as a new peacetime generation arose, they adopted a position closer to that of a big brother. Then, with even younger generations, they switched to a pose not unlike that of a surrogate father. And now, when today's youngsters come of age, they may have to engage in a form of baby-sitting.[1]

The change in the outlook of workers has been drastic and, as far as personnel officers are concerned, hardly encouraging. From year to year they welcome new classes of high school and university graduates and from year to year they find that it is harder to teach them the ropes and make them happy, loyal workers. Even temporary improvements are not always helpful. There certainly was a good deal of relief when the student radicals were replaced by more relaxed types. But screening out the radicals was probably easier than invigorating and motivating relatively soft human material. Employers asked for a blank sheet of paper, not putty!

It was not very hard to direct the remnant of the Meiji generation. They had been brought up on patriotism and hard work. It was enough to show them the task, teach them the techniques, and then convince them of the importance of performing well. The Taisho-generation workers were less tough, after all, they had grown up in the time of thought control and, although they could follow instructions nicely, they sometimes lacked initiative. Even among those born in the early Showa period it was possible to find the essential human material to create good company men. The *moretsu shain* (dynamic employees imbued with a *samurai*-like spirit) performed

Now, sing the company song, recite the company slogans and
go back and work!

Photo credit: Matsushita Electric Industrial Co.

well and are still at the forefront of every production or
sales campaign.

It was not so easy to get the "my-home" and "new
family" generations moving. They were certainly less
interested in the job than the earnings it brought. They
were working more for money than for patriotism or
satisfaction. But burdened down with the cost of a house
and striving to lead a "new family" life style, they could
not slacken the pace much. Anyway, they were at first in a
minority as compared with the *moretsu* type and would
have looked bad if they too obviously showed reluctance
to work as hard.

However, as far back as 1964, the majority of managers
surveyed thought that young employees tended to work
no more than was directly asked of them and that they
lacked eagerness and interest in work. And more such

employees joined the work force all the time. By 1980, a Nippon Recruit Center survey of male freshman employees showed that those who insisted that their main purpose in working was "to create a fulfilling and enjoyable home and family" outnumbered those who said "it is all right to sacrifice family life to some extent in order to put one's soul into the job" by more than two to one.[2] Thus, the workaholics were clearly being replaced by "my-home" and "new family" types.

All this while, things have been getting harder for the personnel officers. First, they had to face the fact that there was a nasty anti-business attitude among many young people. The late 1960s and early 1970s were an era of student revolt and the number of radicals rose considerably. Some of them gave up their views, at least visibly, as soon as the time came to join a company. But others kept them and worked their way into the unions, bringing a new toughness. The end of the student troubles seemed to spell a better period and, on the surface at least, the candidates were very correct and well-mannered. Underneath, however, there was bound to be difficulties. For the newcomers were clearly choosing employers on the basis of what they could get out of them and not what they could contribute. The ideal company was a large, growing and stable one which offered a nice working atmosphere and good wages and welfare facilities.[3]

It hardly looks as if the companies will fare better in the 1980s. Increasingly, the philosophy prevalent among teenagers is that one should follow a life at one's own pace and the favorite life style is regarded as easygoing. These people have been pampered as children, given pretty much what they want with little effort to attain it, then overprotected in most inessentials while dominated in such important matters as education and marriage. They have little backbone and are referred to as the *shirake sedai* (reactionless generation). Some of them were, of course, serious and diligent. But the whole batch had to be integrated in the work process, not only the better elements. That this did not quite succeed is shown by the appearance of Japan's first dropouts.

No one really knows for sure what the following crop will be like. Judging by the indications available, it is even less promising. Brought up neither by father nor mother but largely the television, knowing nothing but affluence in most cases, often living in imaginary dream worlds which their parents allow them to perpetuate, they might be called the Patty-and-Jimmy generation. The late-maturing Japanese have never matured as late and the behavior of these children is similar to that of children much younger in other countries. How they can be turned into a dynamic, or even passable, work force is hard to imagine.

Thus, the time of the workaholics and even the radicals has been replaced by the time of increasingly limp workers and *amaé*.[4] This latter element is particularly important since it draws a sharp line dividing two types of postwar generations. Both of them were individualistic. But the earlier ones did not hesitate to speak out and stand up for their rights, even to the point of engaging in riots. At the same time, they repeatedly insisted that they hoped to contribute to society. The more recent ones have also been individualistic, except more in the sense of doing one's own thing and wishing to be left alone. If it were necessary to conform externally, that could be done. In return, as few as 5.8% replied that they wanted to contribute to society in the 1977 youth survey.[5]

This may explain how, in one way, they could follow in the tracks of their predecessors, while still being quite different. Ever since 1953, the Statistics Institute of the Ministry of Education has carried out a periodic survey asking young people what sort of boss (*kacho*) they would like to serve under. The choice is between one who is relatively lenient at work but is otherwise unconcerned about the life of his subordinates and another who is demanding but "looks after people well outside of work." The latter has always been most popular. But, in 1978, this alternative was chosen by fully 87% of the respondents.[6] This was the highest ever and the *amaé* syndrome would seem to have reached epidemic proportions.

It is hardly surprising that this kind of boss should be desired by a generation of youngsters that has grown used to living under protectors, whether mothers, teachers, older colleagues or others. It is natural that they should look for someone to care for them at work as well. However, the problems that can arise from such an attitude are perfectly clear to some. According to the *Japan Times'* editorialist: "Our interpretation of this desire is weakness. If so many workers want only to be taken care of—their bosses substituting for their nursing mothers, it seems—where are the leadership and initiative going to come from?"[7]

Alas, it is not only a question of leadership but even of suitable followers. For, the *amaé* urge does not always go coupled, as it did in the past, with a desire to reciprocate. Many youngsters feel that they have a "right" to be looked after without a corresponding "duty" to help others. This means they could not be drawn into the traditional Japanese system. Decision-making from the bottom up or work in small groups with relative independence, which are the underpinnings of the system, would have trouble functioning even as much as they do now. It may no longer be possible to count on the ordinary efforts of employees and workers without making correspondingly greater efforts to gain their understanding and fire what little ambition they may have.

On the other hand, there are some trends that show a

positive interest in work. In listing reasons for choosing a job, more and more young people concentrate on the job itself rather than company name or prestige. They prefer it because it is something they like to do, it takes advantage of the skills they have acquired, it is a challenge. Work, although frequently seen as a drab duty, is also regarded as a way of contributing to society or leading a meaningful life by some of them. Surprisingly enough, many young people claim they would voluntarily work diligently "because it will contribute to my self-attainment even if it fails to attract attention."

Even some apparently negative traits have a silver lining. Many students reject work in big companies and say they intend to change jobs or become self-employed in the future. This, of course, looks like a lack of patriotism to the big companies. But it may finally offer a chance to small ones. Indeed, it may actually lead to the rise of new entrepreneurs who create their own companies. Other forms of individualism indicate that it will be possible to maintain a somewhat drier atmosphere in the companies, where people will work for their pay but the company can at least save on its efforts at superfluous human relations. Even while salary becomes the top priority in choosing a job, it is accepted that there be a relationship between pay and what one accomplishes (as opposed to one's seniority).

One could hardly claim that the positive factors outweigh the negative ones. Still, they are promising. The big problem, however, is that they do not fit in very well with the Japanese management system as it presently exists. This means that the good points will be useless or harmful as long as they conflict with the present state of affairs. They can only bear fruit if they are accepted, or at least integrated, in the future system.

Dragged On The Escalator

Young people no longer seem quite so eager to stay on the career escalator. Of course, they want a good job. Of course, they want to get into good companies. This means almost by definition that they will be a tiny cog in a huge machine and that they will get on an escalator that sometimes looks more like a conveyor belt. But what is new is that many of them, after a short ride, think very seriously of getting off. And some of them eventually do.

When they arrive at the company, they repeat pat phrases like "I am here because I think I can serve your company" or "I have come because I think highly of your company." But everyone knows that they make such statements because they want to get the job. Before they came, however, the candidates looked very carefully into the situation of the company, its wage scale, the chances of promotion, its relations with other companies, its hopes of survival. Actually, wanting to serve the company was considerably less important than finding out if it would be able to look after them properly during a long career.

This is shown most by the meticulous way in which they rank companies and the feeling that, although fresh out of school, with no experience and few skills, there are a vast number of companies that rank so low they would not set foot there. Even among those they deign to visit, there is a clear ranking. Their good will decreases as the ranking falls, although they may accept the job. This is mentioned mainly because most freshman salarymen end up in companies that are not at the top of their list. This is quite natural. Since everyone chooses the same leading companies only a small minority can possibly get in while the others go to the second, or third or nth choice.

This me-first attitude carries over to the first few years of work when they wonder if the company is really

The age of job hopping dawns. Share of those visiting government employment offices who wish to change jobs.

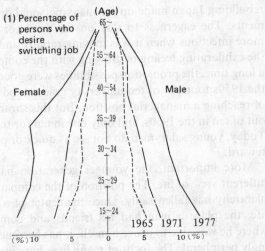

(1) Percentage of persons who desire switching job

Female   Male

(Age)
65 ~
55 ~ 64
40 ~ 54
35 ~ 39
30 ~ 34
25 ~ 29
15 ~ 24

1965 1971 1977

(%) 10   5   0   5   10 (%)

Source: *Employment Status Survey*, Bureau of Statistics, Prime Minister's Office and *1979 Report on National Life*, Economic Planning Agency, p. 134.

suitable for them and not, vice versa, whether they are contributing much to it. (As a matter of fact, they rarely contribute much in these first years.) About six in ten actually think of changing jobs and four in ten do change somewhere along the line.[8] Among young people, three changes—once anathema—is no longer unusual. But they do not go much further since the escalator keeps on moving and the potential losses in getting off begin to exceed the conceivable gains. It takes a number of years, and the accumulation of vested interests in the form of wage increments and promotions, for the salaryman to change from a me-first to a company-first attitude.

This sort of thing has always existed, an older salaryman may insist, if he can remember his youth. But it did not exist to the same extent in earlier years when you needed a job just to survive and when patriotism in rebuilding Japan made up for many personal disappointments. The eagerness to stay on the escalator was also more infectious when it was moving rapidly and one had the exhilarating feeling of growing with the company. For a long time, the promotion possibilities were good. During the 1950s four out of ten university grads stood a chance of reaching a managerial position. But this shrank to two out of ten in the 1960s, and only one in ten for the 1970s.[9] Today, young salarymen do not see as quick or palpable a reward.

More important, the younger generation has a very different view of life. The position of the company in this hierarchy has fallen sadly. Once the center of a person's life, the place a man had his friends and companions, where he was able to prove himself, it has become increasingly peripheral. The focus of many lives has since moved to the home, where a person can be alone and act as he will, and the family, where a new life style that clearly denies that of the workaholic can be fostered. The patriotic young men and eager beavers of yesteryear are being replaced by my-home and new family types, and they in turn by relaxed and easygoing successors.

Meanwhile, the company has become less a sponsor and protector than a competitor or opponent, a body that will keep them away from what they claim—and perhaps feel—they desire. Getting dragged into the old routine of company relations is avoided. More employees stick with their colleagues of the same age rather than entering into *oyabun-kobun* relations. They are less willing to join the race for titular posts. They think little of putting in overtime just to show their superiors how serious they are and often gripe even if the overtime is justified by work that has to be done.

Their distaste for company life is coupled with a growing distaste for hard work, or so it would seem. In official statements, the younger generation is usually praised. In private comments, it is often enough admitted that they do not work quite as hard as expected and they certainly do not show the same old spirit. The workaholics among them are rare birds, not always liked by their colleagues. Even while many work, their heart is not quite in it. But, what else could be expected of a generation that repeatedly lists as its primary goal to "lead an easygoing life" or to "live at my own pace?" Work in a company is the exact opposite of that.

Some claim that once on the career escalator they must conform. Alas, the seniority system only makes things worse. Since everyone will progress pretty much at the same rate, there is much less pressure for an individual to work harder than the others. If anything, he can get away with working less and still not suffer particularly. Moreover, when a growing number of them relax their efforts, this has a negative effect on the others, who find less purpose to working harder or being more dedicated. In the end, the company itself proceeds at the pace desired by those in it. And the time is already approaching when the majority will consist of people who are more interested in slowing it down than speeding it up.

On the other hand, there are also young people who work harder not only because they hope to catch their superior's eye and pull off a *shussé*. They often do so because they find their work interesting or feel that they can do something really special. This is probably one of the best reasons for working hard but one that is neither rewarded nor encouraged by the career escalator. It is geared basically to seniority with the faint hope that by being exceptionally capable one may rise slightly faster. So, in effect, it tends to discourage additional effort.

Thus, the only way to bring out the best in many young workers, although admittedly not all, would be to alter the wage and promotion structure to offer incentives for individual achievement. This is hardly a novel idea. The need was already conceded by many managers back in the early 1960s. By the end of the decade, Japan had supposedly entered the age of "personnel administration based upon ability." First a job classification system (*shikaku-seido*) was introduced in a somewhat modified form. Whereas Westerners paid a worker according to the job he did, the Japanese paid him according to what he was capable of doing, whether he actually did the job or not. Then, to determine the person's right to a given classification, one basically considered his educational background. And thus the reform was diluted to the point where it hardly rewarded special ability. The attempt to reward exceptional effort also failed. Whether it was called a "merit" rating, or payment by "performance" or anything else, it ended up being an evaluation of people rather than what they did. Moreover, the rating a person received tended to be aligned on experience, namely seniority in a given category. When one adds the fact that none of these allowances ever represented a large share of total earnings, it must be admitted that Japan's half-hearted attempt was hardly a success.

There were various reasons why none of these innovations worked. The primary one is the social system in which they functioned. Geared to an individualistic society in the West, they would either be crushed by Japan's group orientation or instead burst the traditional bounds of the company. Adapting them to Japanese circumstances was perhaps the wisest solution. But that meant weakening and distorting them as well. A second problem was that all such systems require a careful and objective evaluation of individual performance. In Japan, it is hard to judge an individual, although by no means as hard as claimed. To do this, however, one needs a proper evaluation body which does not exist even in the personnel division. And one needs a willingness of the subject to be evaluated. The Japanese are amazingly reluctant to undergo evaluation by others for fear they might not measure up. Giving a higher evaluation openly to someone would also spoil the smooth and amorphous harmony of the group. So, most employees have been left to evaluate themselves, hardly a purposeful exercise.

But the biggest barrier has been a combination of the generation gap and the vested interests of seniority. Merit systems of one sort or another have always been strongly supported by the younger employees. It gives them a chance to rise faster, to show ability they instinctively assume they have until proven otherwise, and to reach a position of responsibility (if not yet authority) in a shorter time than the interminably long wait on the career escalator. Those ahead of them, however, are afraid that they may be passed by some whiz kid who has better education but no experience. They have worked hard to get as far as they have and they want their effort and loyalty to be rewarded. Those at the top, and who would have to approve any change in the system, are the ones who have accumulated the greatest benefits under the seniority system and would gain nothing by a change. Thus, the older employees opt for the present system while the younger ones push for change. The president or some director may talk grandly of giving youth and ability a bigger role. But he does not want to rock the boat either.

Yet, if there ever was a time to alter the system even in some of its most fundamantal aspects, that time is now. True, the techniques imported from abroad didn't work in the 1960s. But the Japanese were much more group-oriented then. The more individualistic Japanese of the

1980s could make them work. Equally important, since they are the ones being stifled by the seniority system and losing interest in moral appeals for dedication, it would take palpable material incentives to make them work. This could not be done abruptly or overnight. But there is no reason the techniques could not be introduced gradually, first accounting only for a few percent of total wages so as not to treat those who have accumulated seniority unfairly. Over the years, depending on how things develop, the share could be expanded. For this, our individualistic Japanese would have to have the guts to undergo an evaluation and the human relations-oriented personnel division would have to create reliable and generally acceptable evaluation machinery.

Naturally, there will be dissatisfaction among those who are not singled out for special attention, who do not get early promotions, or whose wages are not enhanced. This can lead to unpleasantness and rivalry between younger and older employees, between more and less successful ones. It may be felt that this should be avoided to maintain harmony in the company. But it would be foolish to ignore that by doing nothing there is also a lot of unpleasantness which arises unavoidably out of the frustration of those who *do* want to work harder, to accomplish more, to rise faster, but find themselves hemmed in. If there has to be disappointment, it would be better that those who work less well or care less are penalized rather than those who could make a greater contribution if encouraged. Also, the very fact of rewarding extra effort and penalizing slackness would get everyone moving in the right direction.

Pushed Off The Escalator

There is a bitter irony about Japan's present employment situation. No country in the world makes so much fuss about loyalty to the company and seniority. Nowhere else is there as much lip service about not firing personnel in general and caring for the older ones in particular. Yet, when the recession struck after years of rapid growth, who were the first to be discarded? . . . the older employees!

It is thus not surprising to find the other most serious problems at the upper end of the escalator. Unlike the problems of younger employees, they do not seem to concern the company so much, at least not at first glance. After all, the company is trying to ease them out, not drag them in. So, after some token support and a few words of encouragement, much of the burden rests on the shoulders of the older men themselves. And those who bore the brunt of this were not the ordinary workers, the rank-and-file, since they were largely protected by the unions. It was the older salarymen, those who did not make it to titular posts (and some who did) and expected the better times promised them when they were young.

Recession or no recession, the Japanese employment system has an anomaly that would make the later years of any employee rather uncomfortable. The decision to make the compulsory retirement age 55 may have made sense back in 1902, when it was adopted and the average life expectancy was only 42. Since then it has increased to well over seventy. This means that the average employee must expect to spend another ten or twenty years trying to get by on funds that were never intended to carry him that far.

A first flaw is the gap of as much as five years until coverage under the pension schemes begins at 60. This was originally supposed to be met by the lump sum severance payment or the newer annuities. But they are not always adequate. The other flaw is that often the pension benefits themselves are not sufficiently generous to cover living costs at today's levels. Thus, a post-retirement job, either

Passing the West with the world's most rapidly aging population. Percentage of people 65 years old and over.

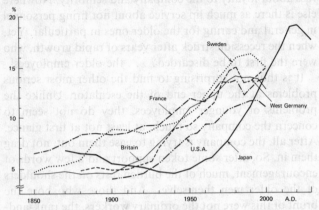

Source: Report of April 1979 for Council on Basic Ideas of Pension System (*Nenkin Seido Kihon Koso Kondankai*).

within the company, at a subsidiary, or outside, is almost a must. Yet, they were never intended to bring in as good a salary as the regular job and some were rather poorly paid. With the present recession, it has gotten harder than ever to find such jobs, more of them are part-time, and the rates are worse. It is not surprising that many old people are worried about how they will get by, what to do if they fall ill and cannot work, and whether their offspring will look after them.[10]

Recently there has been some improvement with the move to raise the retirement age to 60 and even higher. This is the stated goal of many trade unions and there is every reason to believe it will become generalized in a few years. After all, in an enterprise union comprising people desiring long tenure, everyone stands to gain by raising the retirement age. The only losers are those who will not be recruited when fewer posts fall vacant (and in some ways managment). The railways and steel companies have been most prompt in extending the retirement age and Matsushita has again been a pacemaker. However, the limitations of these plans must also be admitted. Under the Matsushita plan, employees have three choices: to continue on in the same job, to work for an affiliate, or to be prepared for self-employment. This is not much different, although more institutionalized, from the earlier system except for a retirement age of 65. That others will be less generous is clear from some railway plans. Those who stay on will first take a cut of 20% in wages, then only obtain half the average annual wage hike, and finally receive severance pay pegged largely to the wages at the old retirement age. It is broadly admitted that most companies cannot extend the retirement age and *also* keep on raising wages without facing severe financial difficulties.

Strangely enough, those in the most precarious positions are the middle managers. Although theoretically enjoying a higher status than the ordinary workers, they are not protected by the unions and are thus more exposed to pressure from top management. It is in the ranks of middle managers that the real "weight reduction" has been taking place. Many of the latest plans, including the railway schemes, have included the alternative of early retirement with increasingly large bonuses the younger one retires voluntarily. But this is just a generalization of the "selective retirement" that has been around ever since the oil crisis. Those who are willing to step down already between the ages of 40 and 50 are offered incentives. To encourage them to go, yet other plans have been increasing the share of efficiency allowance as of the age of 35 or 40 so that there is less advantage to accumulating more years of service. If they do not leave, some managers may be demoted and others given a "specialist" post instead. This is not an honor but a way of getting them off the elite ladder leading to top executive positions.

Despite all the lip service paid to lifetime employment, the companies have found ingenious ways of getting rid of personnel, all of them more sophisticated than Western-style layoffs, but having a similar result. There is the "golden handshake" which allows a man to step down with pride . . . but still no job. When times get worse, there is also the "tap-on-the-shoulder" and the offer of a modest bonus to withdraw gracefully from the company. This, too, accomplishes the task rather well. For the salarymen know that the next time they get a "tap-on-the-shoulder" the bonus will be much smaller and it is even possible that they will simply be fired. If not, they may wind up transferred to an unpleasant provincial or over-seas office, or put in a low-level subsidiary, or sent to the sales division, or demoted to an awkward position with colleagues and even superiors who are younger than they. These steps are usually combined with a freeze or reduc-tion in wages.

There is probably no doubt in the minds of the older men that a method will be found. Thus, many of them have become increasingly nervous and despondent. Those in what the Japanese call the "window-sill tribe," namely tired employees with a desk near the window and no work, seem to await their fate calmly without making any further efforts to prove their value or ability to the company. Other salarymen have begun brushing up on their ac-counting techniques, or learning a simple trade, or study-ing the job market just in case. Those who are determined to make good show a sudden burst of energy and a hitherto unsuspected drive.

Alas, when they do find themselves back in the job market, at the age of forty and over and nothing else to recommend them than that they worked for a pretty big company for over twenty years, the older ex-employees will be in a harder position than the youngsters fresh out of school. Whereas most of the school leavers can expect the equivalent of two job openings each, older people are usually two to an opening. Whereas the younger generation can enter reasonably good companies, the older generation is excluded and must accept the smallest companies and often the lowliest of tasks.

This often is a tragedy. It is not easy to start a new job at that age, especially in a society that looks down on those who change jobs and has trouble absorbing newcomers. It is painful to pass from a big to a smaller company. And it is far harder to accept an often lowly position after having enjoyed the prestige of relatively senior posts, or at least accumulated years of seniority, elsewhere. Young salarymen may joke about the middle managers who have become clerks, or salesmen, or janitors. For those concerned, it is anything but a joking matter.

The basic reason the companies are now trying to squeeze out the older employees is that, with seniority pay, they are earning considerably more than younger people although they lack the vitality, do not always have the same level of education, and their contribution is deemed inadequate to justify the pay. It was, of course, the company that offered supplements for staying with it, and thus the company that is responsible for the wage differentials and which should, in theory, accept to pay these debts now that they fall due. Perhaps it would like to; perhaps it doesn't really care. Anyway, all companies have a perfect excuse to renege on old promises now that hard times have come.

During the high growth of the 1960s, the seniority pay scale was already shifted in favor of the younger workers, since they were in short supply and had to be attracted with a better salary. Now, in the 1970s and 1980s, the companies can be expected to reduce the slope upward until the differentials are less considerable than before. At the same time, the peak is coming earlier, before 50, and then falls more rapidly. Although this, too, may seem unfair to the older employees, it is their only hope of salvation. As long as the financial burden seems higher than it is worth they will run a greater risk of dismissal. When their wages are lower, there will be less reason to reject their services.

Rather than regret these novel measures, many salarymen may be relieved by arrangements that clearly sort out the potential managers from the others at the age of about forty and give special priority to the former, who alone will enjoy the more usual prerogatives of seniority. The others, whose future career is dubious, will at least be given a reasonable choice: either retire and seek another path or stay on with a lower salary or lesser position. In either case, they would seem to avoid the worst alternative which is to be suddenly dropped from the payroll at an early age.

As a matter of fact, an amazing number of salarymen are taking the first alternative, namely to retire and go out on their own. As many as 89% of white collar workers questioned in a recent survey said that they would accept to retire earlier in return for increased severance pay and 45% were actually thinking of doing it. Unfortunately, the employers have learned to their regret that it is usually the most competent and dynamic personnel who leave and not the deadwood. Among those who would rather stay, the "specialist" system has aroused considerable interest. In the same survey, 65% replied that they were possible candidates for such posts.[11]

Nevertheless, this whole situation is extremely perilous because it attacks most directly the foundations of the existing system of lifetime employment. First of all, it makes a mockery of the nation's creed and traditions that unemployment should be most serious among older people. It is particularly ugly because the social security and welfare system was never built up enough to meet the present needs. Thus, older, unemployed persons may be in a financial pinch unless they are aided by friends and relatives. But the depths of Japan's shame is that those who are suffering most are the very ones who were responsible for raising the economy from the rubble and creating the affluence that now permits the companies to prosper and the young people to find work. Many of these people are patriots of a sort. But their reward was to be asked one last service, namely to sacrifice themselves for the sake of the company and a society that would not care adequately for them.

It would be hard to claim that all older employees know more simply because they have accumulated years. Their experience is not always pertinent or useful and perhaps their education is less valid than that of new entrants. But they do possess knowledge that should not be wasted as readily as it now is. In an enterprise-oriented economy, they can only be used purposefully and effectively where they were trained and integrated. What they have learnt is hardly transferable and thus they are worth pitifully little in any other company. (This may explain why they are so little sought after on the job market.) Thus, discarding them is a waste of human resources of a tremendous magnitude.

But this treatment of the older employees affects the whole company system. By discarding first those for whom the seniority arrangements were created, the companies are admitting to both older *and* younger workers that their word cannot be trusted. Whereas once they could call for loyalty and this would seem only fair, by showing their disloyalty to those who had served them longest they will hardly be able to inculcate loyalty in a younger generation for whom such appeals are suspicious anyway. Given the importance of social and human relations in Japanese companies, even the slightest hint that one may be dropped or demoted some time is enough to break the emotional ties and result in worsening performance.

This is apparently realized, albeit with some delay, by top management which is now trying to bring about a more orderly transition to a new system rather than the past frantic efforts to scrap excess personnel as quickly as possible. Some of the elements are an older retirement age but with less advantages, a decrease in seniority pay, and an earlier selection of managers while shifting less promising candidates into other specialized or professional positions. The selective retirement phase may be temporary or periodic, only necessary when personnel must be reduced rapidly. But there is no doubt that whatever reforms are adopted they will result in a radical break with the past and a fundamental change in the personnel system.

Kacho-byo And Other Illnesses

Doubtlessly, the most decisive level in the hierarchy is middle management. Unlike the Western-style pyramid, where top management tries to maintain full control over the workings of the company, much of the power is delegated to the *bucho* (department head), and by him to the various *kacho* (section chiefs), and on down. Not only is the power delegated, in many cases the middle managers are quite simply left to figure out how things should be done and held responsible for the results. Top management looks on, makes comments, but does not really intervene unless there are noticeable difficulties.

The middle managers thus provide the essential level at which overall policy is sorted out into day-to-day activities and where decisions are put on the way toward implementation. Although basic goals and policies come from above, as well as many specific orders, the middle managers also have to liaise amongst themselves to provide a suitable framework for overall action. Below them, power is also delegated, and sometimes just diffused, but there is no one who gathers as many vital strings together. Despite *ringi-seido* and the like, those at lower levels do not have as much leeway or play a crucial role. And they know that they must answer for performance to the *kacho*.

This makes the middle management, and especially the *kacho*, the most important joint in the company structure. They are where everything comes together. And they have a multitude of responsibilities, both administrative and social.

Their normal administrative work is quite considerable and not very different from a Western "boss." They have to decide which individual or group in their section will be entrusted with which task. With the loose job classification that exists, this may also imply helping to decide how the work should be done even in its practical details. They must check on the implementation and results, for they will ultimately win the praise for successful accomplishment or bear the blame for mistakes. They have to see to it that cooperation, as opposed to overlapping, duplication or competition, arises with other sections. But, in addition to directing and guiding, the *kacho* also have their own work to do. They have to deal with customers, bargain with suppliers, or make arrangements for work that is contracted out. In the sales division, for example, the *kacho* not only has to keep an eye on the other salesmen, he has to handle his own clients, usually the biggest and most important.

This is obviously not enough within the social context of the company. In order to get the most out of his subordinates, he has to show a kindly interest in their work and even their personal life. He may have to help them out of some difficulty, in the company or outside. This is then capped by a friendly drink after work or a periodic dinner with his younger colleagues so that they can get to know one another better than the office protocol permits. However, as a salaryman he also ends up drinking with the clients and suppliers. And, as an inferior, very concerned about keeping up good relations with top management, he would not turn down an invitation to dine with the *bucho* or others higher up.

Socializing, as was mentioned, is a very time consuming activity. It is not always a pleasant one, depending on who one sees and how often it must be done. By now many *kacho* regard this as a duty more than a pleasure and a "necessary evil" in the eyes of some. But it is made more painful by the fact that today's *kacho* are among the last Japanese who have much understanding for what Japan used to be like and can suitably deal with their superiors who are rapidly becoming fossils of another era. They are certainly not on the same wave length as their subordinates but at least they recognize the tune. So, they function as a sort of transmission belt between those on top and those near the bottom. But this transmission is hardly easy. They pass along the watchwords of loyalty, devotion, company spirit and the like, but they know the younger employees often snicker. They then try to explain to the stodgy old men why young workers no longer want to put in overtime or sacrifice their home life. It is an ungrateful task and brings them little benefit.

All this makes the *kacho* and some other middle managers the hardest working and most harrassed personnel. They put in long days at work with no extra pay for overtime. They have to put in long evenings at entertainment, sometimes at their own expense. They have to be not only competent in their own job but also reasonably

A staff that drinks together stays together.
If Japan can, why can't we?

Photo credit: Toyo Keizai

popular with their colleagues and subordinates. They have almost no personal life and no real home life. And they do not even take more than a few days vacation. This makes them the last of the workaholics.

A study by Keio University Newspaper Research Institute and Hashimoto Research Corporation compiled from the responses of about a thousand middle managers in several top companies supports this view. Some 45% of them said that they were willing to sacrifice their family life or their own time for their job. A good 30% replied that they were already sacrificing their home life for the company. As to their work in the company, only 25% thought of themselves as just ordinary clerical workers. Fully 69% said they were serving as well as supplementing top management. And 40% said that they were "overworked."[12]

But, what were they getting for this sacrifice? According to this poll, not enough. As many as 53% of them said that they were not satisfied with their present salary and another 9% said they were greatly dissatisfied with their salary. Partly they felt that their work was underestimated. More essentially, they realized that they were carrying proportionately the heaviest burden in the company. They had their normal administrative work. They had the tasks of leadership and social morale boosting. They also bore not only heavy but seemingly the primary responsibilities in the company. The *kacho* must shoulder the blame for a failure beneath them while their own failures lead to criticism from above. Yet, they were not being paid much more than others of the same age class with much less duties nor that much more than those further on down, while their salaries hardly began to compare to those in top management who did not always do much more (and sometimes considerably less).

When this study was made, back in 1975, the *Mainichi Shimbun* claimed that middle managers had the "blues."[13] But the situation became even worse with the years. For that was just before the wage freezes and cuts in managerial personnel. When it came to belt-tightening, top management, which could make little headway with the unions, usually turned the hatchet against middle management which could be eased out through appeals to company loyalty (of all things) sweetened by hefty bonusses.

Admittedly, there was a lot of deadwood in managerial circles at that time. Over the years, the career escalator had been forwarding many middle-aged people onto the level at which one is usually appointed manager. Obviously, no matter how rapidly the company expanded, there was not enough room for them all. So the company began inventing new and often pointless posts, even if they involved no special tasks or responsibilities nor even a rise in pay, but merely gave the man a title. This forest of managers, from assistant chiefs on up, tended to get in one another's way and it was necessary to clarify the lines of command. The easiest way of doing so was simply to get rid of some of them.

The rationalization then went a bit further. Obviously, not all the *kacho* could make it to *bucho*, and not all the *bucho* could become directors, nor all the directors, presidents. Rather than have them swelling the ranks of superfluous staff or kept on the payroll with little to do, a screening was introduced at managerial levels. Those who could progress further would be left on the escalator, the others shoved off. They would then be given the alternative of staying on in the company, often as a specialist or professional with a lower status and salary, or retiring and trying to make good elsewhere. Fitness to become a manager would be determined by informal methods and occasionally a promotion examination. A few companies even experimented with a "term" system whereby managers would be appointed for a fixed tenure and dismissed if they proved inadequate.[14]

So, added to all his other headaches, the middle manager had serious worries as to whether he would succeed. Sometimes he felt he was being watched too carefully by those who would decide his fate. At other times he was really in the hot seat, as the head of a profit center, and if he could not make profits well enough he might be on the way out. With this, the blues turned into the *kacho-byo* (*kacho*'s disease). Although a psychological and moral ailment, it even had a physical reflection. For some reason, men born in the Showa one-digit years had a higher mortality rate than earlier or later groups. It might have been due to their hardship during the war and rebuilding the economy. But much of the strain came recently.

This series of events could not help affecting the company. By making the middle managers the scapegoats for difficulties and putting more pressure on them, the strongest link in the hierarchy was being made a weak link. Middle managers could not perform as they were supposed to under all these demands. It was also hard for them to show the accustomed loyalty if they knew they might not be around much longer. Already back in 1975, 39% of the managers questioned said they occasionally thought of quitting the company and 4% said they would do so "very soon."[15] This was a striking change. And the trend only continued. Whereas those in their forties were still wed to the company on the whole, middle managers in their thirties tended to feel much less that they belong to their organizations than earlier classes had done according to a later Nippon Recruit Center survey.[16]

Meanwhile, the whole career escalator that was powered by successive classes of entrants who felt that they could reach a titular post and thought it worth making the effort was having a harder time in advancing. Whereas once everyone hoped to get a title some day and the theory of seniority promised this, by 1977 only 41% of the salarymen expected to reach section head and 28% department head. There were still more candidates than posts, since according to the Ministry of Labor the probability of reaching these posts was only 23% and 13%. But the competition was letting up.[17]

Since Japan's companies can hardly afford worried or discontented middle managers let alone a lack of people striving to fill the posts, they would be wise to find other ways of solving this crisis. The basic problem is that the *kacho* quite simply has too many things to do. He has his administrative tasks, his own work, and his social obligations. Not only is this too much for one person, some tasks require a different training or personality from the others.

In any other society than Japan, one would be tempted to say that the social aspects should be lessened or completely removed so that he can concentrate on real work. Let him plug at it during the day but at least be free to recover at night. In Japan, however, his primary concern is not to direct people but to motivate them, and this can only be accomplished by spending a tremendous amount of time with them. These demands will only decrease if the general office atmosphere becomes "drier," an existing tendency but hardly a dominant one. Thus, the *kacho* will have to remain someone his subordinates can relate to and trust rather than someone who is merely competent or orders them about. In return, he should be relieved of all possible tasks of his own as regards ongoing business. This could be delegated either further down for the less important assignments or up to the *bucho* for more prestigious ones. Or much of the work could be entrusted to the specialist positions being created. This would leave the *kacho* as a director, with tasks similar to the Western "boss," but an approach and personality that are nearly the opposite.

At any rate, as things stand now, being *kacho* is a killing job for the person concerned and one that few can accomplish to everyone's satisfaction. Something has to give: either one of the *kacho*'s responsibilities will be met less well or the *kacho* himself may succumb.

Heavenly Ascent And Descent

Throughout the world, it is unlikely that one could find normal commercial establishments that are as closed to the outside as the Japanese companies. That is partly due to recruitment at the bottom and promotion through the ranks and it is reinforced by the prevailing virtues of harmony and loyalty. The scattered individuals coming into a company are expected to mold themselves to its environment and, in so doing, form a society different from all others, one in which outsiders feel ill at ease and are rather hard to assimilate. Insiders, accustomed to working in a given manner, do not take to them well and are also worried lest they upset the customary practices or get in someone's way to a promotion.

Nevertheless, it is repeatedly necessary to work with outsiders. This means not only rank outsiders like clients or relative outsiders like suppliers and subcontractors. It also means any number of people who work intimately with the company, day by day, and some who also spend their career with it. For, in order to maintain lifetime employment for the regulars, it is necessary to have casual or temporary employees who can be called in when there is a sudden excess of work and who can be dropped once the aid is not needed. In addition, to keep the wages of regular employees higher, yet other people are brought in as freelance workers or work under a firm to which normal parts of the ongoing process or menial tasks are assigned.

Thus, there can be a multitude of lesser beings related to the company. Some are only partial members of the "family" because they only work on a part-time or temporary basis. Others may be full-time workers but paid and looked after by subcontractors. Whatever the case, they are not granted the same wages or benefits as the regular staff, they usually do not belong to the union, and in most cases they are stuck with the hard or unpleasant tasks. These people do their work, usually quite competently (or they would not last long), but without the same concern and care that management grants to its regular staff. Nor does the union show much interest in their fate. Yet, having seen how much good a bit of kindness and decent treatment does to encourage its own staff, one would hope management would also think of those who serve it in this way.

Obviously, the greatest improvement would come by raising them to the position of regular worker. This has happened in the past, especially at times of rapid growth when the staff had to be expanded quickly and one could not do this with recruitment from the bottom. Nowadays, with reduction of personnel a major concern, that is less likely to occur. However, using mid-career entrants as a tool to cope with slackening demand is certainly better and easier than resorting to recruitment fresh from school. The mid-career entrant is already trained, indeed, he has already worked with the company, and he can be taken in just when he is needed rather than on a rough estimate of when he will be needed made for recruitment at the bottom. Although an outsider, he will still be easier to assimilate given his familiarity with the company. But keeping the old distinctions or limiting his chance to rise because he was *once* outside is not going to help work him into the team.

Mid-career entry can also be offered to employees with no prior relationship to the company. This sort of thing is necessary for highly qualified professionals or specialists who are needed too urgently for the company to train its own in-house. Similarly, it is not a bad idea to take people who are already trained rather than go to the expense of training them because, at least that way, one knows they have the qualifications. It is hard to tell just how fast a young employee will learn the skills or if he will ever be as good as a professional. Once again, such people are liable to perform better if treated fairly and not relegated to a lesser status.

Japan is going to have to live with the phenomenon of people entering the company not only from the bottom but also part way up. Increasing professionalism will cause this. Growing uncertainty about future business and the need to make staffing more flexible will cause this. And especially the recent tendency of people to switch jobs will cause this. It is obvious that if some of the employees are going to leave the company during their career someone will have to replace them. All this will be much easier to handle if the company becomes a less closed society and also to the extent that staff is categorized, utilized, and remunerated by qualifications and merit.

Since entry into the company is so hard in general, one would hardly expect it to occur at the top as well. Yet, this is what happens quite frequently through a practice known as *amakudari* (or "descent from heaven") whereby employees of higher bodies slip into lesser ones, usually near the end of a career. It is most prominent in government, whose high officials retire into state and prefectural corporations or into related private enterprise. Many banks also send their superannuated staff to sit on the board of companies whose financial debts seem to entail moral obligations as well. Within the private sector, larger companies manage to foist their retiring officers on one or another of the subcontractors. The situation is so bad that some subsidiaries, and seemingly also government corporations, are apparently created mainly as a rest home for aged staff.

The higher body, government office or large company, will often claim this is a gift of sorts. Receiving such personnel will make it possible to "upgrade management" or the like. But, in practice, many of the *amakudari* employees know little about how business is conducted when they arrive and few try to contribute. This, for them, is a sinecure. Those from the bank or prime contractor occasionally appear in an even worse light as a kind of "spy." But the biggest problems arise with the rest of the personnel. Outsiders are not welcome in general. So people who pick up top jobs are seriously resented.

The whole personnel system is predicated, at least in theory, on the assumption that a person starts at the bottom, works very hard, and slowly rises to the top. If some of the top spots disappear, this blocks the ascension of the aspiring salarymen and upsets the carefully maintained harmony with the lower level staff. There is considerable annoyance at the appearance of people, with different attitudes and different concerns, and who are certainly more interested in themselves or the body that sent them than in the rest of the team and the company that receives them. Even when they do not take over regular jobs and just become advisors, there is anger that they should be so well paid while others are sometimes retired out early due to financial stringency.

This will obviously have a negative effect on the work will in the company. But most seriously, it will slake the ambition of the up-and-coming managers who, knowing they can only go so far, may decide not to make further efforts or to seek possibilities elsewhere. On occasion, the tension becomes so great, even in government entities, that the staff goes on strike. Nothing much comes of this because, after all, one accepts *amakudari* not because one wants to but because one has to. Still, the anger and frustration remain and spoil the atmosphere.

There is little chance of doing away with *amakudari* because it results from a relationship of dependence. The larger companies and government bodies are in a position to ask this favor of smaller companies or state corporations in return for continued good relations. In some cases, the person accepted has actually rendered considerable services to his new employer in the past and can be counted on to do so in the future. The government official may have facilitated access to contracts, or helped in cases of overproduction, or engaged in setting up barriers to foreign or domestic competitors. The man in the larger company may have helped foster the small one. The bank man probably presided over granting of loans on favorable terms.

The relationship is mutual. The organization on the top wishes to continue its supervision and can best do so by placing one of its own men there. At the same time, the *amakudari* man will be looking out for the interests of his new host, for otherwise he would be too unwelcome. In fact, this concern may be so strong that *amakudari* becomes a double-edged sword. Banks like to send advisors to their clients, but if the advisor was in too exalted a position and can still control his successors, there is some fear that he will obtain too many loans on too good conditions for his new company. Thus, many banks that would otherwise oust senior officials find it safer to keep them on as advisors in the bank.

So, despite any unpleasantness created among the staff, the recipient companies often find not only that they have no choice but that the advantages can be considerable in receiving retired employees from above. The good will and connections they obtain may be otherwise inaccessible and the man may well repay his wages many times over. Even the lower level personnel who dislike the practice realize that. And thus a modus vivendi does set in.

However, even if individual companies can afford the practice, it is uncertain whether Japan can. It is extremely unhealthy in a country where personal relations are already so important to have relations that are as close as that. It may be good for a company to get contracts readily through *amakudari*, but that is certainly the least objective and most dangerous basis for making such decisions. The same applies to bank loans and government support. Personal relations in this context can result in tremendous waste and damage for the economy as a whole.

No Reply From The Top

No matter how important competent workers in the factories and offices may be, or how essential it is to have capable middle managers, it is obvious that one also needs intelligent leadership from the top. Top management must decide on basic and long-term policy that will be implemented by all other levels. And, if it decides unwisely, it is not only the efforts of all the rest of the staff that will be wasted. Since they are schooled in harmony and loyalty, and will implement foolish policy as vigorously as wise policy, the whole company could be endangered.

Descriptions of the Japanese management system usually dwell at length on the activities at lower levels. How the workers are motivated and create QC circles. How the salarymen engage in decision-making and write *ringisho*. How the *kacho* brings out the best in his men and strives for the company's success. But pitifully little is ever said about top management, aside from praising the glorious leadership of such-and-such a president. Very little is known about how he actually directs the company or who in the company actually controls the levers of command.[18] Worse, almost nothing is known about the problems encountered at the top or those directors whose leadership has been merely competent, less than acceptable, or outright disastrous.

Nevertheless, it should be clear from the basic characteristics of the management system that it is extremely hard to control things from above. The fact that the basic unit is the group, as opposed to the individual, simplifies things somewhat since one has to work with fewer elements. However, the group is a very tight organism, concerned with its own success and prerogatives, and thus has to be handled gently. Many of them are relatively independent until they can be convinced to fall into line with overall policy. Should this policy not favor them, then the *nemawashi* can take endlessly long. Moreover, efforts at bringing all groups into line alternate with periods when they are purposely encouraged to compete against one another. Their leaders are also potential rivals in the race for promotions. All this is compounded by the fact that in Japanese companies, groups can be very small and amazingly numerous.

Those particular factors make it hard to impose strong control downward or even routine coordination except in rather special cases or when the entire company can be whipped into a crisis mentality or aligned against its competitors. They also make the whole decision-making process more complicated than necessary. Many top managers do not take hard-and-fast decisions on their own and then simply impose them. At best they engage in careful *nemawashi*. But in far more cases the decision-making process is very dispersed, among the various top managers, the middle managers, and sometimes with an input from below. At the same time, top management not only handles broad company policy but frequently has to deal with quite minor matters that have filtered up from below and need approval. Whereas the diffuse type of decision-making so popular in Japan shows its advantages at lower and middle levels, it is just as likely to reveal its drawbacks at the top.

One reason the weaknesses of top management have not been very noticeable so far is that many decisions during the earlier period of reconstruction and growth were relatively simple and straightforward. It was necessary to enter a given field, make a given product, and sell it actively. The whole staff, from top to bottom, could be geared to this. And the basic slogan was to fight and to fight hard. In an economy with fewer opportunities to be followed up aggressively, where caution is needed in making investments, and balance required to obtain profits, the slogans become more ambivalent—fight as hard as you can, but if necessary hold back and perhaps even retreat. This is not the sort of orders business leaders like to give and they are apparently confusing to their subordinates who are unable to decide when to push and when to fall back. It results in a stop-and-go approach that is very unsteady and hard to maintain.

Perhaps the greatest strength of Japanese managers is to know their company thoroughly. Being rotated periodically, passing from one sector or division to another, they become acquainted with a broad range of activities. They will also get to know many of their colleagues. This creates managers with exceptional ability at using the company machinery as well as obtaining support from their own network of personal relations. This in many ways makes up for any lacks in the decision-making process because close cooperation is much easier among a group of managers who have worked their way slowly up the spiral staircase together.

But it does not obviate all the problems. One is that, although managers know much of the organization, they are still most closely related to one part or another. The *bucho* are obviously best acquainted with their own staff and problems and just as obviously try to defend their department's interest also against those of others. This they continue to do as directors, even though by then they should rather be thinking of the best interests of the company as a whole. Even when they become managing directors or presidents, many executives have been so impregnated with the concerns of the departments they know best and the personnel they have dealt with most that their policy can be biased. They are too busy paying off old debts to think what this may mean to company policy.

In addition, since they have risen to the top through the ranks, few of them know anything about *management* as such. They are often excellent sales people, or excellent production people, or excellent research people, but absolutely horrible managers when they reach a level where running the company as a whole is their primary task. It is common knowledge that the higher a person rises the harder it is to decide whether he can take the next step. Many ordinary salarymen can become quite competent *kacho* and the average *kacho* might might turn out reasonably well as a *bucho*. But a company would be very foolish to assume that more than a minority of the *bucho* could go any further. As of that level, the type of work changes radically and the decisions become so crucial that a mistake can be disastrous.

Despite this, as for middle managers, the present system does not really allow top managers to concentrate on their basic tasks either. The men at the top must also engage actively in the work of morale building and human relations. The managing directors have to maintain very close relations with the middle managers, both to direct and to evaluate them. The president and chairman are often so busy with social and quasi-political activities that they hardly have time for business as such. They must act as arbitrator for any disputes within the company. They have to appear as a father figure at numerous company functions. They spend untold hours entertaining major customers, keeping up relations with dealers, and seeing that subcontractors tow the line. For major companies, especially with government contacts, they join in *zaikai* activities and try to win the favor of influential politicians or bureaucrats.

Here, too, is a job which is so demanding that few could possibly accomplish it well. Either the business side must suffer or human relations must be neglected. It often happens that the top managers shift the burden of day-to-day decisions to the managing directors while they worry about rapport. This policy is a wise one if the other managers are up to the task. But too many presidents and chairmen nowadays neglect, or lack time to handle, what elsewhere would be their primary concern. Rather than controlling or dominating their own company, they become a figurehead for those actively running things. In fact, it is almost as if they had retired and just hang on as a symbol of authority. This can be beneficial by giving those lower down more leeway and encouraging initiative. It can also be harmful if managers do not entirely agree and there is no one person who knows enough to impart unity to the company's policy or force everyone to pull together.

These are problems which affect most companies in Japan, large or small, new or old. They are obviously less serious in companies still under the influence of a founder or the postwar management which built it up. They can be acute for some of the more bureaucratic companies. And that is why these problems can no longer be glossed over today. For, Japan's companies have aged, and mellowed, and grown more bureaucratic with time. Any problems are bound to become yet more debilitating in the future.

The clearest warning signal is the mere age of Japan's top executives. According to the most recent *Oriental Economist* study, in 1979 the average age of presidents of companies listed in the first section of the Tokyo Stock Exchange was 63.1 years. Although we are already in the Showa 50s, only 9.4% of the presidents were born in the Showa era, another 65.4% in the Taisho era, and still 25.2% in the Meiji era.[19] An earlier study by *Japan Economic Journal* put the share of Japanese aged 60 and up in top management at 75% as compared to a mere 37% in the United States.[20]

More important than age is ability. Here, Japan is at an even more crucial turning point. It has reached the stage where the giants of the business world who brought about the economic miracle are disappearing. Whatever some may think, the bureaucratic leader is not typical of Japan's managers. Just after the war, the *zaibatsu* and major companies were disintegrated and many old leaders forcibly retired. Younger men had to take over. And only dynamic managers could restore the company's strength. At the same time, some older companies began to grow, either under the founder or his children. And a number of vital companies were first created. Most of the leaders who have become famous since were in those groups.

However, those strong and dynamic leaders cultivated the present crop of bureaucratic leaders. These are men who followed the slow path upward, who obeyed instructions, who made proper contacts, but who rarely showed initiative, imagination or drive. They are admirable followers, some of the finest in the world. Now the time has come for Japan to find out if they are also capable leaders. There is considerable fear that these men may not meet expectations to judge by the number of companies that cling to their founders or older presidents. There is just as much reason to fear that by the time they become leaders they are quite simply too old.

These various trends have come together most visibly in Matsushita Electric Industrial Co. Founded by a dynamic individual, Konosuke Matsushita, a travelling salesman of electric bulbs with just a primary school education, he would have been the lowliest of staff in anyone else's company and even his own today. Nevertheless, after the war, he got into a growth field and built up a huge company through daring and innovative policies. Yet, he still preferred that his subordinates be good company men who followed orders and hid their "self" so the company would appear more strongly. He held onto power into his eighties as an "advisor" and could not withdraw because there was no one big enough to replace him. The most serious trouble in the company quickly became the fear of what would happen if it were entrusted to old and "senile" managers. In a striking move, Konosuke appointed as president Toshihiko Yamashita, a mere 57 years old, just a technical high school graduate, and ranking 25th among 27 directors.

If such a decision were to set a trend, it could perhaps have rejuvenated management and reinvigorated business circles. But it attracted so much attention specifically because it was unusual and, so everyone agreed, no one but Konosuke could have done such a thing. Instead, most top management will soon be the patient bureaucrats of today or the increasingly pampered children of dynamic fathers who run the privately owned companies. We shall see how many of them match up to a Matsushita, a Morita, a Honda, or many more.[21]

NOTES

1. See Jon Woronoff, *Japan: The Coming Social Crisis*, pp. 155–80, and *Japan: The Coming Economic Crisis*, pp. 198–227.
2. *What do freshman employees think?*, Nippon Recruit Center, 1980.
3. *Employment motivations of university students*, Nippon Recruit Center, 1980.
4. See Takeo Doi, *The Anatomy of Dependence*.
5. *White Paper on Youth*, Prime Minister's Office.
6. *Survey of National Characteristics*, Statistics Institute, Ministry of Education, 1979.
7. *Japan Times*, October 7, 1979.
8. *White Paper on Youth*, Prime Minister's Office.
9. *Japan Economic Journal*, February 8, 1977.
10. See *Survey on Japanese Employees' Life After Retirement*, Ministry of Labor, April 1980.
11. *Asahi Shimbun*, May 15, 1980.

12. *Mainichi Daily News*, March 24, 1975.
13. Ibid.
14. *Japan Economic Journal*, October 23, 1979.
15. *Mainichi Daily News*, March 24, 1975.
16. *Asahi Evening News*, November 21, 1977.
17. *Sunday Mainichi*, November 13, 1977, p. 37.
18. See M. Y. Yoshino, *Japan's Managerial System*, pp. 85–117, and Kazuo Noda, *Executives in Japan*, Diamond Co., 1960.
19. *Oriental Economist*, February 1980, pp. 8–13.
20. *Japan Economic Journal*, October 24, 1978, p. 6.
21. A recent Nikkei survey showed founder-run companies to be among the most successful, *Japan Economic Journal*, September 30, 1980.

This looks like a suitable profession for women.

Photo credit: Kokusai Denshin Denwa Co.

position was increasingly similar to that of men. However, a somewhat closer look will show that this is not quite true. Rather than finding employment throughout these sectors, they were being grouped within a rather narrow range of jobs. In 1975, fully 64.4% of all women workers were concentrated in merely 10 of the 286 census occupations. They were employed as farm, forestry or fishery workers (17.1%), general clerical staff (13.8%), sales personnel (9.9%), accounting clerks (8.3%), cooks (3.6%), servants, waitresses and the like (3.4%), sewing machinists (2.5%), miscellaneous laborers (2.0%), nurses (2.0%), and barbers or beauticians (1.8%).[2]

This revealed a very clear labor stratification that sometimes bordered on segregation or at least sex discrimination. There was, on the one hand, a limited number of jobs which might be regarded as "women's occupations."

They included those in which over 80% were women, such as nurses, midwives, kindergarten teachers, stenographers and typists, key punchers, telephone operators, spinners, doublers, yarn twisters, sewing machinists, canned food makers, packers and wrappers, domestic maids, housekeepers, beauticians, waitresses, bar and cabaret hostesses, geishas and dancers. This image was hardly altered by those professions where they held over 60% of the posts, such as workers in the textile and garment trades, in light industry, clerical and related workers, and insurance agents.

On the other hand, there were a number of occupations in which women were very slightly represented. This included numerous positions in heavy industry, specialized crafts and technicians, where one might not expect them due to the nature of the work and training. But they are also less than 20% of almost all professional and technical workers, such as physicians, dentists, judicial workers, registered accountants, high school teachers, professors, authors, reporters and editors, and scientific researchers. Where they do work, they usually only attain low status jobs, many of which are a dead-end since they do not lead into any promotional sequence. And the number of women who rise to positions of authority is exceptionally limited. There are pitifully few women managers or government officials. That is apparently also men's work.

Equally serious is that many of the women in the labor force are only there in a rather tenuous way. It rarely happens that they enter into a lifetime employment relationship or become regular workers. This is hard to see, let alone determine statistically, since lifetime employment is not written into the contract and women appear to enjoy the same prerogatives during their early years. Nevertheless, there are extremely few who stay with a company until retirement age. Instead, most women are just temporary employees or part-time workers who can be hired and fired at will. This casual nature of the relationship was not always imposed on them. Women often prefer not being drawn into a deeper commitment. On their own, they seek jobs which can be limited to a few hours a day or a few days a week. They may engage in what is known as *arubaito* and do not even regard that as something that should get in the way of their other activities.

To this general picture must be added the fact that, on the average, women are only earning 56% as much as men. This results partly from the fact that their professions are usually less remunerative in general. Even when they are hired by companies which offer equal wages for men and women, since they do not stay as long as men, the seniority-based wages obviously are not able to accumulate as high. For this latter aspect, the women are often

Another good job for women . . . as long as they have a male supervisor!

Photo credit: Foreign Press Center-Japan

as much at fault as the company. But it also happens that, even if they get the same job in theory, its contents are somewhat different and so is the remuneration. There is also less likelihood of obtaining promotions and the financial advantages they bring.

Thus, it is clear that women are not full-fledged participants in the workforce and probably their contribution is not as great as it might otherwise be. Whereas their work on the farms is doubtlessly essential, and their jobs in the factories cannot be done without, in many other cases they appear a wee bit superfluous. One more salesgirl in a shop or one more clerical worker in an office does not add much to the economy. This is particularly true if their tasks are carefully restricted and their role looked down upon. Women—just like men—only perform well when they are encouraged and rewarded for showing greater ability.

Many men may think this is a problem for women. Certainly it is, and women are increasingly displeased about the second-rate treatment they get. But it is also a problem for men and for society in general. Japan cannot afford to use its female labor force improperly, let alone discourage women from taking jobs. In the economic competition, everyone counts equally, men and women. If Japan keeps on neglecting more than a third of its labor force while other countries offer women a more useful role, it is going to be the loser.

Career Escalator For Women

As everyone knows, not all those who enter companies get on the same career escalator. White-collar workers get on ones that start much higher and lead to the top. Blue-collar workers get on ones that start considerably lower and never climb too high. As for women, they get on an escalator that hardly rises at all. In fact, one might call it a moving sidewalk. For, the women get on and are just carried along for a while. Then they get off and walk on their own for a bit. Some will get on again later until, sometime in the future, they are asked to step down or pushed off. Terribly few of them will ride it to any notable destination.

Just how different this career escalator can be is shown in many ways. First of all, and it is perhaps an inauspicious omen, the companies do not use quite the same channels to recruit women as men. While the salarymen-to-be line up at one door and are received by a rather serious committee to test and screen them, the women are received at another door by a much lower level welcoming committee. Personnel officers scout the best universities for male employees. Women are often just introduced by contacts or hired through connections. While men are tested partly at least on ability, women have to show their charms and pleasing personality. This way, if the girls turn out not to be very good, at least the company hasn't lost much and one has done a favor for a useful contact.

The chances of women even getting into some companies, especially the big ones, are somewhat restricted. For, they tend to recruit more men than women and prefer high school to college women. According to Ministry of Labor statistics, in 1977, although 62% of the companies hired both male and female high school grads, and 51% hired male university grads, only 22% hired female university grads.[3] This means that the vast majority of companies are closed to "educated" women. Women are also subject to closer scrutiny as regards their morals (a seemingly more important matter than their ability). Good companies refuse to hire girls who were *ronin* or don't live with their parents. Yet, rumor has it that they are increasingly looking for charming and attractive ladies to grace their offices.

Once having been recruited, women are rarely treated as equals. Thus, 73% of the companies—an amazingly large share of the total—have different starting salaries for male and female employees. The justification for this is that the women fit different job descriptions (75%) or, even if they meet the same conditions, the contents of their work is different (33%).[4] This will explain how a man and woman fresh from Keio University, say, can enter the same company and be addressed as equal members of the team verbally, since standard company rhetoric would not admit a difference, while he does a man's work and she just cleans up for him, at the same wage or more likely a lower one.

Of course, to be of any use to the company, both must undergo a period of training, or so the theory goes. However, although every male gets in-house training and this is sometimes quite extensive, the situation for women differs. In 19% of the companies, there is the same training for male and female employees while in 33% the men and women are trained separately, which hardly indicates the training is equal. And, in 13% of the companies, there is no training whatsoever for females.

The training women get, when they get it, may come as a shock to them, and a surprise to men. It is full of strictures on how one behaves, matters like presentation, how to greet customers, even how to bow. Special attention is paid to how to answer phone calls and stress is placed on the use of polite language. The more solid elements, material of a technical nature, or introduction to a profession are limited. A girl who would demand the same training as a man, and there are a few nowadays, would risk being scorned by her male colleagues and resented by the other girls . . . should the company accede to her wish.

During their stay in the company, on the basis of years of service, women's wages obviously rise. But the escalator they are on is a slow one and there is little hope for any acceleration through promotion to higher posts. In fact, according to a Ministry of Labor survey, more than half the companies (52%) do not give female employees any chance at promotions. The reasons for not promoting them vary. Major ones are: the job they do is of an auxiliary nature (60%); the length of service is short (47%); they have no or low supervisory capability (13%); many legal restrictions exist with regard to female work (8%).[5]

There are, of course, companies which do give promotions to female staff. The only problem is that the women still never rise very high. They managed to reach sub-section chief level in 41% of the companies, section chief level in 27%, and department head level in 4%. It is exceedingly rare for them to rise higher. Much of this progress has only come of late and is more striking in non-manufacturing companies, especially in distribution or fashion-related sectors, than in industry or trading companies. It should also be noted that, according to a recent poll by Nippon Recruit Center, there is a growing willingness to promote women. As many as 30% of a smaller sampling of companies hoped to put more women in managerial positions in the future . . . if only they would show more zeal and responsibility.[6] Whether they will actually do so remains to be seen.

Still, all in all, the results are pretty bad. Women have not really gotten ahead even in those sectors where they could be expected to rise most rapidly, namely ones with many female entrants at lower levels. Thus, although over 50% of the elementary school teachers are women, only 1.4% of the elementary school principals are. About 20% of the civil service employees are women, but only 0.9% of the managerial positions in the civil service are held by women. In the government's deliberative councils, despite the concentrated effort urged by the Prime Minister's Office, the share of female members only rose from 2.4% in 1975 to 4% in 1980, although the target was 10%. This is even worse than the showing in private business, where there was a total of 120,000 women in managerial positions (albeit usually low level ones), representing 5.2% of the total.[7]

So, the first trip is rather uneventful for most women, consisting of a brief visit almost to the business world after graduation and before "entering home life" and raising a family. What they had in most cases could hardly be called a career. Rather, they hopped onto the moving pavement and enjoyed a ride. Some of them got off on their own to get married, others were shoved off to make way for newcomers. But, in few cases was theirs a very long stay. Despite some progress, especially in recent years, the average length of employment has only risen from 4.0 years in 1960 to 6.2 years in 1979.

Not only wasn't the trip very long, it was not particularly pleasant or fulfilling either. This applies both to the female employees and their bosses. Women, even the most capable and ambitious, are rarely given a challenging job and thus do not stand much chance of promotion. They have every reason to be angry about this. On the other hand, since most of them only work a few years (the fault here is shared between the women and society), the employers cannot really afford to give them proper training or entrust much responsibility to women when most male employees will be around until retirement age.

Nevertheless, after having left their job and returned to their home, the women have been coming out in ever larger contingents to hop back on the moving sidewalk. At this point, it can hardly be referred to as an escalator except in very few cases. What they get is a mere job, one unlikely to change much over the years, where salary increments may come due to longer work years or in keeping with inflation. But even the longest stint will rarely culminate in a promotion and, if things get bad economically, they may be the first to be laid off. In fact, this second ride can be pretty bumpy on occasion.

The arrival of so many older women on the labor market can be explained by the basic changes in the life cycle over several decades. Before the war, most women got married at 21, had a fair number of children, and the youngest child only started school when they were 42. Life expectancy then was 50. Thus, their whole life was devoted to raising a family. Nowadays, women get married a bit later, at 25, have only one or two children, the youngest of which starts school when they are 35. And they will have many years to pass after that since the female life span has extended to 79 years.

This led to an M-shaped labor structure, with over two-thirds of women working from the age of 20–24 and an equally high proportion from 40–44. As more older women join the workforce, and stay longer, that category has grown to outnumber the younger women three to one. Meanwhile, the average age of working women (outside of agriculture) has risen from 26 in 1960 to 37 in 1979. And the percentage of working women who are married has reached 67%.

In all too many cases, these women are not even integrated fully in the company and are just working on a part-time basis. What is more serious yet is that the growing part-timerization of women appears so sharply since the recession. By now, it is estimated that as many as 18% of female workers are employed on a part-time basis as opposed to only 9% in 1960. This means that they enjoy few of the advantages of regular staff although it often happens that they put in almost as many hours work.

Rise of the middle-aged working women and an M-shaped female labor force structure.

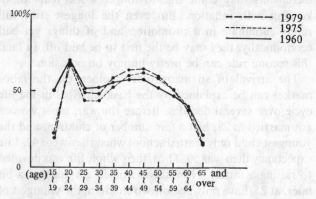

Sources: *Kokusei chōsa* (National Census), Statistics Bureau, Prime Minister's Office, 1960, 1975; *Rōdōryoku chōsa* (Labor Force Survey), Statistics Bureau, Prime Minister's Office, 1979.

Whereas part-time employment means about 20 hours a week in the United States or Great Britain, it runs as high as 30 hours and more in Japan.

One last group of women is even worse off, namely the home workers. Estimated at about 1.2 million, and perhaps considerably more, they are engaged especially in the garment, textile, toy and electrical industries. Not members of the company in any sense, and simply working on consignment, they are bereft of most advantages other workers enjoy. Insurance and social benefits are limited, severance pay or retirement allowances nil, and they can be hired or fired at will. Working at home, usually in crowded quarters shared by children or grandparents, they nevertheless use dangerous machinery and harmful chemical solutions. Paid on a piecework basis, these women earn considerably less than part-timers although many put in six hours or more a day. As if their situation were not bad enough, there has been a tendency for wages to rise slower than inflation while the number of home workers grows.

This combination of circumstances will explain quite readily why, despite anything written into the Constitution or any recommendations of the International Labour Organization, there is no real equality between men and women. Different treatment, as noted, is also expressed by different payment. The average hourly wage of women has for years only been about 55% of that for men in Japan, while it was 73% in Germany, 74% in Great Britain and 86% in France.[8] Part-timer wages are harder to define, but the indications are more alarming yet. Although working nearly three-quarters as many hours as regular staff, the average female part-timer only earned one-third as much as the average full-time male worker.[9] Since the situation has not changed for so long and the positive trends like increased promotion can be outweighed by negative trends like part-timerization, there is no reason to expect much improvement in the near future.

Learning How To Fly

In recent years, there has been a sweeping change in the attitudes of young women toward work and life in general. This can be summed up best by the idea that they should learn how to "fly." This means that they should leave the nest of the family and school and rise by their own force in the work world. They should spread their wings and soar up into the sky. These ideas are widely spread in women's magazines, starting with those read by teen-agers and continued by the new series of magazines for the working woman, the career girl, and the young housewife. Television programs also offer examples of women who have succeeded and more young women are setting their ambitions correspondingly higher.

In a first passage, during the period of education, actually much has been accomplished for women, if not necessarily by women. Higher education has opened up readily for them and there is almost no discrimination or hidden barriers which has allowed females to catch up with males as regards enrollment figures. Over the years, more and more girls have been continuing on at school and reaching increasingly high levels. The gap with boys is now rather small and shrinking. Back in 1960, only 6% of the girls (and some 15% of the boys) went on to college after high school while by 1979 some 33% of the girls (and 42% of the boys) did so. The number of females receiving higher education thus expanded quite rapidly, although admittedly many girls only went to two-year colleges while most boys went to full four-year universities.

The next step, however, has been more painful. The girls now wished to enter one of the careers they had been dreaming about. But this was not so simple. One reason was that too many girls wanted to enter a narrow range of particularly glamorous fields. This included things like fashions and television, travel or government. Like the boys, they also wanted to get into the larger, more prestigious firms. According to a Nippon Recruit Center survey, preference was given by the girls graduating from college in 1981, as per usual, to government and public offices, publishers and mass media, trading companies, service sector, transport and insurance (but not industry or distribution).[10]

But jobs did not exist in such profusion in these sectors and it was impossible for their hopes to be met. More serious yet, even when they landed a job, there was a big gap between the kind of work they actually did and their expectations of how they would be employed. For, the work world was not as willing to open up for them as the universities had been and it was not always easy to use

–124–

them.

Problems rarely arose for the high school graduates. And the situation was even better for those from rural areas, as has always been the case in Japan. Where the expectations are quite moderate it is not impossible to satisfy them to a reasonable degree. Girls from the countryside have continued finding work in factories and lower class girls were quite happy to work in shops or the service sector. Many of the high school girls have been accepted in the offices of companies, large and small, where they accomplish clerical tasks. Indeed, this has become a major occupational category and over the years almost a profession of "office lady," or OL for short.

It is a bit difficult to explain exactly what the tasks of an OL should be. And it looks more as if the actual contents result less from an attempt at determining what women can do than an effort by the men to hive off whatever they dislike doing. In fact, their chores seem to have been shaped by what men regard as women's virtues and capabilities. The OLs are relieved of any heavy work; they are also free from any serious responsibility. They merely look after things the men are too busy, or too important, to be bothered with and help out in general. They answer the telephone and take messages, they neatly rewrite the scribbled letters of their superiors, they tidy up the office, they photocopy documents and distribute them, and they run errands. When they are not busy, they simply chat with one another. But they remain on call in case a visitor comes, at which point they asume the principal function . . . serving tea.

Perhaps the best definition has been given in a rather back-handed manner by referring to them as the "flower of the office" (*shokuba no hana*). They keep things bright and cheerful. However, there is no question but that the job is a rather petty and futile one imposed on high school girls for two apparently good reasons. First of all, since it is assumed that few will stay more than a brief period, the company cannot afford to train them at considerable expense or work them into the normal team of personnel. In addition, all too many of them come with absolutely no skills, not even clerical ones such as typing, filing, or bookkeeping, and thus they are quite useless at first for specifically clerical work. So, the tasks given them are relatively simple or can be learned very quickly. Later on, their absence or retirement will hardly be missed and the company can function anyway.

Lest one think that they are of no use, it must be added that another reason the OLs are accepted—actually needed—in the office is that the men are not able to look after such things by themselves. As children, their mother or sisters pick up after them; once married, they simply yell "tea" and their wife goes to make it. In the office, they need someone to do the menial work and keep things in order. Not only is their time too precious, it is almost beneath them to make their own photocopies or boil water for tea. And someone has to remind them of appointments and look after the desk during their frequent absences for business reasons.

Thus, the real problem of late has not been with high school girls but the rapidly growing contingent of college graduates for whom work has to be found. Obviously, none of them would work in factories, let alone farms. They would not become salesgirls in stores or tellers in banks. But some were willing to look after customers in high class boutiques or make out tickets for airlines. A few even became air hostesses or journalists. But far larger numbers have also been moving into the offices to occupy nondescript clerical posts. Given their higher education and especially connections through parents, friends or school, they have entered the most prestigious firms.

Nevertheless, one may well ask whether it is necessary to have a college education to do such work. After all, even in the most glamorous establishments, the actual contents of the work could be quite commonplace and dull. There is not that much difference between selling cabbage in a grocery store and selling Dior scarves in a boutique or between typing letters for a small businessman or sending telexes for a major trading company. But the college graduates rarely bothered asking such questions and many are known to prefer a relaxed job like OL to a more demanding profession.

The greater problem seems to rest with the company. The personnel division in particular is hard pressed to find some suitable work for these women. The more educated they are, the harder it is to give them menial tasks. Yet, this education is so rarely oriented toward business that it is scarcely useful. So there are constant worries about how to treat them. The relations between girls of differing educational levels are also a headache, the more educated often shunning the high school grads and the latter annoyed about working as hard, or harder, for lower wages. It is a thankless task to train them when so many are leaving all the time. And it becomes very unpleasant when the girls leave with little advance notice or much thought as to how the company will fill the sudden vacancy.

Thus, all sorts of methods are conceived to make better use of the college grads or at least to keep them happy and out of the way while they are there. One attempt that has attracted attention recently was made by Toyota Motor Sales with the "assistant" system whereby each male employee (including the freshmen) is given one or more female assistants. These girls work only for one man and theoretically form part of the team. Yet, once again, the girls are given only rather simple and routine tasks to handle. The same old thing consisting of making photocopies, rewriting documents, taking phone calls and arranging appointments. The glorified title has not really changed the functions and it is clear that the woman is never more than back-up for the man who does the real work.

It has not yet occurred to many companies, or perhaps it was deemed too progressive, that a specific class of girls, without the frills of OLs, be hired to handle the menial and routine tasks at a going rate for such work. After all, it is absurd to have large numbers of staff filling such vague functions at the wages they now get. And, if this is absurd for high school girls, it is doubly absurd for college grads (who are paid more) and triply absurd for the few who continue on as OLs throughout a career (and benefit from seniority). On the other hand, those girls who possess the appropriate clerical skills and have the ability and ambition to become a proper secretary should be hired as such and paid a suitable wage. This is mentioned because the category of clerical workers has already grown to include a third of the female salaried labor force and represents well over four million employees.

This would still not solve the problem of what to do with talented and serious college girls who want to have a career. The ideal solution, which has worked out very nicely in many other countries, may appear far too revolutionary for Japan. It is simply to hire them on the same basis as male college graduates, to give them the same training and put them on the same career escalator. If this were done, many Japanese companies would be amazed how many succeed. Certainly not all will do well. But the less promising ones can be weeded out or will probably quit soon enough anyway. Similarly, girls who have taken technical courses or received training for various professions might be given an equal opportunity with their male colleagues. Where that has been done,

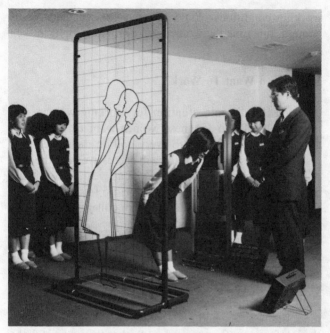

The very latest in training for young ladies.
A "bowing machine" to get just the right angle.

some excellent female professionals have come to the fore.

In such ways, Japan could finally start benefiting from the huge effort and expense that has gone into educating its young women. But little has been accomplished so far and rather few females have been given a chance to "fly." At best, they were lucky enough to get out of the nest for a while. Thus, despite any hopes and aspirations, women do not really expect much change in the future. According to Nippon Recruit Center, 81% felt that for the coming decade men would continue to obtain better jobs, higher wages, and faster promotion. Not even 4% thought that working conditions would improve for women.[11] Sadly enough, this time the women were probably right in their forecast.

Do Women Want To Work?

Given the difficult situation for working women, one might well ask, do Japanese women want to work? The answer so far, according to every poll on the subject, is a resounding yes! In fact, with each successive year the level of job consciousness seems to rise. Last year, according to a survey by Nippon Recruit Center, no less than 88% of the female students graduating from college were seeking employment.[12] Unfortunately, as in the past, only about 60% of the four-year college and 70% of the two-year college grads would eventually find a job. But at least the vast majority was showing good faith.

This latest batch seemed to be the most serious so far. Fully 29% of them wanted to stay on the job until reaching the retirement age and no less than 51% hoped to stay on the job for more than ten years. Rather than a brief flight, this was meant to be a genuine career. And, as such, a fair number hoped to rise through the ranks. About 21% of the university grads and 15% of the junior college grads claimed that they wanted to hold a supervisory post some time.

The only thing that might leave one dubious as to their true intentions was that the most popular company for these young women to work at was Japan Air Lines. True, the ambition of many modern women is to "fly." And by joining JAL, some of them would certainly be flying more than otherwise, if not in the cockpit, at least in the galleys. But that is hardly the kind of job a serious career woman would seek nor can many of them be accepted by JAL.

Although the results of such surveys are indeed promising, it is hard to accept them at face value. For the trends with regard to job consciousness appear to have little effect on actual performance on the job. It is much less encouraging to see what many of these young ladies do once they have gotten into the work world. Here, it is not necessary to restrict oneself to observation or stoop to mere gossip. Another poll by Nippon Recruit Center issued shortly after enables us to see what other young ladies, who graduated just a few years before, were doing with their chance at a career. The answers, gathered from 8,000 unmarried working women, aged 18 to 29, living in and around Tokyo, allows them to paint their own self-portrait.[13]

Although these girls are now at work, only 15% of them were most concerned with things like work and study. The rest had other things uppermost on their minds. Some 49% found the meaning of life in associating with friends and another 35% by engaging in leisure activities. The favorite ones were tennis, driving, reading, listening to records, and especially travel. Even though these girls were only earning between ¥1 million and ¥2 million a year, this did not seem to cramp their style (especially not since most lived quite cheaply at home). As everyone knows, career girls are immaculately dressed and can be found in the finest restaurants. Their travels take them very far afield. In this group, many had gone to Hawaii and Guam while others made it to Europe.

Does the fact of working get in their way? Hardly. According to these working women, they were able to take vacations or days off whenever they wanted to without any objection from their employers. They just had to ask. As for overtime, 30% did none, and the rest only put in a few hours a month. Now that they have an opportunity to seek promotion, what do they do? Some mentioned study as a major concern. But what they study has nothing to do with business. Rather, 46% were busy learning flower arrangement, 30% were immersed in cooking lessons, and 25% practiced tea ceremony. Anyone who sees this curriculum will know very quickly that they were preparing for marriage. Most of them want to get married before the age of 25 which does not leave much room for a career.

It is with respect to this particular question of marriage that the gap between dream and reality seems to be greatest. The latest report by the Prime Minister's Office, drawn up for the Women's Decade Conference in Copenhagen, announced that according to a poll 25% of single women claimed that they preferred to remain unmarried as opposed to only 14% in 1972. But there has been no noticeable decline in marriages over these years. And the standard reason for women leaving work is to get married (*kekkon taishoku*) while for all too many it is clear that working in the company was only a *koshikake* (temporary sitting chair) until marriage. A look at the graph of women working by age group shows that the tendency to leave work after 25 has actually grown.

We know that today's women have great pretensions of being different, of wishing to lead a more fulfilling life, of wanting to have a career. This is highly commendable. And some people, even grouchy old personnel officers in staid companies, would be willing to help them attain their goals. But, when they see how the young ladies behave once they have gotten a job, they tend not to want to repeat the experience. Nor can the young ladies, most of them at least, expect much respect or support from their male colleagues as long as they behave this way. No matter what they may say, if what they do turns out to be completely different the situation regarding female employees will not change.

But these women are not the only ones on the labor market and other categories show a markedly different attitude. The biggest gap in one sense exists with the older women, those who return to work after marriage and child raising. They have few illusions about what they will find and do not make a fuss about job consciousness and such notions. A survey of women working part-time at chain stores showed that they had very specific reasons for doing so. Either it was to get out of the house and obtain some "social participation" (17%), or to earn money to pay for their children's educational expenses, reimburse housing loans or cover other living expenses (nearly 50%) or, for the somewhat better off, to earn leisure expenses and pocket money (17%).[14] These women worked almost as long and sometimes as well or better than their young colleagues.

The final category, perhaps the most important, consists of women, both young and older, who really do want to have a genuine career and regard work as an essential part of their life. There are many female students who, rather than attend pointless classes at school, took up courses that lead to real professions. They often engaged in *arubaito* even before graduating to get a taste of work. And they have shown that a career is more important for some, about as important for others, as marriage. At any rate, they are no longer willing to let marriage become an absolute obstacle to a career.

Thus, more and more girls are taking vocational courses in or after high school and more and more students are choosing technical majors at college. The number of women sitting for government exams has increased rapidly. Some women have begun entering professions that were previously closed, or at least very unusual for women, such as working on ships or in the Bank of Japan. They are particularly numerous in the few branches where women can get ahead more rapidly, such as fashion, or sales, or retailing, or translation and interpretation. But they can be found elsewhere. Meanwhile, those who are raising a family do their best to keep at least one foot in the work world and work at home or engage in part-time activities.

But it is not easy for women to succeed. Like anyone else, they must work hard and show ability to advance. But they also encounter all sorts of opposition no man faces. This comes from the company management, their fellow workers (both male and female), and society in general.

Companies, and especially the larger and more conservative ones, often have formal policies, or at least long standing practices, that discriminate against women. This reaches much further in their case than for men. For example, companies are even concerned about the personal life of female employees to the extent that a woman not living with her parents would have trouble finding a job. Yet, why should such a rule apply to a woman who is mature and shows her independence or quite simply happens to be working in a different city from where her parents live? Once having been recruited, the job allocation procedures are such that women rarely get positions where they can show much ability and win recognition. In most cases they are unpersons to the extent that, unlike the men, they do not receive any business card (*meishi*). Since training is necessary to handle more important jobs, and they rarely get much training, again they are excluded.

Should the company be fair enough to give them a chance, the women will find that other companies they deal with may still not take them seriously, making it very hard for them to accomplish their work properly. If they engage in sales, the customers may regard it as second-class treatment that a woman is sent to them. Even in advertising, where women elsewhere have become particularly prominent, it would still not appeal to clients that their account should be handled by a woman. This even goes to the extent that suppliers might not wish to deal with them. One woman manager was amazed to find that the securities company salesman who dropped in regularly to sell to her male colleagues was not really interested in doing business with her.

Other problems may arise with the male employees. Here, the trouble is double. Frequently, the men look down upon their female colleagues because most of them are not working as hard and accept very little responsibility. They find that women are not sufficiently serious and sometimes quite egoistic. But, if they encounter a woman who is different, the reaction may not be much better. There is already more than enough competition among salarymen to get the few managerial posts available. They do not usually regard women as competitors. If there were to be more dynamic women, trying to get the same top jobs, that would only increase the competition and perhaps worsen the relations.

Thus, the most serious problems arise in connection with promotions. Women are not really put on the track to promotions unless they insist on it, and most do not seem to care. If they do show much interest they will stand out noticeably and attract a not always positive attention. They will also become the subject of criticism as to how poor managers women are, that they would not know how to deal with major problems, and so on. It is also clear to all concerned that it is not easy for women to give instructions to men. It is even more unthinkable for a woman to give orders to a man than for a younger man to give orders to an older one. This is often not because the men are too strong and proud to accept them but—in both cases—that they are too weak and insecure to bear the shame of receiving orders from those who theoretically should be beneath them.

But it is hardly as if women who seek improvement are backed up by other women. If anything, the problems career women encounter with other women are more painful. First of all, they must prove that they are different, since the image of women at work is so bad. They must show that they are not among those for whom it is a pastime or hobby and that they are not doing it just for pocket money. More seriously, the women they try to distinguish themselves from are in the majority, and they react. They proceed to push the career woman out of their social circles, to give her less backing, on occasion to bitterly criticize and antagonize her. Or they try to bring her back to the true path, which seems to be not solely motherhood but frivolity. It is hard to work more diligently while the others are relaxing, chatting, or preparing for a pleasant lunch or evening in town. It is not much fun being their supervisor either if that is the kind of promotion one is most likely to get.

The standard (apparently "fair" and "neutral") reason for not promoting a woman, since it is less obviously biased and unjust, is to claim that women are bound to quit soon anyway. Since so much of the case against women is based on the "fear" that they will retire at marriage, it is essential to take a closer look at this and see who, if anyone, is at fault. For, in an economy where so much is based on seniority, this is the crucial decision. By failing to put in more years of continuous service it is inevitable that a person's pay, promotion and prestige will suffer.

According to the most recent Survey on Women by the Prime Minister's Office, 53% of the unemployed or part-time employed women who had worked before had to leave their jobs to get married and another 21% to have or bring up a child. Whereas one can argue that, in a modern age when housekeeping chores are limited, a woman could work well beyond marriage age, it must be admitted that child-rearing is another matter. This is especially true in Japan, where day-care centers are few and a woman who entrusts her child to one is not highly regarded. Yet, as many as 18% of those who quit to bring up a child said that they would not have left if they had access to a day-care center.[15]

While in many cases women do leave on their own or because it is materially impossible to bring up a family otherwise, there is clearly a degree of pressure from the employers which may involve either the company management or the rest of the staff, men and women. When asked about the situation in their company, 11% of the employed women said that for marriage, and 14% for childbirth, "women have to quit their job here," or "it is customary" for women to quit, or "there is an atmosphere which makes it difficult for women to continue at work."

This helps explain why the situation in Japan has remained so backward as compared to other places. Negative comparisons have been made by many women leaders and professionals, including Fusako Fujiwara, a staff writer for *Nihon Keizai Shimbun* dealing with women's affairs. "In the United States, even in private enterprises, women are being appointed vice-presidents of major department stores and presidents of advertising firms. Compared with that, I am most disturbed by the situation in Japan. There is the preconception that women cannot be trusted with positions of responsibility since the danger exists that they may quit. That must have considerable influence on their acquiring rank and promotions."[16]

Conservatism, fear of innovation, respect for precedents only make the vicious circle in Japan that much more vicious. As Tomoko Shibata, Cabinet Councillor for Women's Affairs of the Prime Minister's Secretariat pointed out, the Japanese system makes the same problems as elsewhere even harder to solve:

"For either sex, rungs cannot usually be skipped on the ladder of the Japanese system. From the time one enters a company, one gradually receives training and advances one step at a time while accumulating experience. However, as in the past, the system has men and women follow different courses from the start except in extraordinary cases. Thus, women amass different experiences than men and never have a chance to display their abilities. For that reason, many women retire at the opportunity created by marriage or child-birth. The consequence is the repetition of the vicious circle that builds a wall against entrusting women with work."[17]

Recycling Female Labor

Although—in theory at least—considerable efforts were made to enhance women's position in the work world, it looks as if relatively little has been accomplished over the past decades. In some respects, actually, the movement has been in the wrong direction. The fact that the number of female workers has kept on growing should not make us forget that the share has not. For example, the percentage of working age women holding a job is significantly lower today than in the 1950s. The participation rate, which stood at 57% in 1955, has been falling steadily to 51% in 1965, then 46% in 1975, after which it rose slightly to 48% in 1980.[18] The latter gain is misleading due to the trend toward part-time use of women, meaning that more women were in the labor force but working fewer hours.

This drop of about 9% in the participation rate of women is part of a general tendency whereby more women (and men) enter the labor force later after longer studies and more older people leave work and retire. But, in the case of men, the decrease was only about 6%. Since this was a period in which women sought work and there were valid tasks for them to fulfill, such a decrease must be seen as a regrettable loss to Japan. Over recent years, millions more of them could have been employed if jobs had been available or proved attractive enough to hold them longer. A few million woman years of work lost every year is a tremendous waste. When you consider that the female participation rate is yet higher in some countries, the imputed loss may be much greater.

The loss is aggravated by the fact that many women who appear in labor statistics are not really integrated in sensible working processes where they make the greatest possible contribution to the economy. Vast numbers of women listed as working are just helping out in family enterprises. Others are giving lessons of one sort or another. Only 61% of working women are employed for wages, implying employment in modern sectors, as opposed to well over 90% in America or European countries. Until this situation changes any claims about the integration of female labor must be taken with a grain of salt. Their employment is frequently marginal, sometimes a duty to the family, and occasionally just a remunerated hobby.

Finally, as we have seen, even when Japanese women are employed in normal jobs within the companies, the tasks that are entrusted to them can be petty or superfluous. At any rate, all too often they are not very productive in any meaningful sense. Thus, further millions of Japanese women are underemployed or underutilized. This is a serious loss both when they are paid more than they are worth and when they are poorly paid. The only proper solution is to make the best use of them at a proper wage.

This can apply to the vast overutilization of female

labor in the retailing and services sectors. But it is worst with regard to clerical staff of the OL type because this is one of the few real attempts at recruiting women into modern companies, because so many actually hold this kind of position, and especially because it is now attracting more educated women as well. It is hard to understand how personnel can be used so pointlessly. It is no less difficult to understand how women who have gone through two or four years of university could accept such work. Whatever the reasons may be, it is impossible to justify such a poor use of personnel combined with relatively high salaries.

Still, squandering female labor has a very long history in Japan. Its roots go back easily to Meiji days and beyond into the Tokugawa period. But the persistence is harder to grasp in this day and age. Of course, the matter has been brought to the attention of the public. It has been regretted officially by business and government bodies. But the progress has been slow to say the least. It has been so slow, so half-hearted, and so unconvincing that one wonders whether improvement will ever come. Yet, if it does not, millions of women will be lost to the economy, other millions misused or wasted, and untold millions of female employees will remain neglected at best, frustrated at worst.

There are still some who claim that there is no need for women to enter the work world. Women have traditionally ruled the household and found their fulfillment there. True as this may be, it is hardly relevant today. With the change in women's life cycle, they now have many more years when they are not needed to raise a family. The amount of housework has also decreased sharply with modern appliances and fast foods. In many cases, with the children at school or grown up and the husband at work and returning late, the crying need for women is something to fill their free time usefully. Work is certainly one of the better solutions.

However, to make proper use of women, either during the first period right after finishing school or during the second phase after having raised the children, it is necessary to bring about major changes in the present situation. The ones responsible for this are the companies, the government, and society in general. But there is little hope that much will be accomplished unless women also play an important role in the process.

Change can come through company efforts. Some have realized the situation and, for moral reasons, tried to give a boost to women on their staff. Others are using women more intelligently for perfectly good commercial reasons . . . because this is the only way to beat the competition. Two alternate paths seem to be open. Companies can either use the female employees better to justify their wages or they can lower the wages to what the actual work is worth and, if need be, just dismiss women from the staff. Unfortunately, more seem to be doing the latter than the former. Taking women on as part-timers seems to be a popular compromise and an easy way out.

In retailing, which seems most advanced in the use of women, there is much less hesitation about letting women assume responsibility and offering them promotions. Of course, the fact that so much of the staff is female makes this easier. But the positive treatment, where it is offered, seems to have aroused the enthusiasm of the employees and improved performance. More recently Seibu has taken steps to build on, rather than cast away, the first period of employment by registering its better female employees so that they will get preferential treatment later when they return. This has a double advantage for the company: the women work better during the earlier period since they know it will be rewarded; their experience is used again when they return, somewhat more mature, for the second period. For the women, it is a precious link with the work world and an encouragement.

For the women who are hired in major companies, either in manufacturing or trading companies, this sort of encouragement is rarely offered. The transformation of OLs into "assistants" was largely a verbal one. The solid contents and prospects did not change measurably. Nor is there much chance of improvement as long as women are not accepted as full-fledged members of the team. Since it may still be too revolutionary to create a race of salary-women on a major scale, the companies could at least decide what they want of the OL. If she is simply to do dull routine tasks, she should be recruited specifically for such and given a rather modest wage. If she is recruited just like the men, on the basis of education, she should be given the same job and the same pay. But then she should also be given a fair chance to succeed.

That change may finally be coming was shown recently when a few companies began hiring female graduates of engineering schools. This meant, one would assume, that they were now recruiting women for what they could do. Only on the basis of a true merit system, rather than one that adds sex to age and education as the primary attributes of an employee, can women possibly make much headway. If this is not granted, there is reason to fear that the OLs will also disappear with increasing office auto-mation and that there will be no outlet for educated women. It might be mentioned that the trading com-panies, which have no particular respect for the skills of most women, have been doing that in a big way. Maru-beni, for example, reached a proportion of 44% female employees in 1966, but as clerical work could be mecha-nized the figure fell to 30% by 1979. If such trends were to continue there would not be much hope for women except as salesgirls and waitresses (or bar hostesses).

By rights, the most prominent initiator of change should be the government. After all, it is dedicated to watching over the interests of all citizens, half of whom are female. The Constitution provides for equality of men and women and, to make things perfectly clear, it has signed a number of ILO conventions providing for equal pay for equal work. Yet, the fact that equality is non-existent is most blatant in the government itself. There is a grotesque underrepresentation of women in the Diet, where they only hold a few percent of the seats. In the civil service, despite the number of educated women now sitting for exams, the situation is only somewhat better and promotion for women still poses some problems. But it was not until the International Women's Decade, that began in 1975, that the government gave this any priority at all.

Nevertheless, society does seem to be coming around to a slightly different view of women. This can be judged by a recent survey in a district within commuting distance from Tokyo. It shows, like many other polls, that the general attitude is in flux and has become increasingly favorable to a work role for women . . . although within certain bounds. Only about 8% of the respondents thought that women should not work. Of those who approved, 13% thought women should work until marriage and another 12% until childbirth. Fully 38% thought that women should quit at childbirth and start working again when the children had grown up. And as much as 21% felt that women should work throughout their lives.[19]

Given the new life styles developing among young people, it would have been expected that the attitude toward women working would quickly swing in their favor. But there has also been an unsuspected countercurrent as regards the men. Although the young husbands speak of equality much more than older men, they have become enamored of a vision of happy married life that rises out of the my-home and new family concepts. They dream of having a cozy little home, with a sweet little wife, and a cute little child, to which they can retire when they have finished a long painful day at the office. Whether this pleases their bride, who may be dreaming about how to "fly," does not seem to concern them. And, although they would hardly threaten or browbeat her to stay at home, they might just buy her off with gifts and pamper her into fitting the happy home image.

But the trends among women are far more important. One can speak as much as one will of what society must do for women, nothing much will be done unless they do more for themselves. It is not enough to dream of "flying" nor to express fine sentiments about work. Women must go out and work . . . and work seriously. Only by increasing their stay with the company can they earn the seniority that is necessary not only for wage increases but promotion. Only by showing their responsibility and loyalty to the company can they expect much back, although they will obviously still have to fight harder than men for whatever they do get.

One would expect the lead to be taken by the university graduate girls. They have two years more education than the junior college grads and four years more than the high school grads. Their universities are frequently among the best known. And, due to the Japanese system of recruitment and promotion, this gives them an entry into the better companies as well as the chance that, in theory at least, they can gradually climb the promotion ladder to the top. In the 1960s and 1970s, many of the women were very serious about a career and they have managed to rise despite any resistance. But they have found more recently that the present generation of women is not taking the same path and that they can expect little support from them.

Rather, today's "educated" women are frequently lost in the same dreams of a happy married life, one replete with the comfort of a nice home, the use of the family car, and great expectations as regards leisure and good living. Rather than work until childbirth, or marriage, many quit shortly after getting engaged to enter into bridal training. This further cuts down their career which most employers realize is terribly short to begin with. The rule of the thumb is still that high school girls will work six years, junior college girls four years, and university girls two years before getting married. And who would bother training or promoting someone who will be around such a short time? Thus, the hope for improving the status of women falls on the shoulders of the older career women, the professionals, and the less educated women who at least make an effort to be of some use during their employment.

This is not to say that there is no sign of change. Change is bound to come slowly anyway—although it could have been much faster—due to other general trends and the material circumstances. If, for example, men show less loyalty to the company and engage in job hopping, this will already increase the relative stay of women in the company proportionately. Since they are so eager for improvement, it would make sense to train women more than before and increase their responsibilities. Should the companies themselves switch more to job classification and remuneration by merit rather than seniority, then women would have a bigger chance. They would still have to earn their promotions by better educational background, more training, and greater skill. But at least sex and years of service would not give them an automatic handicap.

The recession is liable to do the rest. The more difficult it is for companies to offer a lifetime commitment, the more opportunities open up for women. True, the advantages of part-time or temporary employment are hardly as good. But they often fit in better with women's time schedule and have at least given them more jobs at a time when they were drying up for other categories. Lower wages for women also aid them, albeit in a rather negative way, as cheaper women are hired to replace more expensive men. The biggest opportunities will come, however, when the Japanese finally realize that they cannot continue wasting the energy and good will of a third of the work force. Competition from foreign countries, more than local trends, will make even the most conservative companies as well as government stop and wonder whether they are using human resources as well as they could.

NOTES

1. *White Paper on Women's Labor*, Ministry of Labor.
2. Yasuo Kuwahara, "Occupational Structure by Age and Sex in Japan," *Japan Labor Bulletin,* October 1, 1979, pp. 4–8.
3. *Keiei to Jinji Kanri*, No. 217, February 1980.
4. Ibid.
5. Ibid.
6. *What do OLs think?*, Nippon Recruit Center, 1980.
7. Mariko Bando, *The Women of Japan*, Foreign Press Center, Tokyo, 1977.
8. Labor Force Survey, Prime Minister's Office.
9. Japan Institute of Labor Magazine, No. 6, June 1980.
10. *Employment motivations of female university students*, Nippon Recruit Center, 1980.
11. *What do OLs think?*, Nippon Recruit Center.
12. *Employment motivations of female university students*, Nippon, Recruit Center.
13. *What do OLs think?*, Nippon Recruit Center.
14. *Japan Times*, August 10, 1980.
15. *Survey on How Japanese Women Feel*, Prime Minister's Office, November 1979.

16. *Look Japan*, April 10, 1980, p. 2.
17. Ibid.
18. *Labor Force Survey*, Prime Minister's Office.
19. *Keiei to Jinji Kanri*, No. 217, February 1980.

5
Burdening Down
The Economy

Shift From Primary To Tertiary

When the recession struck, some companies, in a very humane gesture, rather than drop redundant factory staff had some of them transferred to the sales division. Others, to avoid dismissing labor, sent engineers to work with the dealers throughout the country. These measures did more than just keep people working for their pay, they helped to upgrade the knowledge of products among the distributors and doubtlessly created closer links with the manufacturers. However, although they solved the problems of the producers in some ways, they certainly did not solve many problems for the distributors.

To the extent that the distributors had to bear any share of the cost, they were probably unhappy to have more people working for them. Even if the seconded personnel were free of charge, they only added to the already large staffs dealing with sales. But the worst complication was that many manufacturers began increasing their own sales staff instead and taking over a larger share of the sales activities. There was a gradual shift of personnel within the companies from the factory floor to the sales division. And many companies have started either duplicating or cutting into the competences of their former independent distribution networks.

The recession also had a strong impact on the job market for university graduates. There has been a gradual increase in the number of companies seeking personnel, but relatively few of them have been in manufacturing. According to Meiji University, last year fully 80% of the openings received were for sales-related posts and many of them came from small or medium-scale companies in the tertiary sector. More and more graduates have ended up working for supermarkets, chain stores, small securities firms and even fast food outlets. The trends on the job market have continued from the secondary to the tertiary sector, from larger to smaller companies and from clerical and engineering jobs to sales and distribution jobs.[1] This means that gradually the university students can look forward to becoming not salarymen but salesmen.

These various movements triggered by the recession were only symbolic of much broader changes that had already been taking place in the labor force and seem to be occurring with even greater vigor today. Basically, there has been a massive shift from the primary sector to the secondary sector and now from both into the tertiary sector. The primary sector has been shrinking ever since industrialization began and will continue to do so for some time to come, although it is already quite small. In the meanwhile, the secondary sector has also peaked. This normal transition was probably hastened and aggravated by the oil shock. So the time has apparently come when only the tertiary sector can be expected to grow markedly.

Already, from 1955 to 1975, while labor engaged in the primary sector dropped sharply from 37.5% to 12.7%, in the secondary sector it grew moderately from 24.4% to 35.2%. But the bigger rise was in the tertiary sector, going from 38.1% to 51.9%. And the trend is expected to continue, leaving the primary sector a mere 8.8% of the work force, the secondary only 35.6%, and the tertiary

More people than ever find employment in the tertiary sector. But, will they earn their keep?

Share of labor in %

	1965	1970	1975	1980	1985	1990
Primary	23.5	17.4	12.7	10.4	8.8	7.4
Secondary (Manufacturing)	31.9 (24.4)	35.1 (27.0)	35.2 (25.8)	34.8 (24.7)	35.6 (25.6)	34.8 (24.7)
Tertiary	44.6	47.5	52.1	55.6	55.6	57.8

Source: *Labor Force Survey*, Prime Minister's Office, and *Japan's Industrial Structure*, MITI. 1980.

sector as much as 55.6% in 1985.[2] Thus, Japan, like other highly industrialized countries, now has over half its working population in branches like distribution, finance, insurance and real estate, transport and communications, gas, water and electricity, government, and especially services.

Although this phenomenon is a seemingly "normal" one, it cannot simply be accepted at face value. According to some economists, there should—in any economy—be a gradual shrinking of the primary sector, as fewer farmers are needed to feed the population. There must be a growth in the secondary sector with increased manufacturing. Then, a new and dynamic tertiary sector, replacing the old-fashioned methods of merchandising and the traditional services, should appear to lead the economy into the postindustrial era. This theory, admittedly, has never been tested objectively and may simply be derived from the fact that most "advanced" countries have such a labor structure. That this structure has made them more modern and dynamic, as opposed to leaving them burdened down by superfluous services and encumbered with people doing less useful things, is far from certain.

In Japan, the advantages of the shift are doubly suspect. There is reason to believe that this was not a natural movement in which the tertiary sector expanded because it provided things of value. Rather, it seems to result more from a push than a pull, the shift being produced partly by the downturn in industrial employment. The increase of labor in the tertiary sector may thus arise from the need to find alternative employment in a sector that is easier to enter because it is loosely organized, broadly dispersed, and can readily absorb more people. The second reason for doubt arises from this last characteristic, namely that it is too easy to absorb more people without their necessarily making a corresponding contribution to the economy. It remains to be seen, even assuming a larger tertiary sector can be purposeful, whether the right branches are being developed in Japan.

More simply stated, a bigger tertiary sector does not in any way guarantee a more modern or a more useful tertiary sector. And it certainly does not guarantee a more productive tertiary sector. This can be seen from the fact that the shift in working population from the secondary to the tertiary sector has been more rapid than the shift in production. It is also shown by the fact that the two biggest branches of the tertiary sector, retail and services, have managed to record the lowest productivity growth of all, especially of late. The improvement has actually been so small as to be almost marginal. From 1975 to 1978, according to the Ministry of Labor, productivity only rose 1.6% in retail and a bare 1% for services.[3]

Putting Farm Productivity Off For Tomorrow

In the case of Japanese agriculture, it hardly makes any sense to speak of productivity because the sector is plagued by both by low and high productivity. This may seem strange at first, for Japan is incapable of growing enough agricultural produce to keep its population alive and its industries supplied with raw materials. It depends very heavily on imports to make up the difference, so much so that this is a heavy financial drain. But its most serious problem lies not where it cannot produce enough but where it produces too much.

Much of the present agricultural crisis arises through rice production, where the farmers have done too well. From year to year, the demand for rice has fallen as people have a more varied diet and especially as bread replaces the old "staple," rice. This, however, has not prevented the farmers from growing more rice and showing great ingenuity in raising yields per hectare so as to produce almost unbelievable amounts on their miniature farms. Unfortunately, even using the finest methods and the best inputs, Japan's farmers cannot compete with the poor peasants of Southeast Asia and local production is considerably more expensive than imports. The cost even seems to be a bit too high for the Japanese population so the government has had to take a position between the suppliers and the purchasers.

Unlike most middlemen, however, the government does not make a profit. It is obliged to sell the rice at a relatively low price to keep from fueling inflation and so that it can be purchased in reasonably large quantities by the average person. At the same time, it has been obliged to pay a rather high price to the farmer in order to cover the rising cost of inputs and to keep farm incomes up to a "decent" level. This subsidy is not quite the end of it, since production has outstripped demand so much that the total stock of rice ran into as much as seven million tons which have to be stored at great expense. Even exporting the rice, aside from upsetting foreign suppliers, still involves a loss since the government pays more for the rice than the going international rate.

These subsidies, which mount from year to year, have proven to be a heavy burden on the government and, of course, on the average citizen and taxpayer. They are also a perfectly futile exercise since the government is in effect paying the farmers to produce rice no one wants. To cut back on this burden, measures have been taken to bring about a "production adjustment." In this way, the farmers would keep some of their land out of rice production in return for a different kind of subsidy. If they were willing to grow other crops instead, the government would help subsidize that venture. Since wheat was replacing rice in the people's diet, one prime target was to boost local production of wheat. However, since wheat is best grown in a highly mechanized and extensive manner, Japanese producers could not possibly compete with American or Canadian producers. To encourage them properly, a wheat subsidy was introduced that is rapidly growing in size and has added to the burden of the rice subsidy.

The situation for a number of other crops is just as bad, although it takes a slightly different form. Japan's fruit and vegetable growers are rarely as cheap or productive as their competitors abroad. This applies to many things, including cherries, oranges and bananas. Thus, in order to keep the local price high enough to be remunerative, quotas and tariffs are raised to keep foreign produce out. At the same time, since local production is not enough to meet demand, imports are channelled through government purchasing agencies and private distributors in such a way that they are bought cheaply abroad and sold more expensively in Japan in order not to depress the market price. The most extreme case involves meat purchasing, which has already caused quite a scandal both domestically, due to the exorbitant prices charged, and abroad, since major trading partners sell their produce at the low

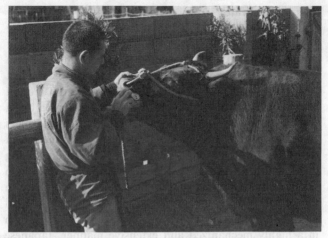

The consumers are milked so that Japan's cattle can drink beer.
Raising Kobe beef is not a very cost-efficient process.

going rate but can only export smaller quantities due to
quotas or artificially high prices.

Some of the money collected by government buying
agencies is channelled back to the producer in the form of
assistance to raise productivity. In theory, the higher
subsidized prices for beef and wheat should also help the
farmers raise productivity . . . if they want to. But the
results have been rather modest. Although quantities
produced have risen, the costs apparently have not fallen
enough to end subsidies and protection and in a number of
cases there is good reason to doubt whether Japan could
ever be competitive. As long as the farms are small and
there are limits to mechanization, it will be impossible to
go much further than today. Presently, agricultural productivity per person is only 29% of that of industry, which
is by no means surprising since each farmer uses far less

machinery.[4] But the gap is getting wider rather than narrowing, which means agriculture is losing whatever edge it had.

Only a radical change could reverse the situation. If each farmer were able to cultivate a larger area, he could do so more efficiently. And this would not necessarily create a serious problem for the other farmers to the extent that most of Japan's farmers already have one foot in agriculture and the other foot in industry or another sector. Only 13% of all farm households are engaged exclusively in farming while the rest are divided between 18% which are engaged predominantly in farming but have a side job and another 69% where the side job is more important. Since this latter group actually depends more on other sources of income, and is more affluent for it, the effort at rationalizing agriculture is lacking. If some of them were to sell, lease or otherwise transfer management over their land to full-time farmers, a big step could be taken. Younger farmers, with more land, and a different concept of farm management, might be able to resume the upward curve of productivity and become more efficient with the ultimate goal of producing what is needed at internationally competitive prices.

Obviously, not much of this has happened—or could happen—unless there is a strong desire for it among the farmers. So far they have found that it was much easier to remain under the protection of the state. As long as they received subsidies for some crops and were protected from foreign competitors for others, they saw no advantage to keeping costs down. Rather, if costs rose too high, they would agitate for higher subsidies. The farmers quickly learned that their livelihood did not depend on farming well, or producing what the market needed, or producing it at prices the consumer could afford as much as their ability to rally political support. Due to the wide dispersion of the farm population throughout the nation and their relative strength in the outerlying areas with disproportionately high representation in the Diet, they could mount the biggest lobbies in the country. Each group, the rice farmers, the citrus farmers, the cattle farmers, has its own organization. And between them they could easily rally a hundred "agriculture Dietmen" (*Norin Giin*). Since they usually voted LDP, and the Liberal Democratic Party has been in charge for a long time, their political support was richly rewarded.

The farmers were also encouraged by the solid backing of the Ministry of Agriculture, which not only channelled considerable assistance and subsidies but singlemindedly pursued a policy of increasing domestic production. While Japan has pleaded the case of free trade for its industry, those dealing with agricultural policy have constantly demanded greater self-sufficiency. They warned about the dangers of being dependent on the outside world for food or agricultural raw materials and tried to promote as many crops as possible locally. The incipient threat of interruptions of trade was repeatedly played up as when there was a temporary shortage of soyabean or wheat. But the likelihood of all suppliers for all products holding back was very slight. And the cost of realizing such a policy is incalculable.

Although not usually recognized by the Japanese, protection has not really helped them very much. Despite one of the most complete and intricate systems ever seen, none of Japan's farm sectors has really improved its performance greatly. If anything, protection discouraged measures such as land consolidation and diversification that could have improved the situation because the farmers were doing well enough as is. The effect on the rest of the economy was disastrous. High food prices reduced sales and farm income. They also contributed to a higher cost of living for all and this had to result in higher wages, making Japanese goods that much more expensive. Higher taxes have siphoned off money that could have been invested in new industries that offered greater potential and have cut into consumption expenditure. The funds used to subsidize rice or beef, for example, might have done more good if invested in industrial R & D. Finally, the refusal to purchase foreign agricultural produce has prompted some countries to raise protective barriers against Japanese industry.

Bloated Bureaucracy

Although in a capitalist economy they are only expected to play a supporting role, the bureaucrats began proliferating during the period of high growth when the country could afford it and social services were expanding. However, even as low growth set in and when it could least be afforded, the number of personnel in the various administrative bodies kept on rising. It has gradually assumed very considerable dimensions. By 1980, there were 1,199,000 national government employees, 3,167,000 local government employees and 940,000 government-affiliated corporation employees.

More striking yet, even when the nation's private firms were forced to cut back on personnel and sometimes reduce or hold wages down, this movement was not carried over to those whose patriotism was counted on to run the state. There was a basic principle that state employees should enjoy a wage level equivalent to that in the private sector and their wages were geared to that. But this ignored the aspects in which they were well ahead. The most prominent advantage, in an era of vanishing lifetime employment, was that they faced little chance of being dimissed and could stay on in one post or another almost indefinitely. Moreover, with larger severance payments and pensions, their total earnings were greater.

Whether this number of rather well paid people was really necessary to handle the tasks assigned them and what they were worth has been a major issue. Although there was relatively little complaint about the central administration's staff, it was clear that personnel on the prefectural and local levels had been expanding at a terrific pace and it also became known that they were earning about 7% more. This made little sense when one considers that the educational level of the central civil servants is much higher and the very functions of some of the prefectural and local ones were anything but essential. On the other hand, there have been a few categories that were understaffed, such as teachers and welfare workers.

Even when justified, there is room for doubt as to whether the civil service is making the best use of its employees. The "bureaucratic" mode of operation is obviously pushed to an extreme here. The candidates are taken in through educational background and tests, where things are done properly, and through personal connections with local politicians or bureaucrats, where they are not. But, although the degree of specialization has been increasing elsewhere, those chosen are still the generalists, at most with some legal course work. The fact that they then undergo a period of rotation, moving about from section to section, prevents further specialization. Promotion, ruled more rigidly by seniority, is even less likely to result in the best man making it to the top here than in business.

Moreover, anyone who has dealt with the bureaucracy knows, already from what can be witnessed, that the organization is not always rational or carefully integrated.[5] It is easy to get shunted from office to office before finding the right one, should it exist. Those in some of the offices seem to have little effective work and any number can be seen reading newspapers, chatting with one another, or having tea. Many seats are empty with their occupants off on uncertain duties. The flaws that could be compensated for by the zeal of officials in earlier days are more likely to be harmful now that few apply for patriotic reasons and most candidates really want just a secure job. Most unpleasant, a phenomenon rarely encountered in the private sector, there is a lack of courtesy toward the caller or applicant which is incomprehensible coming from a civil servant, namely someone paid for by the public to serve the public, but quite understandable coming from a "bureaucrat."

A major task of the bureaucracy seems to be producing forms to be filled in by the public. If all these forms are necessary, then there is little reason for complaint. But many businessmen (foreign and national) who have to deal with them find that the forms are unduly complicated and unduly numerous. Indeed, it often takes an expert to know how to fill in a form and the bureaucrats tend to get impatient with amateurs. This paper work which justifies their existence can have a deadening effect on those who get bogged down in the red tape. Although rules and regulations have not encroached as much on business as in the United States, for example, many bureaucrats also live to fulfill regulations and the more the better, for them at least. This trend is not lacking and, if it were to continue, could easily get out of hand in a nation with a bureaucratic tradition as noble as Japan's.

The fact that the bureaucracy, especially at the lower levels, is not only a machine to accomplish specific tasks but rather part of the general political process, means that it can become a center for brokerage as well. Civil servants are beset with requests from contractors for work, by pressure groups demanding services, and even by influential citizens seeking special favors. That all of them cannot be rejected is evident from the results. The bureaucrats give in most readily when politicians enter the scene and promote a specific project or request. Thus, various bodies are created that serve little useful purpose for the general public despite their great value to special interests. There are often more public works than strictly necessary or, rather, too many projects for those with political clout and too few for the rest. And the whole operation saddles the administration with additional staff it does not quite know how to use, although some job is always found.

Even in rather straightforward activities, such as one might expect from public corporations, the situation is hardly encouraging. The mere fact that they are either financed, subsidized, or protected by the government means that they are not really under pressure to perform, let along make a normal profit. This can be seen with the JNR, which is providing the same type of operations as the private railways, but regularly makes a tremendous loss. It is, among other things, burdened with lines that are inadequately used and has to keep the services going for political reasons. But there is no excuse for it to permit the degree of feather-bedding allowed so far. Nor could it pay its workers as much as it does if the money did not come from the public budget. The Japan Housing Corporation has shown itself capable of both allowing substandard housing to be built and then accepting the work of contractors because its own inspectors did a poor job. Nor could it survive without subsidies. The Livestock Industry Promotion Corporation has spent a fortune to increase production with little success to date. And there are many other corporations of equally doubtful value.

What is harder to understand is how similar practices could occur in semi-public organizations that are under government control but expected to live off their earnings. Here, the problem is not a lack of profits but that profits are too large for companies working in the public interest or accrue due to an ability to set rates that guarantee profits. KDD, which managed to boost its telex and telephone rates above any reasonable level due to relations with the government and the supervising ministry, certainly has not fulfilled its responsibility to the public. And there is little likelihood its inflated profits were used solely for the professed purpose of improving service. NTT has come under scrutiny lately because of American complaints that it was contracting for goods only from a limited number of suppliers. In fact, only a few percent of its purchases were even open to many major Japanese companies. This sort of practice may be permissible for a private company, but not a public one which must get the most for its money and be open to offers from all possible suppliers.

Nevertheless, throughout the administration, central, prefectural, and local, the agencies and corporations, there is a blatant disregard of the most basic commercial rules. Competitive bidding is not resorted to enough and there are too many cases of negotiated deals. Land is not purchased carefully enough and it too often happens that the exact location is leaked in advance to speculators. There is not even proper control of the quality of work done. But inefficiency comes as less of a shock than learning that the civil servants in a number of agencies and ministries had engaged in dishonest practices like filing fake travel claims or overtime to obtain additional pay. If this could occur in the central administration and remain hidden for so long, one can only fear what is going on at the local level.

The various governments have also been prolific in creating special corporations, such as those referred to, as well as others of a social or research-oriented nature. Some are engaged in tasks of major concern, such as seeking alternate sources of energy or promoting industries that should come to the fore later in the century. Yet, the efficacy of all these bodies is seriously open to doubt when it becomes evident that a major reason some are created is to provide post-retirement jobs for bureaucrats. About 80% of the directors in public corporations are said to be former senior government officials and the situation is not much different in prefectural or local government bodies. The next level of personnel is often also *amakudari*. Only further on down, where the work is actually done, are there genuine employees.

Moreover, given the high wages and retirement provisions of the top management, there is reason to wonder how well the money was invested. In this sort of arrangement, where the general staff stands little chance of rising to the top, the atmosphere can be very unpleasant and there is considerable friction. When those getting the worst deal are the only ones young or educated enough to accomplish the aims of the organization, there is little hope that they will give of their best. They are also tied down by all sorts of bureaucratic rules and regulations that do little to enhance their initiative or imagination. Under such conditions, it would be hard to assume much effectiveness or efficiency. And it would be very foolish to think that Japan's future will be promoted essentially by such bodies.

This state of affairs was unpleasant, but bearable, during the period of rapid growth when Japan had a relatively small government sector. Now that the economy has matured, it can carry a heavier burden and actually this will be very hard to avoid due to increasing welfare needs. Japan is thus being propelled into the age of "big government." One sign of this is the growth of expenditures, which were kept under 20% during the 1960s but rose quickly toward 30% of GNP in the 1970s. Once far behind the United States or Europe, the Japanese level has been catching up. The other aspect where the trend toward bigness is striking has been the growth of personnel, which was most notable in the local administrations and certain public corporations. By now, government's share of the labor force has risen to about 10%.

With a budget and staff that size, it has become more urgent than ever to seek greater productivity in government as well. The standard concept makes most sense in specialized agencies and corporations like JNR, NTT, KDD or the tobacco monopoly. Yet, as we have seen, performance does not always compare well with the private sector. It would not hurt if the more commercial bodies, which occupy a large share of the work force, were either subjected to strict commercial discipline or turned into private companies. For the more administrative bodies, it is hard to talk in any other terms than an increase in efficiency since output is a very vague concept here and what is most needed are intangibles like wise decisions, fair treatment, or concern for the public good. Nevertheless, there is a general feeling that the bureaucracy is much larger than it needs to be and could accomplish as much with fewer personnel and fewer statutory bodies.

This feeling has run so strong that as far back as 1962 a committee was set up to promote administrative reform. Most recent cabinets came up with vague plans to streamline the constantly growing bureaucracy. Prime Ministers Miki and Fukuda never got very far with this task. But the Ohira government made administrative reform a major plank due to the need to overcome the financial crisis. A look at the various proposals provides a good idea of what could, and probably should, be done. The Administrative

Advisory Committee urged the government to stop recruiting any new employees in principle, to recommend that employees aged 60 or over be retired, and then not to fill these vacant posts. In that way, it would be possible to reduce the number of central government employees by about 10% in three years. The Committee also suggested that similar efforts be made to reduce the workforce in local government by 10% in five years, if need be by withholding funds. The Ohira cabinet actually approved a realignment program to ultimately cut personnel by 37,600 (about 3%) in five years. And it hoped to consolidate or abolish 200 local offices of 11 ministries and agencies as well as to do away with 16 of the 112 special corporations by merger, abolishment, or change to private status.

But these plans were never fully implemented, any more than the previous ones. When Suzuki came to power, he was also under pressure to reduce the burden of government (since it was hard to increase taxes) and appointed Yasuhiro Nakasone as director general of the Administrative Management Agency to carry out the necessary reform. Instead of taking up the old plan, however, Nakasone went off in a completely different direction. Rather than eliminate staff, it was hoped to eliminate work by abolishing various laws creating tasks for the civil service, indirectly limiting growth. It was obviously painful to cut back ruthlessly. But this plan only offered a very tenuous hope that the same results could be obtained more gently and over an undetermined time.

Just when it looked as if the issue was being forgotten again, a mini-taxpayers' revolt caught the government off guard. The decision to boost taxes in fiscal 1981 was roundly criticized by the opposition parties, posing as defenders of the people. Yet, those who had been hit worst by the new taxes were business circles and administrative reform (*gyosei kaikaku* or *gyokaku*) got a new lease on life when Toshiwo Doko, former head of Keidanren, was made chairman of the Second Ad Hoc Committee on Administrative Reform and warned the Prime Minister that big business was tired of "big government." With this, Zenko Suzuki buckled under again, pledging not to raise taxes in 1982 but rather save on administrative costs. He even said that he staked his political career on the success of this reform.

Unfortunately, although the prospects were better than ever, even the verbal support of the whole cabinet did not guarantee that the measures would be adequate or implemented. The first projects mooted included transfer of government monopolies to the private sector, a decrease in certain subsidies, sales of assets and land, and not hiring enough teachers to have classes of forty. But many of them only implied a one-time saving while others already involved some hardship for the public. More substantial, long-term gains, could only come from a thinning out of personnel done more through selective recruitment than the proposed "freeze" on hiring . . . while maintaining a proper level of service through increased efficiency and productivity, a matter that has been entirely neglected so far.

The most important question, however, is whether the program will be implemented vigorously. In the past, there has been no shortage of proposals, only of action. And there are reasons to wonder whether that much will be done. In Japan, to begin with, it is hard to dismiss staff and this is particularly true in the civil service where tenure is often guaranteed. Only by attrition, not hiring new people, can much be done. Yet, even this is hard to obtain and the various bodies have gone about increasing staff with impunity. This is largely because of the overly close relations between the politicians and bureaucrats. There is a tendency for local politicians to recommend their supporters to the local administrations which may hire them. The bureaucrats are no better, engaging in empire building that would shock executives in private companies and finding room for their own friends hired through connections. Some of the special agencies were also established either by LDP politicians as a means of obtaining campaign funds from those favored with contracts or by bureaucrats to provide retirement jobs.[6]

In the central administration, it is even harder for the government to move the top bureaucrats to cut down on their own budgets or staff because it leans heavily on them in its day-to-day work. Moreover, the bureaucrats have their own special supporters among former bureaucrats who have entered the LDP or other parties. Even the socialist party would not be too keen on a reduction in personnel since the lower level staff, where unions are permitted, most often join Sohyo-related bodies. Nothing much can be done by the public to impose its wishes aside from showing a reluctance to pay more taxes, a mood that already prevails. But some of the local bodies have escaped even that constraint by floating bonds which have accumulated as perilously as the central government's own debt and will have to be paid by the taxpayers, or their children, in the future.

Defeat Of The "Distribution Revolution"

Many Japanese feel that the distribution sector has been drastically transformed in the past decade. This may be because there is so much loose talk of a "distribution revolution." Or perhaps they have seen too many articles on Isao Nakauchi, recounting his successes as founder and president of Daiei. Starting back in 1957, with a small shop and only 13 employees, he managed to build Daiei up into a huge empire. It has hundreds of outlets and was the first to break through the magic barrier of ¥1 trillion of annual sales. From there, Mr. Nakauchi plans to open another dozen stores a year and boost sales to ¥4 trillion by 1985–86, when the company hopes to have sales representing one percent of gross national product.

Equally impressive are Masatoshi Ito of Ito-Yokado, Seiji Tsutsumi of Seibu and Seiyu, and Noboru Goto of Tokyu. It is nothing short of miraculous that such people could have cut through the maze of distribution channels that make doing business in Japan highly complicated for Japanese as well as foreigners. It was because of the sector's very complexity that new techniques had to be introduced and new chances arose to expand rapidly in certain directions. But the success stories of certain businessmen or their ventures should not blind us to what is happening in the rest of the sector.

There have been many such "revolutions" in Japan that burned fiercely and then somehow just died out or were contained. We might remember that when Mitsukoshi, the largest department store chain, came into existence about three centuries ago, it was also revolutionary. Since then, the number of department stores has grown to over 300 and they have become quite conventional. The more recent booms began with the supermarkets, of which there are almost 3,000. Then came all sorts of self-service shops and the chain stores. The most impressive form has been the "superstore," with the Japanese creating a unique merchandising structure to meet their needs. It may not be long before there are a thousand of them. And now come the "box stores."

For a while it really looked as if the old distribution network would be rooted out and nothing would remain but the giant retail outlets. The "mom-and-pop" shops seemed condemned to disappear. The public clamored for lower prices and the only stores that could compete on that were the larger, more efficient units. They introduced new merchandising techniques, updated the management systems, and trained their personnel better. They started using computers and labor-saving devices. They could purchase in much larger quantities, often directly from the supplier, and even took to importing. Some of them developed own brand products. And the prices did come down . . . at first.

But, when it comes to cost, it is amazing how resilient a small outlet can be. Mom, and pop, and the kids, if they have no other source of earnings, will accept to make less money simply to keep alive. They don't care how many hours they work and overtime does not upset them. In fact, some hardly recognize any difference between private life and commercial activities. Their rental is usually cheaper when they are not simply running the store out of their own home. They also offer accessibility, living in the same neighborhood as the shoppers. If you compare that with recruitment of high school (and now college) grads, trouble in getting people to work long hours for anything but good salaries (and paid overtime), the cost of the gadgets used by modern management, and the astronomic rentals of large premises in choice locations, you see why the new units are not *so* competitive.

The real problem of the more modern units, however, is that they seem to be fighting with one another more than with the small retailers. Department stores sell more and more food and daily necessities to compete with the supermarkets. The superstores compete with the super-markets and the department stores by adding leisure items, clothing, and some furniture. Popular items are on sale in large outlets and small ones. And the various units tend to concentrate in specific areas, with a superstore opening just opposite another and down the street from the department store. The customer has a broad choice and may visit them all a bit. But, when pressed for time or too lazy to go out, the neighborhood shop is the winner, especially if it also offers delivery service.

In this tight competitive situation, the more modern units found it increasingly difficult to make a profit based on greater sales capacity. Defensively, they also tended to offer more "service" to hold on to customers. And with it they began to lose one of their prime advantages . . . low price. At one time, department stores had sold on price. But they decided that the better path was to provide breadth of selection, elegance of environment, higher quality personnel and other frills. The superstores, once regarded as low-price, mass-sales outlets also slipped into the same rut and began increasing the margin. It rose from about 15% in 1967 to 22.3% in 1978, for the bigger chains, not far from the 24.5% margin of the big city department stores.[7] It is uncertain whether the convenience stores will offer many bargains. And the box store is as yet unproven. So, if prices are not that much better, why buy there?

Thus, although the new merchandising units have grown, the limits are already in sight. By now, the department stores account for some 9% of sales and chain stores another 16%. But this has stabilized largely and growth is small, aside from growth at the expense of one another. Opening another dozen stores may—or may not—add proportionately to Daiei's sales, but it is likely to cut down on someone else's. Whereas the growth of sales for department stores and supermarkets used to be as high as 39% in 1973, it fell to 13% in 1978 and was a mere 7.7% in 1979. This was not much, especially not in a year when most of the gain represented inflation. On that basis, it will not be easy to expand in the aggregate.

Not only is their expansion slowing down, the newer units are being faced with a "counter-revolutionary" offensive. Small retailers have done much to modernize and presently offer a wider assortment or use improved methods. But they have also resorted to political means of resisting change. This was possible for the simple reason that they were so numerous and had so much staff. The nation's *tofu* makers, rice merchants, grocers and the like, mom, and pop, and the employees, and their families, added up to a tremendous number of votes. They brought pressure to bear on the Liberal Democratic Party, and the other parties, and found considerable support. In an economy that is not strictly liberal to begin with, and where it is natural to protect one interest or another, they won out against the innovators. And there were few consumer interests to complain.

As of 1973, legislation was introduced to control the opening of new stores with a sales floor area over 1,500 square meters, later reduced to a more modest 500 square meters. To open such stores, superstore and supermarket chains must obtain building and business permits from the authorities. And the authorities have to consult the local commercial activities coordination council, in which the small shopkeepers have a substantial voice. Although not always blocked, they usually have to accept compromises regarding size which hamper economies of scale. Other rules restrict business hours and sales over weekends. With this, the distribution "revolution" petered out.

The much touted distribution "revolution" was also hampered, just like every other transformation, by the incredible conservatism of the Japanese. They clamored for lower prices, but they also wanted convenient location, broad selection, luxurious surroundings, and especially personal service. They demanded at least a show of the honor and respect Japanese consumers have been getting from mere shopkeepers ever since Tokugawa days. They expected to enter any shop and have people greet them, look after their needs, and carefully wrap their purchases. On occasion, they wished to be served at home rather than making the long trip to the store.

Moreover, as income increased, there was an interest in the exceptional, the unusual, the exotic, something that would make a person stand out or give a taste of luxury. Mass produced cheese, or kitchen utensils, or canned food was all right. But clothing, or cosmetics, or leisure articles had to fit one's personality. It was essential to look just right and any number of boutiques, novelty shops, sporting goods stores, knick-knack corners, and the like sprang into existence for these very special people the consumers were becoming. This moved merchandising in the opposite direction from the earlier trends, away from the mass market and towards the personal touch. The urge for individuality and diversity resulted in a fragmentation of the market that saved the smaller units.

The situation in the rest of the distribution sector was somewhat better, but considerably less so than had been hoped. As long as one was dealing largely with things and not people, and the further one was removed from the final purchaser, the more could be accomplished. It was possible to modernize and rationalize physical distribution quite rapidly. Despite the shortage of space, room was made for larger, well-organized centers to channel goods from the makers or importers to the rest of the nation. In the warehouses, modern techniques were introduced for inventory control, billing and collection. Computers were used more often to handle these operations.

However, as one moved from the primary, to the secondary, to the tertiary distributors, everything became more complicated and the degree of efficiency dropped. It had been assumed that another "revolution" would consolidate the large wholesalers and undermine the smaller ones, many of whom were expected to disappear with time. Instead, throughout the 1970s, the number increased steadily. The small units were more solidly implanted than expected and the manufacturers, by entering the wholesale sector, added new firms to the old and competed largely with the bigger, more efficient units.

The most revolutionary move has had less to do with scale of operation or sales than the radical attempt to get away from providing physical premises and personal service by going over to mail-order sales. This particular innovation has caught on and the number of companies is growing. More significantly, a number of larger chains and some manufacturers are also entering the field. But the growth has been less than in the United States and parts of Europe, where mail-order sales account for 5% or so of total sales. In Japan, they still do not represent 1% and it is not yet certain the customers will take to this. It is equally uncertain whether the form can maintain its advantages. With a tradition of service as well as the need for after-sales care, personnel costs may grow. Advertising will be terribly expensive. And much will depend on whether big brand name articles can be added to the range of goods.

So, here we are, entering the 1980s, and one could hardly say that things have changed drastically or look like they will keep on changing even as rapidly as before. To those who let themselves be impressed by the Daiei story, it may come as a surprise to learn that the distribution sector, which was grossly overstaffed and inefficient in the past, is even more extensive now than a decade ago. That, nevertheless, is the case if one will take a look at some simple statistics. The following figures are from the Statistics Bureau of the Prime Minister's Office, but all sources give similar results. And they cover what was regarded as the period of most rapid advance.

Back in 1966, there were 9,112,116 employees working

for 2,085,857 establishments. In 1975, there were 12,368,240 employees working for 2,635,991 establishments. This means that during the time that population only grew by about 12%, the number of employees in the wholesale and retail trade grew by about 35% and the number of establishments by about 26%. The number of employees in the distribution sector actually rose as a share of the total population from some 9% in 1966 to over 11% in 1975.[8]

Thus, in Japan, one person in ten is still tending shop, looking after the customers, picking goods up from the manufacturer, or bringing them to the retailers. This does not compare very well with the situation in other countries of a similar economic level. For example, although the Japanese population was only half, and its GNP about a third, that of the United States in 1975, it had about as many wholesalers and even more retailers. The average Japanese retail store served 70 households as compared to 109 in Britain, 134 in America, and 179 in West Germany.[9] And there were two persons working in wholesale for every three in retail, showing how clumsy the pipeline was from maker, to wholesaler, to retailer, to purchaser.

This rather extravagant use of personnel has been criticized for many years now. But it is certainly not coming to an end. Ever since the recession, the growth of personnel has continued, rising 6% from 1975 to 1978. The growth in productivity has been very uneven. In wholesale, where innovations could be made and personnel used more rationally, there was a substantial improvement of over 27%. In retail, however, people were being used about as poorly as ever with a mere 2% growth during this time.[10] The fact that distribution is still absorbing new staff faster than other branches arouses serious concern as to whether it will ever take the quantum leap that is necessary.

Low productivity and large staffs have inevitably affected costs. Despite all the effort at streamlining distribution, little has been accomplished and the balance between manufacturing and distribution was further upset. Whereas distribution costs only represented 27% of the commodity costs in 1962, by 1977 they had risen to over 33%.[11] It was becoming ever more expensive to move goods as compared with manufacturing them. This has had a negative effect on the profits of industry. But there was also a worsening of the profit situation for wholesalers and retailers during much of the period. The simple reason is that, although personnel in this sector work a bit longer and are paid a bit less than in industry, they are so numerous that the wage burden is hard to carry.

At the same time, the growing costs of distribution are affecting the sales price and adding to inflation. Wholesalers manage to pass some of the costs on to the retailers. Then the retailers pass along even more to the consumers. There are, of course, periods when business is slack or resistance is felt. But, on the whole, the consumer price index rises faster than the wholesale price index. This may not even be due to retailers taking a bigger margin, although they are often quite substantial, but because there are too many retailers around. The final victim, at any rate, is the consumer who finds prices are increasingly out of reach. In fact, according to Masatoshi Ito, president of Ito-Yokado, due to agricultural protection, lack of imports, and low productivity in distribution, the level of consumer prices in Japan is double that of the United States.[12]

At this point one may well wonder whether there is any chance for Japan to throw off this burden. Two decades of innovation and rationalization, repeated "revolutions" of one sort or another, and serious efforts to boost productivity have left Japan with a distribution network that is still one of the heaviest. Rather than cast off unnecessary links and shed superfluous staff, there are more establishments and personnel than ever. And the weight of all this is hurting the manufacturers, the consumers and the distributors themselves. The future looks less encouraging than before and there is no solution in sight.

From Old Services To New Services

Japan is still firmly convinced that it will lead the world into the postindustrial society of the 21st century, perhaps treading on the heels of the United States, or in more optimistic moments even hoping to get ahead through knowledge-intensive industries. That these hopes may be misplaced must already be clear from the progress, or lack of progress, in the distribution sector. That sector is growing in sales and personnel, but more rapidly than wise in the latter which is making it hardly more efficient than before. The situation for the more specifically defined services is not much better, although there are some promising trends.

The various items listed under "miscellaneous services" in the inter-industry relations table have been growing quite rapidly over the past decade and are expected to do even better in the future. Whereas they were expanding at an annual average rate of 8.7% between 1969 and 1979, they should accelerate to a growth rate of 10.2% between 1979 and 1989, according to Nikkei's NEEDS. This will boost them from the 7th most rapidly growing sector to the 2nd position. And the weight in gross domestic product should rise sharply from 7.2% in 1969 to 12.8% in 1989.[13]

This is the sort of news the Japanese like to hear, for it heralds a big step toward the future. However, within this sector it is necessary to make a clear distinction between different categories of services. There are some which serve the economy directly and are related to business, including advertising, data processing, market surveys, information supply, legal, financial and auditing services, building rental and equipment leasing. Others are related to individuals and meet needs such as amusement and entertainment, restaurants and bars, laundry, barber and beauty salons, or bathhouses. There is a third group which will be dealt with later and basically serves the community, such as education, health care and social welfare.

If Japan is to move resolutely into the postindustrial society, it should be concerned more with the first category than the second. The big difference between it and the United States, as well as some European countries, is that the role of the business-related branches is still quite small. The second category, especially the branches related to leisure, are also symbolic of a higher standard of living, but they can only be sustained by maintaining a reasonably affluent society. In the recent past, the progress has been encouraging since business-related services have been growing more rapidly. From 1970 to 1975, they increased at an average 28% while services related to individuals grew by a still considerable 19% per year.[14]

One branch which has done particularly well is leasing. Although it only got started in the early 1960s, the leasing business has been progressing nicely. It offers considerable advantages by making equipment available to companies that could not afford an outright purchase as well as those which do not want to buy either because the material is only needed occasionally or, as for computers and some office equipment, because it is possible to keep abreast of technology as new models come out. The chief items handled so far have been, for this reason, general office equipment, facsimile machines and computers. Car and truck lease or rental have done less well. Still, leasing has grown quickly, with an annual sales contract volume that rose from about ¥200 billion in 1960 to over ¥1,000 billion in 1979. But it is still far from reaching the American level, with only 3% of the total amount of plant and equipment investment in the private sector against nearly a quarter of all such investment in the United States.[15]

There has also been a growth in software services and expertise. The number of calculating centers has increased briskly. Business consultants have made their appearance and more law, accounting or auditing firms have arisen. Market surveys are being made. And advertising has expanded at an impressive pace. By 1979, advertising expenditures passed the ¥2,000 billion mark. An even more striking development has been the supply of Western-style temporary outside workers. It was almost impossible to launch this sort of activity a mere decade ago, when it was introduced by foreign companies like Manpower. Now apparently as many as 16% of all companies employ "temps" or *haken-shain* and the figure rises to 75% of the companies with over 5,000 employees.[16]

For various reasons, however, it has not been that easy to make headway. The company being a relatively closed and compact unit, it likes to impose its control very firmly on everything related to it. For reasons of prestige, or to inflate assets, it tends to purchase its own equipment and even today many Japanese companies buy computers while most American companies would only lease. Dealing with outside personnel is even harder. Sometimes the barrier is social, that one does not have the habit of dealing with newcomers or assigning them tasks. To the extent work is accomplished by small groups, an individual who comes briefly or irregularly can hardly be integrated. For more specific tasks, especially highly specialized ones, the situation is much easier. An accountant, a lawyer, or simply a typist, has a given job to do and can be hired to do it. This is preferable to taking on regular personnel if the needs themselves are limited. And now the impetus is far greater since, with uncertain economic prospects, many companies do not really want to add to their commitments under lifetime employment.

At the same time, there has also been a growth in services directed at individuals. Some branches have done better than others. There has been a boom in the fast food business. Both foreign franchises like McDonald's and Kentucky Fried Chicken, which initiated the move, and Japanese imitators like Yoshinoya or smaller *ramen* or *sushi* chains, showed that the techniques could be applied to Japanese as well as Western foods. But they have surprisingly not driven the more traditional categories out of business. New ones were simply added to the old in many cases. Tea shops, beer halls, pubs, bars and the like did nearly as well. In fact, this whole branch has shown a strong growth rate so that eating and drinking establishments clearly surpassed the sales even of the automobile industry by 1978, reaching a level of over ¥13,000 billion. The situation in the leisure sector was more varied with movies in a slump while amusement centers burgeoned. In personal services, laundries and bathhouses did poorly while Turkish baths and massage parlors were more successful than ever.

There is no doubt that rising personal incomes, changing tastes and the huge company expense accounts for entertainment contributed to the various "booms." Future growth, however, seems less assured. Since the recession, consumer spending has grown quite slowly and people are worried about the future. Even businesses have begun to realize that they cannot endulge in the high living and lavish entertainment spending of the past. The other danger to this sector is that many establishments are directly or indirectly competitive. They are fighting for the consumer's money and, if this does not expand, some are bound to be hurt. The fast food boom was partly a result of increased spending, but it also involved the disappearance of less efficient establishment. Price wars and competition for customers not only drove others out of business, it frequently hurt the fast food chains themselves by constricting profits or leading to overborrowing, which caused the bankruptcy of Yoshinoya. In leisure, one fad drove out the other. A person was unlikely to play—or be able to afford—tennis, and bowling, and golf. And an hour spent with the "space invaders" was one less hour devoted to pachinko. Both eating out and leisure should increase, if affluence does, but not all the firms or branches will benefit from the growth.

The progression in sales, moreover, is only one side of the question. The other is the use of labor. There is no point to an expansion of the service sector if it does not utilize its labor force wisely and efficiently. And there are more than enough grounds for fearing that this is not being done. Services, just like distribution, already employed too much staff and it was assumed that the introduction of new management techniques would cut at least the person-related services down to size. Yet, it did not. Many new firms were merely added to the old ones and the overall labor force grew. From 1975 to 1978, the sector absorbed 18% more labor and reached a total of about ten million employees (while productivity stagnated).[17] This means that by now almost one Japanese in ten is engaged in services and sometimes doing things people or companies could just as well do for themselves.

The reason personnel has grown is not unlike what happened in the distribution sector. The vast majority of the establishments, actually nearly 99%, are small or medium-scale companies although large companies have managed to absorb nearly 30% of the total labor force. Even if far less efficient, the smaller operations have shown an ability to rationalize to some extent. They also often work out of premises that belong to them and are less subject to high rentals. But their biggest advantage is that the staff, frequently consisting of family members, is far less demanding with regard to wages and working conditions and more willing to put in countless hours of overtime. Proper companies, on the other hand, have to pay quite substantial wages. Despite the rather low status or perhaps because of it, service units must have reasonably well trained and particularly courteous personnel. Yet, the wages paid in this sector are higher than in manufacturing and seriously compound the disadvantages of having too much personnel, making this the chief burden of most service companies as well as a strong drag on the whole economy.

It may be argued that there is no other place for labor to be absorbed. But that is only true in an abstract and general sense. What is important is just where those engaged in services are occupied. It would be more useful for them to be in the advanced, business-related sector, for example, than the older service trades. And, indeed, there has been a gradual shift. Those in the business-related sector have increased from 13.5% in 1966 to 23.8% in 1975. This was balanced by a loss of almost 10% by the service trades related to daily life and a minor gain in the leisure trades.[18] But the situation still lags behind the United States, and parts of Europe, as regards professional services and leasing.

There is also an amazingly large gap as regards areas like education and health care. For these two headings, the United States has more than twice as much personnel proportionately. These sectors are clearly in need of expansion. By now, health care has become a major "growth" industry. The nation's medical bill, handled largely through the state health insurance schemes, has been growing by about 19% a year for well over a decade and has already broken through the ¥10,000 billion barrier. Medical expense already represent 6% of national income. Yet, with an aging society and the rising costs of medicine, equipment, hospitalization and personnel, it is bound to increase steadily. At the same time, government will have to provide all sorts of other services to care for the aged, to look after the handicapped and disabled, and to provide welfare to the destitute or troubled. At the other end of the age scale, there have been calls for more day-care centers. A growth in costs and personnel can hardly be avoided here.

Meanwhile, it seems as if everything is being done to prevent an equally necessary growth for education. Although the amount does rise from year to year, the allocation for education remains at about 10% of the national budget. And the schools, many of which are old or have inadequate facilities, are not renewed as rapidly as, say, factories and hospitals. More seriously, many of the schools are clearly understaffed. There has been a long standing pledge by the Ministry of Education to bring classes in public schools down to a maximum of forty pupils, but the progress has been painfully slow. The teacher-student ratio was only 1:25 in elementary school and 1:18 in secondary school, higher than many European countries. The overall average for universities of 1:16 was misleading, since it was low for public colleges and high for private ones, some 1:31. If Japan is to progress toward a more sophisticated society it must have more teachers at all levels as well as more researchers. But there is not the slightest chance of catching up here for some while.

Thus, we find a very mixed picture, one which does not put Japan in a particularly good light. The more essential business-related services are growing and absorbing more personnel. But the person-related sector, including old and highly inefficient branches, has only been growing somewhat less rapidly. And it will take time to reverse the proportions. Public services crucial for entering the 21st century properly have been seriously neglected. The next century will need highly educated people which cannot be provided without more and better teachers. Japan will then be inhabited by a population with a vastly increased share of aged. Yet, no provision has been made to cover the vast costs this will entail (the health insurance schemes are in deficit and many pensions inadequately funded) or supply the highly specialized personnel that will be required.

If the service sector is supposed to be the springboard for an impressive leap into the postindustrial society, Japan is liable to fall flat on its face. At best, this sector has been absorbing excess labor in order to make manufacturing more productive. But insufficient efforts have been made to develop the specific branches that can directly promote industrial growth and make the whole economy more dynamic. Services related to persons have largely contributed to an often spurious improvement in the quality of life. And the public sector has yet to prepare suitably for the essential tasks of creating a highly educated society or one able to care for its population properly in the future.

A Surfeit Of Personnel

Japan is blessed with extremely courteous and helpful service and distribution establishments. They receive the customer with a bow, look after any needs most diligently, provide a pleasant atmosphere during his stay, and then follow up to maintain a good relationship. They are frequently rewarded with continued patronage. Japan is also blessed with very persistant and very successful salesmen. They will come singly or in groups, they will come once or a dozen times. And usually they end up making a sale.

In the tertiary sector, as its name implies, "service" is the most crucial element. No effort will be spared to make the customer feel he is the center of everything. A prime example of this can be found in the department stores which carry on the proud traditions of Edo times. There is not only a very large staff, with more than enough salesgirls so that no customer will have to wait long, there are many assistant managers strutting around to see that everyone is looked after properly. There may be a place to leave the children and perhaps an art exhibit to while the

Two salesgirls for one customer.
Only in Japan can service go that far!

Photo credit: Foreign Press Center-Japan

time away. To make the customer feel like royalty, there is one young lady, dressed in a fancy uniform, to help him (or more likely her) into the elevator, another to push the button and call out the floors, and a third to bow low over the escalator.

Stories abound about the hard work and devotion of the sales staff. One, told in many variations, refers to the eager young salesman who finds that a certain shop had already bought from the competitor but who nevertheless tries to win the client. If no one has time to talk to him, he sticks around to observe the shop. Perhaps he gets to know the shopkeeper's staff, or his wife who runs the cash register. He does his best to make friends with the family, even offering to take the little boy for a walk. He comes with gifts now and then. Finally, one day, impressed by his persistence, the shopkeeper agrees to see the product and, although he may not be thoroughly convinced of its value, he is very impressed by the earnestness and sincerity of the young salesman. Thus, he gives a trial order and the path is opened to bigger and better things.

All this is obviously done to increase sales. Almost as obviously, there seems to be a close correlation between the number of people used and the eagerness to increase sales. Thus, when things get bad, rather than cut back on staff, one will frequently hire yet more and the salesmen will be sent out more often. It is felt that there is a relationship between the amount of time physically spent with the customer and the amount sold. So the customer will find himself approached more often than ever. The number of salesgirls in a store or hostesses in a bar may increase as well. And they will put in more hours or make greater efforts than ever.

But there seems to be much less interest in, or even awareness of, the cost side of the equation. Providing the sort of "service" that is necessary is a very expensive proposition. First, it is essential to have the right premises, located in a suitable place and with the kind of decor that inspires confidence, promises comfort, or meets some other psychological need of the customer. The other basic requirement is to provide the staff. Since service implies proper treatment, it is usually necessary to hire more than just enough personnel. It is preferable that there be a bit more, once again to show the solidity of an establishment, to keep a constant eye on the customer so that he not be kept waiting, and to tend to his every need. In addition, the staff must be trained just right, show a proper demeanor, know how to fulfill its role with suitable humility. Premises and personnel are very costly requirements nowadays. And since not just any premises and not just any personnel will do, they are proportionately more costly than in many other countries.

The situation can be worse when it comes to sales personnel sent out to deal with, or to find, customers. For they will be making far more pointless visits than fruitful ones, having to try many potential customers before finding one that is even interested in what they have to sell. Having come to the customer, rather than the other way around, it is up to them to arouse an eagerness to buy. This is often a rather lengthy process and can involve numerous repeat visits. But, in Japan, once having sold a product the relationship does not cease. The sales personnel must still return periodically. This is not only for the necessary after-sales service or repairs. Many salesmen make calls just to keep in the good graces of the customer, checking that there are no problems, coming by to deliver any refills in person, or just dropping in to say hello . . . and see if there is not something else they can sell.

In normal times, the amount of "service" is quite considerable. But it is nothing compared to what happens when business is slow or when there are too many goods in stock. Then the attempts at sales become frantic. More staff is taken on, people are switched from production or clerical tasks into sales. Often, rather than just send out individual salesmen, they are unleashed in teams of two and more. They increase the number of visits and the length of the stay. And they come bearing all sorts of gifts, many hardly of interest to the customer. Finally, they are also willing to lower prices if the customer knows how to deal with salesmen. This does not apply so much to private individuals as companies. Smart buyers with a good eye to the situation will know when the competition is sharpest and will wear away the salesman's resistance on each further visit until he makes the price sufficiently low.

It would not really matter too much if this situation were exceptional. Unfortunately, it frequently happens that the salesmen are under tremendous pressure to sell. This may be because there is a link between sales and their earnings, if they work on a commission basis, or their prestige and chances of promotion, if they receive a regular salary. It also happens when the companies are competing over new products, which occurs a lot since Japanese companies tend to come out with the same product at about the same time and try to carve out a big market share, fighting over each additional percentage. And it arises because there seems to be a rather loose connection between production and sales. Rather than check on the market situation, and produce as a function of normally expected sales, many companies think first of the production side. They have a given staff, a given capacity, and a desire to produce at economies of scale. So they may rush into greater production than can readily be sold. They then mount strong sales campaigns to move the merchandise.

During this process, not enough thought is given to

costs. The fact that so much personnel has to be used inflates the company's expenses. The fact that the personnel has to be well trained, sometimes also well educated, and know how to behave suitably, makes the wages of such personnel quite high, just below the industrial average for distribution, but well above it for services. If it is necessary, in times of surplus production, slow sales, or greater competition, to increase this already considerable cost, then something will give. It is possible that the company itself will find its profit margin getting slimmer and slimmer. Or it may shift some of the burden onto the consumer who will find prices inching up.

Neither side is really well served by the present situation. The distribution and service industries are burdened with too much personnel. They repeatedly made efforts at rationalization and then fell back into the old trap of hiring more staff. Over the years, they have found it impossible to make major progress in cutting down on the use of personnel and thus productivity is low. Not only is it much lower than the more dynamic manufacturing sector. It is low compared with other countries and quite simply low considered in any rational terms. According to Gregory Clark, author of *The Tribal Society*, whereas the productivity gap between the most efficient manufacturing and less efficient service industry is about fifteen to one in the United States, it is around eighty to one in Japan.[19] And everybody in Japan knows that there is a shameful waste of people.

Nevertheless, the consumers are equally guilty, for they impose this burden on the tertiary sector. They frequent department stores which they know are using more personnel than necessary because they find them more pleasant. They go out of their way to visit fancy boutiques or high class shops of all sorts even when they know the goods will be more expensive. On the other hand, many avoid discount shops as unreputable or refuse to go out of their way to visit places like Akihabara where they know the same goods can be obtained more cheaply just because the "service" is bad. Too many Japanese find it flatters their ego to be received as very select customers whose patronage is highly desired. The men who belong to exclusive key clubs, bars and the like find it impossible to wean themselves from the craving for servility and the treatment that makes them feel every inch a VIP when they enter such establishments.

Far less comprehensibly, Japanese businessmen still make purchases from their favorite salesmen, those they have known for years or grown accustomed to, whether their merchandise is better or not. There are still many tradesmen who fall for the tricks of the young salesmen making a show of exceptional sincerity or zeal. In this, they are hardly better than housewives who, knowing nothing whatsoever about the stock market, will buy shares in a company because they like chatting with the salesman. Even the more business-related services are faced with the sort of problems that sellers of kimonos have known for centuries. They must also come frequently, see that everything is running well, bow low and apologize humbly if anything is wrong, and see that repairs are made instantly. The fact that this service personnel may be costly trained personnel rather than just merchants is disregarded. Anyone caught up in the tertiary sector has to place human relations above all other concerns.

This has resulted in a cycle which some might term a vicious circle but is clung to like a beneficial lifeline by the Japanese. To sell, one uses personnel; to sell more, faster, or at higher margins, one uses more personnel. Thus, there is always a tendency for prices to rise as well. If the opposite tack were taken, it is just as conceivable that the problems could be solved as well or better. By using less personnel, it would be possible to lower costs and eventually prices. By lowering prices, it would be possible for people to buy more cheaply, benefiting the consumer, and to buy in larger quantities, benefiting the sales outlets and producers. This is the cycle usually resorted to outside of Japan. It also began timidly in Japan but gradually faded out. Each new type of merchandising unit, for example, started by using less staff only to end up with more, raising its originally lower prices in so doing.

There does not seem to be much chance that things will change for the moment. This is shown by a MITI survey of store managers and shopkeepers asking how they hoped to improve their sales techniques in the future. They overwhelmingly stressed the need "to take good care of human contacts with the customers," the top priority for about half of them, who felt it was most important to secure regular customers by increasing familiarity and contacts. The last measure thought of by any of them was "to lower the selling price," a tactic adopted by less than 9% of the small and medium shops. But, what is no less amazing, the large stores placed even greater stress on taking good care of human contacts and were less concerned about lowering prices, a mere 3% desiring this.[20]

Unless there is a serious review of the use of personnel in the tertiary sector and a gradual change in attitudes, it seems impossible for Japan to increase the productivity of these industries significantly. They will be forced to continue absorbing large numbers of people, some of them for essential tasks, many more for rather superfluous ones. And those working there will continue in an inferior social status which does nothing to encourage them personally to raise efficiency or modernize the sector. The fact that Japan could afford this in the past does not really help. For, the future is going to be quite different from the past

The golden rule of retailing: "Don't lower prices, increase service!" We plan . . .

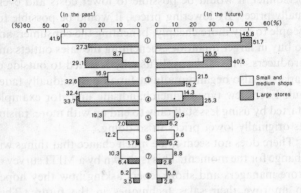

① To take good care of human contact with customers
② To place importance on having a better assortment of merchandise and on strengthening of merchandising
③ To remodel the shop and elaborate the display of goods
④ To enrich knowledge merchandise of to give advice to customers
⑤ To provide such services as taking orders by going the rounds of customers, delivering goods to the homes of customers, etc.
⑥ To stay open for long er hours
⑦ To lower the selling price
⑧ No particular measure

Source: Small and Medium Enterprise Agency. *Kourigyō Keiei Jittai Chōsa* (Survey on the Actual State of Management in Retailing Industry). November 1978.

and the cost of using more of this type of personnel than ever will be a luxury it can ill afford in the harder times to come.

NOTES

1. *Asahi Shimbun*, July 30, 1980.
2. *Labor Force Survey*, Prime Minister's Office, and *Japan's Industrial Structure*, MITI, 1978.
3. *White Paper on Labor*, Ministry of Labor, 1979.
4. *Trends in Agriculture*, Ministry of Agriculture, April 1979, p. 5.
5. See Albert M. Craig, *Functional and Dysfunctional Aspects of Government Bureaucracy*, and Yoshihisa Ojimi, *A Government Ministry*, in Vogel, *Modern Japanese Organization and Decision-Making*.

6. *Japan Times*, October 26, 1979.
7. *Marubeni Business Bulletin*, February 1980, p. 3.
8. *Census of Business Establishments*, Prime Minister's Office.
9. *Focus Japan*, December 1979, p. 9.
10. *White Paper on Labor*, Ministry of Labor, 1979.
11. Finance Ministry.
12. *Keidanren Review*, April 1980, p. 10.
13. *Japan Economic Journal*, October 16, 1979.
14. Ibid.
15. *Marubeni Business Bulletin*, June 1980.
16. *Toyo Keizai Weekly*, June 14, 1980, pp. 88–91.
17. *White Paper on Labor*, Ministry of Labor.
18. *White Paper on Small and Medium Enterprises*, Small and Medium Enterprises Agency, October 1979, p. 23.
19. *Japan Economic Journal*, April 22, 1980, p. 24.
20. *White Paper on Small and Medium Enterprises*, Small and Medium Enterprises Agency, October 1979, p. 23.

6
Education For What?

Education And The New Era

There has never been a period since the early Meiji days when so much fuss was made about education or when it was expected to play such an important role. Most of Japan's leading goals at present are tied up intimately with it. This nation is supposedly the possessor of an *information society* and its success is explained by ready access to all sorts of knowledge. It is actively promoting *high technology* products to replace more traditional ones. And it is groping toward *knowledge-intensive* industries in which knowhow and creativity will be the most important elements. All this should usher in the *postindustrial* age of the 21st century.

It has been assumed by optimistic Japanese and gullible foreigners that this big stride forward should be relatively easy for Japan given its apparently superior educational system. By now it has the second largest contingent of college students in the world and the exams taken to enter college are widely known for being exceptionally difficult. But it is not only a question of numbers of students that will determine the future nor any particular test. The students must be taught subjects that are most essential for the new technologies, they must learn skills that are most needed by the new industries, and above all they must develop a new mentality that will be decisive in creating tomorrow's society.

So far, the indicators are not very positive. Although nearly 40% of today's students continue on to college, many of them, especially the girls, only attend two-year colleges that add little to their education and are sometimes hardly more than a finishing school.[1] Although it is clear that science and technology will be crucial, over half the college students still enroll in the humanities and social sciences while only a quarter take up agriculture, engineering or natural sciences. At lower levels, there will be a need for increasing numbers of technicians and specialists but it is only recently that any effort has been made to promote technical colleges and special training schools. Research workers and scientists at the highest level have certainly not been a priority of the educational establishment either.

Japan's universities and colleges fill up as more high school students prefer higher education to work.

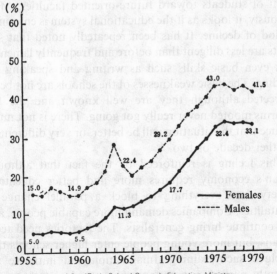

Source: *Gakkō kihon chōsa* (Basic School Survey). Education Ministry.

Quite simply, the school system has kept on producing the same basic types of graduate it produced just after the war . . . . and also before the war, for that matter. The secondary schools turn out potential blue-collar workers and simple clerical employees. The colleges turn out salarymen and bureaucrats. But they do not even offer products that can be used directly by Japan's companies and government offices. Any education must be supplemented with in-house training of one sort or the other before the new employees and workers can do an honest day's work.

Obviously, something must be done to improve the educational system if Japan intends to employ the highly talented and knowledgeable people who will be needed in the 21st century. Yet, there are no signs of an impending reform. There is little upgrading of school facilities, slight changes in the teacher-pupil ratios, and no great movement of students toward future-oriented faculties. More seriously, it looks as if the educational system is entering a period of decline. It has been repeatedly noted that students are less diligent than before and frequently lamented that even basic skills such as writing and speaking are eroding. The basic weaknesses of the schools are not being corrected although they are well known and the few reforms mooted never really got going. There is not much chance that the situation will be better, or very different, in another decade or two.

This feeling is reinforced by the fact that although Japan's economy requires more and better education, society does everything to block a parallel change in mentalities. Companies demand more capable people, and still continue hiring generalists. The factories need technicians, but more young people enter higher schools that preclude such training. Imagination and initiative are urgently needed, yet anyone who stands out from the crowd is more likely to attract jealousy than respect. It is impossible to create a generation of highly motivated pioneers in a society that clings tenaciously to notions like "a nail that sticks out should be hammered in."

Education For Examinations

In nearly every other educational system, students start at the bottom and work their way through grade school, into the university and then on to graduate studies. The most accomplished students are usually those who have gone the furthest and many of them possess doctorates. There is really no cut-off point and a person can study throughout a career, often returning to school later to take supplementary courses or an additional degree. Examinations exist to select those fit for continuation but no one examination, aside from the highest, becomes an end in itself since there are so many others along the path.

Japan's educational system is rather unique in running counter to the usual pattern on two crucial points. First of all, it is not built upward, with all striving to reach the highest level, but rather downward from the end of high school when students are sorted into two categories: those who will attend college and those who are sent directly into the labor force. And much of education focuses on one crucial examination, the one taken to decide which category a high school student falls into.[2]

Although the educational pyramid in Japan looks quite similar to those elsewhere, there are very distinct and subtle differences. In much of the outside world, there has been a tremendous burst of growth at the higher levels. Postgraduate education has come into its own and most intellectual leaders boast a doctorate or perhaps two. Those who do not go as far usually have a masters. And nearly all college graduates have taken some advanced courses or continue their education by attending occasional lectures. The most hopeful movement in recent years has been lifelong education which is materialized by vast numbers of colleges or special institutes which open their doors to those who wish to learn more, including former dropouts and retired people. It is not particularly hard to find evening or correspondence courses to fit in with any schedule.

In Japan, for all practical purposes, a college education is the end of the road. Very few students carry on to graduate school and a pitifully small number obtain a doctorate. In fact, to date, not even 5% of college students continue their studies. The reasons for this are quite obvious. Higher diplomas are not demanded, nor even appreciated by the companies, which prefer taking in students with fewer academic qualifications and a relatively blank mind. If further study is necessary, this will be offered later on within the company or outside (and at its expense). Government bureaucracies do not give any preference to those with such credentials. Nor even does academia place undue stress on the need for higher studies. Thus, there is very little glory or monetary reward to be expected for the additional effort. Worse, many graduate students find it harder to get a job. Meanwhile, the small number, and relatively backward state, of postgraduate schools in Japan often lead those seeking more knowledge to study abroad.

Added to this is the fact that many subjects which are taught at graduate level elsewhere have been watered down to undergraduate courses in Japan. In the United States, for example, one would first attend college and then move on to special schools to study medicine, or business administration, or law. In Japan, after two years of general courses, there would be a bit of specialization in the last two years giving one a major. Yet, such a major can hardly be compared to what is taught in the specialized institutions. For "elite" bureaucrats, in France, it is necessary to attend a specialized Ecole Nationale d'Administration while Japanese merely attend any college and perhaps take a major in law. Teachers elsewhere undergo lengthy theoretical and practical training in special teacher's college and professors have to keep up-to-date and publish regularly. Neither face such stringent demands to enter the profession most crucial in training the coming generations.

Equally serious is the attitude observed among many college students that the mere fact of having passed the entrance examination is enough. They do not even bother obtaining what is offered by Japan's colleges. Relatively few of them devote their time primarily to study while most lead a varied life in which clubs and social relations are at least as important. And there is a rather considerable group which seems to regard the academic side of college as nearly superfluous. They throw themselves wholeheartedly into sports, or social, or political activities. For many, college is a time for relaxation. Thus, many graduate from it with only a slight addition to their knowledge and very bad study habits. This they can do because the college entrance examination is the last tough barrier in an educational career. By choosing easy subjects, lenient teachers, and cramming a bit, nearly anyone can get a diploma.

No wonder the stress is so intense among those preparing for the college entrance examinations. This one event will determine their whole future lives and, once succeeding, there is no need to fear other equally difficult tests to prove their ability. So, the Japanese educational system is built downward from, and as a function of, the college entrance exams. Students, often at the behest of their parents, attend special high schools known for their success in getting one into specific colleges. They may follow the line yet earlier by attending primary schools that are feeders to such high schools. And there has been a massive influx of children into kindergartens to begin preparing as young as possible. While graduate schools only grew to embrace 5% of those leaving college, kindergartens now have over 65% of those moving into primary school. The expansion in the school system has been grossly unbalanced, to say the least.

The pressure to pass the college entrance exams, however, has not only affected the numbers of young people attending various schools, it has also transformed the contents of the education and style of teaching. Although the Ministry of Education has standard curricula that should be observed by all teachers, each college has its own idea of what should be learnt. And, the closer one gets to exam time, the more this influences what students study. Many schools cease general education and begin drilling their students to pass given tests. In addition to this, students spend as much time studying on their own or attending cram courses and prep schools. Since what is necessary to pass exams is not knowledge or understanding but a vast collection of isolated facts that can be entered as quickly as possible on exam papers, that is what students learn.

The most significant phenomenon in the life of many young Japanese is therefore not education but "examination hell." They have acquired not generally useful knowledge but many assorted facts and figures memorized in a state sometimes bordering on terror. This is followed by an examination in which they pass or fail. If they fail, their hatred for this supposed educational experience will grow while their ego is shattered. Such people will hardly wish to pursue education much futher. Those who pass and enter the relaxed and permissive atmosphere of most college campuses are no more likely to seek further learning. They wish most to recover from this first unfortunate experience. Then, discovering that a diploma is all they need as proof of wisdom, they may lose any remaining respect for education as such. Education in Japan is quite likely to create a dislike or fear of learning that hardly offers a foundation for a knowledge-oriented society.

This is why many critics of the educational system have not concentrated so much on the actual gaps in the store of knowledge as the whole approach to learning. Some note a pervasive weakening of scholastic ability, the ability to obtain an overall grasp of a subject so as to relate whatever information one may possess or acquire and insert it in a useful whole. And the most conspicuous flaw is of not having a critical mind which is essential to move beyond the present level of knowledge and forge ahead into the unknown. Such criticism has often come from the highest academic spheres, by people who know the system from inside and want it changed.

According to Michio Nagai, Todai professor and former Minister of Education, the schools in Japan "came to be characterized by the easy adaptation to the practical needs of society rather than by their long-term contribution to the formation of culture through the detached pursuit of truth. Education designed to develop men who think for themselves has already been abandoned."[3] And former Minister of Labor Ishida complained about the age of "low academic level-high educational background society."[4]

Professor Tsutomu Ouchi, dean of the economics faculty and later president of Todai, admitted: "any university professor will share my lament that the scholastic ability of today's students has decreased markedly." Moreover, "the critical abilities of today's students are very weak. Whether in oral or written reports, the majority of students today fail to clearly present what they have found issue with and their solutions. What bothers me is their lack of a critical frame of mind that must precede the tackling of technical problems. And this is what is responsible for their choosing common subjects and relating what others have already said."[5]

Education For Employment

In some countries, education is used to inculcate rather abstract knowledge, in others to propagate a philosophy or ideology, in yet others to place students on the labor market. Japan, in many respects, fits into the latter category. This could hardly be made clearer than by the degree to which the schools and the potential employers cooperate. It is normal elsewhere for companies and the administration to take in the products of the school system. But only in Japan do the school guidance counsellors and the personnel offices work hand-in-hand to see that youngsters flow from school to job with almost no interruption.[6]

The relations between the prime suppliers and users of labor, namely the elite schools and the big companies, have been not only close but almost incestuous. There is a very strong tradition in certain companies or bureaucracies to accept, or at least give preference to, students from certain schools. And the schools have become regular feeders for certain employers. The situation is so tight that other companies often find it almost impossible to get referrals of students while the *sempai* in related companies enter the schools even before the official job hunting season to tie down the best candidates. The same sort of relations exist further down the line, with the personnel officers receiving candidates from junior colleges and high schools, while guidance counsellors send potential clerical staff or blue-collar workers to companies they have been dealing with for years.

These relations have destroyed the rationality that exists in most other countries where a person is evaluated on his own abilities and companies are frequented for what they offer not only in material terms but also a challenge. However, since the relations are old and the methods hallowed, there is no reason to expect much change. The employers also cling to the advantages of the system. If one receives freshman employees from the same feeders they are likely to be more compatible with the classes that went before. By receiving them regularly, the schools are more likely to send their best elements. And, by coming under the auspices of the school rather than on their own they are under greater pressure to behave properly.

This being the case, it is a bit disconcerting to see the apparently poor interface between the two. For, the schools hardly seem to be turning out the kinds of products the companies seem to need most seriously. Japan is an advanced nation with a high level of technology and it obviously needs more technicians, specialists and professionals of every sort. Yet, the schools keep on churning out salarymen for the big companies, law majors for the top bureaucracies, and nondescript female clerks to join the ranks of OLs.

One of the most surprising features is the continuing acceptance —actually a preference —for generalists over specialists. In Meiji days, when there were very few specialists to begin with and the degree of specialization was almost small enough that an intelligent person could quickly make up for any gaps in training, this made some sense. It also makes sense within the framework of the Japanese system which stresses an all-around knowledge of the company more than an ability to do a specific job. But that day and age is rapidly passing. Companies are

Educating women. What for?

Photo credit: Foreign Press Center-Japan

becoming too large, complex and sophisticated for a generalist to accomplish very much. And it takes someone with at least a degree of specialization to even understand what the specialists are trying to do or how to use them properly.

Nevertheless, companies still recruit their potential managers from among the generalists with little regard to what they have studied. They do not even insist on general subjects of some relevance like economics, business administration, or science if they are in a technical field. Philosophy, linguistics, ancient history will do equally well. On the other hand, the fields that should be of most interest, including engineering, do not get as high priority as they might. Surely, an engineer can develop as general a view as a law student, if that is what is needed. But these hints of specialization already put many of the students beyond the pale of administrative posts and on the path to a specialized job, which will give them a technician's career, but rarely bring them into the "line" and onto the career escalator for management.

Only slowly have the companies realized that it can be useful to have people in specialized fields work at other tasks. Yet, this seems perfectly obvious elsewhere. In the West, engineers, financial experts, marketing men, specialists of one sort or another have climbed to the top as their particular field of expertise became most essential. In Japan, at least some companies in engineering sectors, like NEC, have seen the light and begun recruiting among science and technology students rather than liberal arts students even for potential managers. And Sony is known for its strange way of giving opportunities to mere technicians to become managers. But this is far from a general trend to date.

And there are a number of solid reasons why the system is not likely to change rapidly. The first is that Japanese companies still give preference to their special style of doing business over everything else. They want, and this has been repeatedly expressed, a person who is a blank sheet of paper so that they can write whatever they wish on it. They do not want a person who is too set in his ways, who has his own views of how things should be done. Furthermore, they dislike people who are too active, take too much initiative, and might rock the boat. Japanese companies, even the most dynamic of them, lead a rather placid existence in the sense that promotion is by seniority and harmony prevails over other virtues. Finally, by forming a person in their own inimitable way, they run less risk of that person learning something he can use elsewhere and thus leaving them, breaching the most cherished virtue of loyalty.

The second reason will explain why, even if they did want a change, most companies could not bring it about very readily. Although specific jobs, for which specific skills exist, can be found in the factory and some few places, most of the administrative personnel do not fit any job description. The bulk of the managers have no clear distinguishing marks and merely apply whatever skills they happen to posses to whatever situation they may encounter. The salarymen under them merely figure out what best can be done. This applies also to jobs that are specializations elsewhere, such as public relations, marketing, finance, or secretarial work. These are just employees taken into the company like anyone else and given a bit of training. It can usually be assumed that they will hold the post for some years before moving to another.

Finally, the system of in-house training seems to obviate the need for education beyond a rather low level and one may wonder why companies bother taking university graduates at all if it is not that four years allowed them to relax after high school, work off their frustrations, pass through young adulthood and be ready to enter the long grind of lifetime employment. Of course, if they learnt something during the four years, this was not harmful. But most companies are ready to make up for any lacks. In fact, they don't have much choice. The material they get from the schools is hardly able to function as is.

Having a person on the staff for a career of thirty years means that one can more readily afford the cost of training him. Since every company is different and the needs will vary from time to time, it must be assumed that few graduates will have just the right skills. (Of course, the companies could have chosen their candidates on the basis of such skills, had this occurred to them.) So they first offer an introduction to the company which may entail a brief period in a broad range of activities, just to know what they are and how they are done. This almost always includes some menial tasks so that one will have a complete view and also feel particularly pleased when that stint is over. Further on, when a real specialization is needed, the company will be more willing to hold courses on company time or even permit a stay abroad at a specialized institute.

The main problem here is not that the employee has wasted his four years in college because they are not taken advantage of in the normal course of a career, since the need may not exist, but that they are not even considered as being of value. Surely the company must have some idea of what its employees will be doing in the future and could thus select those who have the ability, and have shown an interest, when the screening is done. And, even if the subjects were not particularly relevant, they could be taken advantage of later on. For example, a trading company might gain by hiring an economics major from a lesser school rather than a humanities major from a top one. Or, in deciding who goes to which subsidiary, it might at least send the person who studied German to Europe and one who studied Spanish to Latin America. Yet, even such simple practices are not always observed.

Similarly, although much can be said for the rotation system, it could be improved upon. The progression of jobs is not always rational. In a trading company again, one may switch from a division dealing with steel to another dealing with foodstuffs, from one geographical area to another, from sales to accounting. There are, however, some products which are more closely related to others and geographical areas with greater similarities. Certain tasks have something in common no matter what the division. Thus, by carefully planning a career more could be obtained from the salaryman and he might also have a feeling that there was some logic to the path and some purpose to the career.

Instead, all too often, jobs are filled simply because the time has come for a given person to be rotated and there are a few vacancies around. If the schedules were coordinated more rationally, the vacancies could be arranged so that one moves according to a sensible pattern. From the steel division, one might go to shipbuilding, or raw materials used in steel making, or export of steel plants. One could be transferred not from Belgium to Brazil but to other French-speaking countries or within Europe. One could stay with sales but move to sales in a different division. Thus, at least some of what had been learned before would continue being of use.

By being moved around like a pawn, an employee gets the impression of helplessness and dependence on the company. But it is not certain that this will be translated into loyalty. It could also take the form of anger or frustration. If one is left in doubt about the future there is always an uneasy feeling not only for the individual but throughout the company when transfer time comes and until everyone knows his fate. Instead of this, a person might at least be given an alternative, to feel he can still choose a lesser evil. Or better, he might sit down and chart a series of advances into the future that could be mutually acceptable to the company and the employee, although recognizing that it might not be followed to the letter. When transfers imply not only a different job but a different location, an employee, especially a married man, might be given more alternatives or at least warned well in advance. The old system, where salarymen did the company bidding like soldiers, is likely to be less effective and possibly counterproductive for new generations.

Academic Background Society

Although the educational system does not really seem to be creating an academic or scholastic elite that can lead Japan into the future, it is creating another sort of elite that has been with Japan for a long time. This is the elite which arises out of educational background on the basis not of what one knows but to what level one studied and at which school. It creates the gulf between the high school and university graduates and between those from top schools and those from lesser schools.

There is serious doubt whether this sort of stratification is very helpful to Japan's economy or society. Class formation was a serious bane in the past and traditionally slowed down progress. It was purposely played down by meritocracy as of Meiji days and more sharply rejected for equality during the postwar mood of democracy. But it is coming back in this other guise. Despite all talk of middle class consciousness, people are striving to climb into the elite by the fastest possible channel, namely education. Middle class people are ruining themselves to educate their children and this seems to pay off as the offspring enter the elite themselves. As the class differences become more solidly entrenched there may be unpleasant social consequences for Japan.

Normally, there should be no particular relationship between class and education if not for the fact that educational background is used so unimaginatively in recruitment policies. To even apply for a job in the upper bureaucracy or big companies, one must have graduated from college, and preferably a good one. And to take the test with any chance of success one should have had the kind of training given there. Some colleges thus turn themselves into training grounds for certain types of company or government exams rather than objective learning just as most high schools have abdicated normal education to become prep schools for college.

By a process of elimination, the junior high and high school graduates are accepted into lesser positions. They end up by and large as blue-collar or clerical workers, often for smaller companies. More serious, even in the posts they are assigned to, they are hemmed in with regard to how far they can rise. The prewar distinctions between white-collar (*shokuin*) and blue-collar (*koin*) have become less sharp. But it is clear that the career patterns diverge substantially. If there were any true meritocracy, the fact of limited education might imply starting low but with no ceiling as to how far one can rise. Yet, it is known from the outset that a high school grad will only make it to foreman or supervisor or at most *kacho*, and this much later than a college grad.

This is very unfortunate for the high school grad. For, it condemns him to a sort of lesser life no matter what abilities and skills he may develop later on. It also arouses in many a "second-rate mentality" since they know that, try as they may, it will be hard if not impossible to escape their fate. Thus, if they will not rise, some are bound to take a more lackadaisical attitude than otherwise and will hardly show ambition. This is a serious loss since blue-collar workers also accomplish more if encouraged to perform to their best rather than being held down. Others may become outright disgruntled and engage in activities directed against the company. It is known that blue-collar workers who have risen to their peak are often the toughest union leaders. Whatever the reaction, whether a waste of talent and good will or an incipient class confrontation, it does Japan little good.

The college graduates are usually destined for white-collar jobs and managerial posts, from middle management all the way to the top. During part of their career, they may also be the direct supervisors of blue-collar workers. A rather valiant effort is made to erase any distinctions by having college grads start off on the factory floor or engage in menial tasks just like the others. They wear the same uniforms and eat in the same canteens. But everyone knows that this is just a passing phase and the college grads will soon rise above the high school grads who will remain in subordinate posts for life.

The gap between blue-collar and white-collar is perhaps not so ugly for the moment. But it has the potential to deteriorate in the future. The wage differentials are still there whereby a college grad with less seniority earns more than a high school grad. When they are both working in the same or similar jobs, this can be very painful for the latter. As the administrative headquarters relocate to Tokyo or other big cities while factories are moved out into the suburbs or more distant provinces, the gulf between factory and head office will become greater. And the fact that the contribution of white-collar workers to the company shrinks proportionately as their number grows, while the factory shows high productivity and the office low, may lead the rank-and-file to ask which of the two is really more crucial to success.

If the educational system causes considerable waste by instilling a feeling of being second-rate in the high school grads, it does another disservice by inflating the ego of the college grads. By virtue of entering a college, any college, they are clearly put into a superior category. But they would by very unwise to regard that as proof of superior competence. The ability to pass tests, as we know, is an irrelevant one and hardly conducive to a more inquisitive mentality or more dynamic approach. The time wasted by many in college hardly raised their level from high school. And what they have learnt in college, assuming they made an effort, can be largely extraneous.

Nothing is more harmful than the feeling of belonging to an elite and having the "right" to a more brilliant career. If it was comprehensible when only 5% or 10% of the population obtained a university diploma, it becomes absurd when the proportion rises toward 40%. Nor is the situation altered much when the prestige accumulates most with those who attend a smaller number of "elite" schools. Those who graduated from universities like Todai, Kyodai, Keio or Waseda would be very foolish to assume that they necessarily know more or work better than graduates of other schools. Yet, such is the status they enjoy and the general respect of the populace that they tend to make this mistake.

What, however, has ever shown that mere enrollment at a given school is a valid guarantee of worth? Those who studied harder at lesser schools, perhaps because that was the only way they could get ahead, may well be superior to those who relaxed more at the big name schools. Even high school grads who try to make up for their lacks can easily compensate for the little one learns in fours years of college. The fact that this does not receive recognition does not mean that they have not caught up. And it is not only them, but society as a whole, which is the loser if late developers or those with the will to succeed are kept down.

This sort of thing does not exist to the same extent elsewhere. Neither the American "Ivy League" schools, nor Oxford and Cambridge in Britain, nor the Grandes Ecoles in France, enjoy quite as much prestige as Todai and Kyodai. In the United States especially it is possible to catch up through evening school or correspondence courses. In countries like Korea, Taiwan and Hong Kong, still in the pioneering stage of their development, the lack of a diploma cannot stop a person with drive and business sense. Some of their top businessmen have not even gone to school. In Japan as well, the great founders of enterprises in the Meiji days and early postwar period were often less educated. Today even, more than 100 presidents of the top 993 companies are non-university graduates. They include some of the biggest names in Japan, led by Konosuke Matsushita.[7]

Will this still be possible tomorrow? Those who succeeded in business know that there is pitifully little correlation between academic knowledge and the talents a businessman really needs. Many entrepreneurs found that the best school was not an elite university but the "school of hard knocks." But there is little reason to hope the such dynamic individuals will rise again in Japan. They are being phased out by the graduates of top universities like Todai, Kyodai, and Hitotsubashi among the national and Keio and Waseda among the private universities. Just these five schools now provide 557 of the presidents of the top 993 companies. This makes it certain that they can perpetuate the situation by manipulating the connections that exist among old boys and the intimate links between schools and companies.

This means that, for a long time to come, Japan will continue suffering from this traditional but pointless method of categorizing people. It is a terrible waste to have people who do not try to improve because they feel it will get them nowhere. It is equally unfortunate to have people who, once having attained a high ranking, squander their ability because they do not have to perform better. Both types are less able to make the maximum contribution either to their own lives, to their employers, or to the nation.

Time For Professionalism

We have all heard the old story told to demonstrate the different wave lengths of Japanese and Western employees. A Westerner will introduce himself by saying: "I'm an accountant, or engineer, or executive . . . ." The Japanese will respond: "I'm a Mitsubishi-man, or a Mitsui-man, or a Toyota-man . . . ."

It is likely that in the future most Japanese will still refer to themselves as a member of a given company. But more and more of them will have to be something else in addition. The time may be coming when they will not have a function that changes every few years and is so secondary they hardly bother mentioning it. Then the age of professionalism will finally have reached Japan.

As the world becomes increasingly complex, it becomes more necessary to find people with specific skills to meet the varied needs. As each one of these skills itself requires new knowledge and a higher degree of specialization, it will be harder to acquire them quickly when needed and wasteful to discard them later. Even companies with the broadest range of activities will find that it pays to keep most of its personnel constantly involved in certain aspects rather than to move them around like pawns. Even those who are today the elite generalists, namely those who work their way up the promotional ladder, will have a specialization of sorts . . . manager.

It is hard to understand why Japan has withstood this trend so long. Professionalism has been a major force in the world for centuries already. It is not just a fad or a passing fancy. And many specializations have existed in Japan from the outset: doctor, dentist, teacher, engineer, and so on. This could be tied up with the traditional crafts, such as pottery or sword making, where a person spent almost a lifetime studying before becoming a master. Moreover, the Japanese seem to realize that a lack of professionalism can be a weakness. While looking down on American assembly line workers, for example, Japanese businessmen are full of praise for American professionals.

Yet, they hesitate to press for professionalism in their own companies. Some of the explanation comes from respect for the traditional management system in which a person does not have a specific task but blends into the whole. This way, one does not have a skill that distinguishes him from the rest and creates a differentiation that might upset cooperation or harmony. Perhaps equally important, if one had a skill that was marketable elsewhere and could thus survive without the company, he would be somewhat less reliable and at least potentially disloyal. Companies apparently find it safer to avoid the moral problems deriving from professionalism than to encourage it for its material value.

There certainly is a grain of truth in that view. The bane of the West has been professionals who were nothing more than mercenaries, who hawked their skills where they could and sold out to the highest bidder, who even while working for one company kept an eye open for another that could pay them more. When pushed to this point, the advantages of professionalism have so many drawbacks that it proves unattractive to Japanese. It is far cheaper to train one's own specialists as needed and keep them at their normal salary. Since they know others can be trained to replace them and their training might be of little use to another company, they tend to stay.

The traditional system did not require much improvement during the period of high growth. After all, the whole economy was in such flux that one really never knew what might happen and what skills would be needed then. A rapidly growing group could go into different sectors so suddenly that no one in the company really knew where it might be expanding next. As it turned out, it would have been foolish for Kanebo to encumber itself with textile engineers and designers when, in so few years, it moved its strong point into a completely different specialization like cosmetics. The same thing happened with the domestic and foreign offices, setting up shop in a region or country a company had never dreamed of entering before.

Under such circumstances, the skills slowly acquired in one field could not only prove not transferable but become a psychological barrier to entering another field. A generalist, with no vested interests but a good background, could enter the new field more easily. If a company never knew where it would be sending its employees next, it didn't really matter which foreign languages they spoke, if any, because they might well be starting from scratch in the next place anyway. But it was extremely important to be able to get along with other company employees since a number of salarymen might be thrown together suddenly and find that this common ground was the only thing that held them together during a period of exceptional stress.

That these days have passed, by and large, is clear. Relative stability has set in and the changes will be less rapid. Thus, it is time to take advantage of what one knows and probably also to deepen it. Companies are competing on a more stable front and they have to muster whatever superiority they have. That can now be an in-depth knowledge of their field. Moreover, faced with professionals in other countries, they would be at a disadvantage not to know as much.

The trends are certainly moving in the direction of greater professionalism. More companies are increasing their intake of graduates of technical schools at the lower level and the more technical or business-oriented fields at the university level. This applies not only to male person-nel but females as well. The fear of hiring mid-career entrants, unpleasant at any time, is at least being waived in the case of those possessing useful technical knowhow. There is apparently even some poaching among major electronics companies. The idea of job classification and merit payment has come up again and would obviously work to the advantage of professionals. But it will take some time for this trend to affect the managerial ranks. There the preference for generalists is still very strong, perhaps because, according to the *Oriental Economist*, about 74% of the presidents of top companies are the product of humanities and social science faculties.[8]

Even the tasks of the generalists are likely to become more professional in the future. They will have to know more about their own field. For example, sales people, in addition to visiting clients and knowing the company's products well, will have to engage in more market re-search. The personnel division, aside from maintaining close relations with the schools and freshman staff, will have to fit employees into the right slot a bit more scientifically. Managers, when not busy arousing en-thusiasm, will have to know how to direct—and manipulate—their employees for the long haul. Profes-sionalism will also arise because a generalist cannot even communicate with specialists, such as computer programmers or advertising reps, without himself knowing something about how these specializations work.

This does not mean that professionalism may not be quite different in Japan. In particular, it is more likely to take place within the company. Specialists abroad often work as free-lancers or for specialized firms such as consulting engineers, law firms, auditors and accountants, soft-ware suppliers, and so on. The Japanese companies, preferring to contain as much within their own perimeters as possible, are more likely to set up specific divisions for this than to depend on outsiders. Within the divisions, though, the specialization will have to be far-reaching and good enough to compete with specialized firms.

But, for professionalism to be meaningful, it must be recognized as a positive contribution. If it is only a

Male university students, already in suit and tie, trying to explain: "why I want to work for *your* company."

Photo credit: Foreign Press Center-Japan

necessary evil and professionals feel they are not really appreciated, or listened to, they will soon lose interest in their tasks. If the generalists, their superiors, do not develop the ability to understand what professionals are telling them or fail to give it due thought because, after all, they are just specialists, then much of the effort will be wasted. If professionals are regarded as less reliable and loyal than others, and for such reasons fail to be promoted or included in broader or higher level activities, they will notice it and hardly wish to give of themselves unstintingly.

This is mentioned because it already looks as if the role of professional will be a subordinate or secondary one in many cases. After all, that is the alternative being offered the middle-managers who are not deemed good enough to rise further. They are shoved off the "line" and given "specialist" posts. A professional, however, is not just someone who lacks the ability to direct others but a person who possesses more ability than others in a given field. Still, although for the wrong reasons, the call of professionalism may be welcome to older employees who cannot expect a promotion and must increasingly think in terms of a second career. Such employees are not likely to get very far at the age of fifty, or even forty, if they have nothing more to sell than the fact that they once worked for a big, prestigious company. They will only stand a chance if they have some marketable skills.

Yet it would be a pity if professionalism developed in that way, for then it would be a rather sickly and negative phenomenon. Rather, professionalism should be encouraged for its inherently positive elements. To become a true professional takes more than just ingurgitating a certain amount of information. If takes a genuine interest in the subject and a desire to push one's knowledge as far as possible. In addition, it implies having pride in doing a good job. There is no reason for employers to fear that this must compete with pride in working for a good company. Indeed, the two can go together. Professionals will be working as hard or well as anyone else, and perhaps a bit more, if they feel that their professionalism gains them recognition.

Admittedly, they might conceivably go somewhere else if a market develops for specific types of expertise. But that is not likely to happen much in the near future. Japanese companies in general do not like to hire "unreliable" personnel from other companies and it is hard to be accepted as a person. The most usual direction for an employee to move when he quits is downward, toward smaller companies, or outward to foreign firms. Neither of these alternatives is attractive enough to compensate for anything but a major, and somewhat improbable, increase in pay and prerogatives.

The risk of losing employees is a price that must be paid to obtain the quality of employees that will be necessary in certain sectors at least. So, if one cannot do without professionals, it is doubtlessly wiser to admit this and use them properly. There is no reason this should not work out reasonably well within the Japanese company system. Then, one day, employees may have the right to say: "I'm a Mitsubishi-man *and* an accountant, engineer, or executive."

Too Many "Educated" People

Japan's educational system has gotten into a rather unexpected predicament. Although there are serious lacks in higher education as regards quality, the biggest problem is arising due to quantity. There are simply too many university graduates. Like so many things in this country, production has managed to exceed demand and created an unpleasant paradox. On the one hand, there are too few "educated" people in the sense of those who possess essential knowledge, on the other, there are too many "educated" people in the sense of those who possess some diploma.

This problem has arisen because, for some time already, the colleges and universities have been churning out more graduates than the labor market is in a position to absorb. This is partially a result of the recession, due to which there are fewer good jobs. But the crisis would have come anyway given the rapid expansion of the school system and a much slower expansion of the economy. Under no conceivable conditions could Japan ever provide university-type jobs to all its graduates.

Whereas in 1965, college graduates only represented 10% of those coming onto the labor market from school, by 1975 the figure had risen to 30%. And it is expected by the Ministry of Education to hit 43% by 1985. Given Japan's rather strict division of labor, where certain jobs are filled by high school grads and others by college grads, there was bound to be trouble if the job categories did not expand as rapidly as the supply of graduates. But, how could they? It was absurd to assume that high level managerial, technical and professional positions would replace simple manual, clerical, service and distribution jobs at such a rate.

Thus, the college graduates have been encountering serious difficulties when they try to match their assumed abilities to the jobs they think they deserve. That is why, in a bad year like 1977, there were about 220,000 college students actively seeking the 60,000 jobs offered by some 3,000-odd big companies and national and local government offices. With only one chance in four of getting such a job, the other three candidates obviously had to be accomodated elsewhere. Possibilities were opened up in medium and small businesses with less than 500 employees and about 70% of them expressed interest in taking on students while many big companies ceased doing so. Yet, even as better times returned, there were still not enough "good" jobs in "good" companies to go around.

This has meant not only that students are forced to enter smaller companies but many have to accept jobs that in no way resemble the traditional occupations: not salaryman but mailman or taxi driver, not manager of a trading company or bank but of a fast food outlet or retail store. In theory, this may have been an adequate solution; the students got jobs and finally smaller companies could get "educated" staff. But, for the simpler jobs at least, this would seem to be a terrible waste of education. Who needs a college degree to drive a taxi or deliver mail?

This has already led to a slight drop in the number of those continuing on to college from the peak of 38.6% in 1976. The cause was probably the less favorable result of the calculation of what education costs and what it brings in. After all, getting an education is far from cheap. Only a minority is lucky enough to attend public universities while private college tuition has been rising at a tremendous pace and become a serious burden even for middle-class families. Those residing outside of the major cities also have to cover travel and living expenses. Sending a child to college also implies a loss of several years' earnings. So, education becomes a rather poor investment when good jobs are hard to get.

What has been more critical, however, is that the extra years spent in higher education often did not increase the intellectual ability of the future employee or just did so marginally. Thus, even more amazing than to learn that nearly 20% of the candidates for the post of mailman in 1978 were university or junior college graduates was to find out how they did on the examination. The exam was relatively tough in the sense that only about one person in twenty qualified. Yet, despite their higher education, only one in ten of the college grads passed and the other nine proved inadequate (and worse than many a high school grad).[9]

Speaking to the personnel section of the Ministry of Post and Telecommunications one hardly gets a good impression of the school system's products. "Who cares if you graduate from a university or not? Even if you do go to college, there are thousands of college graduates who do worse in 'common knowledge' and 'composition' tests than high school people. The fact that college graduates and high school graduates take the same test doesn't mean that the high school graduates are put in a disadvantageous position. The academic level of university graduates is quite low nowadays you know . . . ."

Is the Ministry overjoyed to finally have college graduates delivering mail? Hardly. According to one supervisor, "I said to myself looking at these people, 'the economic situation must be really bad.' After all, it is not the kind of job that requires college education. They do their work more or less satisfactorily. There are sometimes people who are slow and clumsy. But we can work together. It's all right." And another added: "Now I know that there is nothing particular to worry about with them. Their bosses are naturally high school graduates so I thought there might be uneasiness among them. But the college graduates themselves claim that their 'educational background' is really worth nothing and I think they are actually convinced of what they say!"

The college graduates themselves do not often defend their superior education. According to one mailman from Chuo University School of Economics, not a top rate school but still good enough to expect better, "It is understandable that the university graduates and the high school graduates are on the same level at work. It's only mail delivery. But it is worth noting that when they go drinking after work, the subject of conversation still remains on the same level. Is it because university studies have become 'popularized' or was the four years at school a complete blank?"

And a female graduate now working as an OL appeared even less convinced of the value of studies. "I feel that under the present circumstances it is rather natural that university graduate girls find it difficult to obtain good jobs. Not only is their average years of service to the company shorter than junior college graduates, most of these girls have spent four years pursuing leisure and fashion and the fact is that their academic level is not much higher than that of the junior college graduates. Nevertheless, they go around claiming that the companies should open the doors for them. This is indeed an *amaé*."[10]

But there are many employers who find college graduates not equally good but rather worse than high school graduates. They have to be paid more but do not produce more. And they often have an attitude or hang-ups that make harmonious relations in small companies difficult. Thus, one manager complained: "Many of the medium and small companies want junior high and high school graduates. However, since the number is limited, some companies reluctantly hire college grads. But the good people are already taken by the good companies and the leftovers are usually very good at quibbling. Their salaries are higher than the high school grads so human relations within the company, between the college grads and high school grads, don't run smoothly."

That such comments are not just griping by dissatisfied employers is shown very clearly by the actual situation on the labor market. Over the past years, there has consistently been a greater demand for junior high school graduates than for high school graduates, and the lowest demand has been for college graduates. The figure in 1978 was 1.5 posts offered for each college graduate, 1.7 for each senior high school graduate, and a much higher 4.2 openings for each junior high school graduate.

And there is reason to fear that the situation will get even worse. According to a study by the Japan Economic Research Center, by 1990 only 30% to 40% of the university graduates will be employed in managerial positions as opposed to nearly 70% today.[11] The others will have to go into professional, clerical, blue-collar and lesser posts. That, of course, assumes that the university graduates will accept such jobs and the potential employers want to hire them. Meanwhile, those they really desire, junior and senior high school grads, will have become exceedingly rare.

Improving Education

How does one solve the problem of too many college graduates as compared to the needs? What can be done about colleges that are so bad they should not exist? Why are there so many students who spend their college years doing little of value? And what does one do to help the large numbers of students who are not "good" enough to get into college? These are very important questions now that the period of high growth has passed and Japan can no longer afford to waste its resources, human and financial, as it did in the past.

With regard to the huge gap between supply and demand, one company director came up with a very sensible—if somewhat shocking—suggestion that many others probably have in mind. According to him, "the situation during the high economic growth period was

-223-

abnormal. I think that a normal employment or job seeking situation can be obtained only when three or four universities collapse each year and there are less surplus college grads."[12]

An equally radical solution could be proposed with regard to the bad colleges. If they do not meet certain standards, they should be closed. As for the students, both those who are substandard and cannot really benefit from higher studies and those who are perfectly capable but take advantage of the lax situation to waste their time, the best solution might be to throw them out.

But there is another solution which is so simple and yet so positive that it is amazing the Japanese have not hit upon it. It is to improve the educational level of the universities through the easiest and cheapest method imaginable, namely examinations not only for entry but for continuing one's studies and then for graduation. (This implies serious examinations, not the kind that are given now.)

Although the entrance examination for most colleges is quite stiff, once that has been passed there are few further barriers to graduation. In fact, graduation is so readily obtained that just about every student who sets foot in a Japanese college is almost guaranteed to receive a diploma. The figures indicate that a mere 5% or so do not get one after four, or five, or six years. This compares with some 30% to 50% of the entrants who never manage to complete the more stringent requirements of American or European universities. It is hard to understand how Japanese students can get away with things that appear absurd in most other nations. Nor can one understand why Japanese universities think so little of their diplomas that they are granted to people who obviously do not deserve them.

It would not cost very much to institute a system of

examinations that would make the Japanese students work for their diplomas and skim off, say, the worst 30%, while awarding the remainder a diploma that has real meaning. If this were done, the results would appear very quickly. The students who do not want to be dropped would study much harder than now. They would attend their courses and make social or sports activities a sideline of higher education rather than a primary purpose. Overnight, without hiring new teachers, printing new textbooks, building sophisticated laboratories or expensive facilities, the degree of diligence and level of knowledge that could be expected from a graduate would shoot up.

The solution is so elementary that one finds it hard to explain why it has not already been implemented . . . unless one knows something about Japanese student and parent psychology. In this age of *amaé*, it seems cruel and inhuman to make a student who has suffered so much to get through examination hell and into a university take more tests as opposed to relaxing and resuming a normal life. The students thoroughly hate tests. And the professors do not always have the courage to impose them. They, too, would rather be popular than respected. The parents, who have to pay such large sums for education, would also be extremely annoyed if that investment were wiped out by a failure. The private colleges, which are still in the majority, are afraid of losing revenue from those who drop out.

However, the laxity would seem to have more social than financial roots. Even the national and prefectural universities, whose funding is assured, adopt pretty much the same approach. It isn't only a fifth-rate college in the provinces that fails to disown its poor students. First-rate ones like Todai and Kyodai allow their students to hold on until graduation as well. A Todai or Kyodai diploma, just like any other, means more that a person passed the entrance examination some years earlier than that he has learned a tremendous amount since then. An attempt to squeeze out the worthless students, they fear, would arouse more antagonism than any other act, no matter how justified it is.

But it seems unfair to base a system on what is desired by the lazier students or wealthier parents who can afford to keep their offspring at school whether they study or not. The advantages of a reform are far greater. First of all, if more students were let into universities to begin with, this would widen the "narrow gate" and relax the competition somewhat. If they knew that it would take not only an entrance exam but continued strict discipline to graduate from the top schools, doubtlessly some students would desist. The others, unencumbered by less motivated colleagues, would be able to gain more. The universities would have a more serious student body and the professors would be encouraged to make a greater effort at training them. Finally, the potential employers would know that anyone receiving a diploma has at least reached an acceptable minimum.

This, however, could only be the first step. The role of the university has been heightened so much over past years, and respect for its products so artificially swollen, that there has been a corresponding atrophy and distortions at the other levels. There is not much point in graduating more people than can be used by the employers while failing to produce other categories that are more in demand. This means that more funds, more teachers, better facilities should be provided for them.

Once the primary and secondary schools cease being regarded as nothing more than feeders for the colleges, they can return to the task of providing a general educational foundation. This would be helped infinitely by replacing the myriad of entrance exams by a single test that could be taken by everyone, everywhere, and would be acceptable to all colleges. It should be a test based on what is normally taught in school rather than the peculiar ideas of what each college wants. Equally important, rather than caring only for the students who are academically inclined and will be moving on to college, there must be a sustained effort to prepare others for the technical skills which are no less important to society.

Finally, in recent years, the message has gotten through and an increasing number of vocational and technical schools are being opened. They include technical colleges which train proper technicians and special training schools for specific professions or trades. Their enrollment has been rising substantially, to take in about 10% of the high school leavers, but they are still far less popular than full-fledged universities or even junior colleges. More worrisome is that some of these schools seem to have become a dumping ground for less capable students and actual troublemakers. Giving them anything but a worthy position in the hierarchy would be most unfortunate.

At the top of the school system, namely the postgraduate level, we also find that there has been much neglect. Despite its advanced status, Japan has been producing very few graduates of higher studies. Even now, only a third of the nation's research workers have doctorates. This makes it hard for them to provide the high level manpower that will be needed in the future or to carry out the sort of research work that is normally assigned to the universities. At present, they are engaged in considerable R&D, as well as fundamental research, and they have the major share of research workers. But too many of them are busy teaching, or have taken second jobs to earn a living, and cannot devote themselves to their essential work. Nor do the higher institutes have sufficient funds to make a decisive contribution.

A reform is definitely necessary. If it does not take this shape, then perhaps another. But, what hope is there that any reform will come? The failings have been exposed and the need for improvement proclaimed repeatedly while little has been accomplished. For, the colleges and even lower schools are very conservative bodies and the Ministry of Education is certainly not the most dynamic. The sweeping changes noted in other countries are rarely emulated while people cling to the traditional educational system as dearly as the traditional management system, despite, or perhaps because of the endearing defects that they have grown accustomed to. If this continues, rather than give Japan the needed impetus, the educational system may drag it down.

NOTES

1. *Handbook of Statistics*, Ministry of Education.
2. See Jon Woronoff, *Japan: The Coming Social Crisis*, pp. 109–54.
3. See Micho Nagai, *Higher Education in Japan*.
4. *Mainichi Shimbun*, December 3, 1977.
5. *Japan Times*, December 16, 1979.
6. See Koya Azumi, *Higher Education and Business Recruitment in Japan*.
7. *Oriental Economist*, February 1980.
8. Ibid.
9. *Shukan Shincho*, February 2, 1978, pp. 120–7.
10. *Asahi Shimbun*, October 6, 1977, p. 14.
11. *Japan Times*, April 12, 1978.
12. *Shukan Shincho*, September 29, 1977, p. 23.

7
Underemployment And Overemployment

There Is Unemployment In Japan

One of the reasons there is so little concern about the threat of automation and other phenomena such as early or selective retirement that have a negative effect on employment is that most Japanese are blissfully unaware that the country faces any real unemployment problem. That is hardly their fault. For, the government certainly does not go out of its way to inform the public of the situation. Back in 1978, when the unemployment rate peaked at 2.6%, there was a clamor, since this level was about twice as high as it had been during the period of rapid growth. However, since then it has fallen to about 2% and this seems acceptable to many.

Unfortunately, the situation is sorely understated. One reason is the somewhat restrictive definition of unemployment used by the authorities. First of all, the Ministry of Labor defines the unemployed as people who have not worked *at all*, not even one hour, during the survey week. This is a standard definition. But it is less helpful in a country like Japan, where many people engage in part-time jobs which occasionally only add up to a few hours a week. It is not quite fair to define this as "work," although the person is clearly not unemployed in the strict sense. At the same time, the definition excludes persons on layoff, a

-229-

less usual practice and not one recommended by the ILO. More important, Japan lists within the total labor force, thus enhancing it considerably, unpaid family workers working less than fifteen hours a week. Although many of them later leave the labor force, including a hardly negligible three million female farm workers since 1960, few would ever show up as unemployed.

A more significant objection is related to the restriction that the persons must be actively seeking work. Once again, a standard condition, it is somewhat less effective in the Japanese context. Seeking work can be shown by visiting placement offices, company personnel offices, and so on. However, in Japan, many job seekers would not go through official channels and prefer trying to find something through the old company or friends and relatives. If they cannot find anything, some would just stop looking for the moment and try again later, while the students have a brief job hunting season once a year. Others, although clearly in need of a job, would be none too proud of this and might hesitate to admit such a social inadequacy even for a labor survey or, more likely, would pick up a few hours work here and there just to get by. This is a very fine attitude and one that must be respected. But it also contributes to producing unemployment statistics that are not as alarming as the true situation.

If we want to know how many people are out of work because of the recession, it is almost easier to find out indirectly. One method, although hardly flawless, is not to count the unemployed (since many will not admit to that) but to count the employed. Thus, if we look at the employment statistics for the past few decades, we find that there has been a steady increase in the working population of about 600,000 to 700,000 persons per year. This is the outcome of an annual increase in population of over a million and roughly two-thirds of them entering the labor force. Normally, the figure should not vary much from year to year. So, it was highly unusual that only 110,000 were added in 1974 and 130,000 in 1975. Even taking the whole decade of the 1970s, the good years with the bad, we find that the increase in the labor force was only 4,066,000.[1] This is the lowest growth rate since the war. And it is a couple of million short of what it should have been.

If we take a look at the working population before the oil crisis, in a relatively normal year like 1970, we can find the number of people 15 years old and over who were working and get a participation rate of 65.4%. By 1976, it had fallen as low as 63.0%, before rising to 63.4% in 1979. This means that during the post-oil shock years suddenly more than 2% less of the population was working than before it. Those are the couple of million workers who disappeared. Admittedly, some younger people decided to continue on to college since it was hard to find a job and

There is no unemployment in Japan, just less people working. Labor force participation rate by sex.

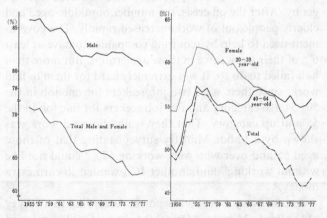

Source: *Labor Force Surveys*. Statistics Bureau. Prime Minister's Office.

there were more older people who decided to retire. But this cannot explain the whole difference since we have met many of these jobless and know they would be happy to work.

Just who are the uncounted ones? They are not the unemployed covered by the government's definition. But they are clearly people who, in a better economic situation, would be out working. They include some for whom work is superfluous and were thus quite willing to withdraw from the labor market. But they also include people who gave up in despair because they knew they did not have the necessary skills or got tired of looking for work. We can call them the "latent unemployed" or the "invisible jobless." If they were living in another society, however, one in which it is not shameful to admit being unemployed or where, in fact, one could collect benefits for that, it is certain they would appear in the official unemployment figures.

One of the largest contingents among those who would have accepted work if it were available are older men who have retired—voluntarily or not—and still need a job to get by. After the oil crisis, the number of middle-aged and elderly people out of work increased rapidly. The government tried to help by requiring companies to have at least 6% of their work force in those age groups. But more than half failed to do so. It was extremely hard for them to find work, since there were two job seekers for one job in the 50–54 age category and five job seekers for one job in the 55 and up category. That they really did need work was shown by a Labor Ministry survey stating that of those aged 55 and over who were working 67% "could not live without working" and another 16% wanted to earn extra money.[2]

Another major group is women. According to a survey of the Prime Minister's Office, the share of jobless married women who desire to work has risen sharply from 21% in 1965, to 32% in 1971, and 36% in 1977.[3] Obviously, if actually offered a job some would turn it down. But not all that many, since about two-thirds sought work to earn an income and there has been a steady influx of women in their thirties and forties to the labor force. It must also be remembered that many female college graduates looking for a job never find one. Anyway, this pool of women who claim they would like to work amounts to over five million and is far too large to be ignored or wasted.

If these latent unemployed or invisible jobless were the end of the problem one could be relatively satisfied with the situation. For, then it would only be necessary for employment and the economy to improve somewhat for them to be absorbed, or at least those who want work most urgently. But there are many others who come first. As we saw, Japan's use of people was very sloppy in the past and there are numerous sectors with more personnel than necessary and where either financial difficulties or new possibilities of rationalization could lead to further dismissals. There are plenty of sectors where companies are still slimming, not by dismissing workers but by refusing to hire new ones. Thus, the present labor force will have to be used properly before much expansion comes.

In the past, either because many companies had been counting on continued growth or because, with lifetime employment or even modified systems, it was necessary to hire employees at the bottom to have them in middle and higher levels when they were needed, most companies recruited personnel not on the basis of present require-ments but what they expected to need in another ten or twenty years. With expansion at a rate of 10–15% a year, companies often hired 15–20% more personnel (just in case). When the growth slowed down to about 5% for most companies, they found themselves with excess personnel or "hoarded unemployment." They had put aside workers for the time when they would be needed only to find that they were not needed at all.

Similarly, with the traditional method of hiring not to fill specific jobs but first recruiting and then allotting jobs to those on the staff, there was much inefficient use of personnel and what in other countries would be called "disguised unemployment." It is quite impossible to know how many such people exist at the present time or earlier. But the figures mooted some years back, none of them with solid evidence, are nonetheless quite extraordinary. They were put at two to three million which is a massive army of poorly employed people which could have turned into another 4% to 6% more unemployment.[4] That some of them probably did join the ranks of the unemployed was shown by the way the companies no longer referred to them as loyal workers who had to be protected but rather as "the unemployed within the company."

One further way in which the employment situation is getting worse without leaving the slightest trace in the unemployment statistics relates to hours worked and status. Obviously, if the definition of employment involves working at all, merely one hour a week, it will hardly be noticed when the amount of overtime falls even though this cuts into the workers' livelihood. Moreover, when a full-time worker is replaced by a part-time worker, there will be no increase in the unemployment figures. As a matter of fact, a gradual shift from full-time to part-time workers might well show up as an improvement if it takes more part-timers to do the same work. These are already major trends at present.

The most insidious threat is the tendency of many companies to turn from regular workers to temporary or part-time workers. The number of regular workers in all industries has remained stagnant ever since 1974 and regular workers in manufacturing has fallen by more than 10%. At the same time, the share of part-time workers has risen sharply from 6.7% in 1970 to 9.6% in 1979.[5] It is particularly noticeable for women who are taken on this basis even while older men are dismissed. These trends can be expected to continue since the major companies, those which usually hire regular workers, are recruiting less actively than smaller or medium-sized companies. This will strike a further blow against lifetime employment which is strongest in the larger companies. For, it subtly alters the very nature of the work relationship by making it more fragile for many people and allowing employers to more readily shed their unwanted personnel during any future recession.

Even those who feel that such an unconventional method of measuring unemployment by reference to the "latent unemployment" or the "unemployed in the company" inflates the figures unduly will probably admit that both phenomena do exist. They will also admit that elsewhere some of those desiring work but not actively seeking it would be clamoring for unemployment benefits and thus be counted. Moreover, the only reason many of the employees were not dismissed is that they could be looked after Japanese-style, namely by staying with the company or being retrained thanks to government subsidies. Left on their own, the companies might have been more ruthless. Thus, at least some share of each category would have been included as unemployed in a social context like that of the Western countries (one Japan is increasingly resembling). That would then bring its unemployment rate to 5% or 6% which is also pretty close to Western levels.

This leaves us with a few rather embarrassing questions. What would happen if those who were not counted as unemployed but face much the same problems stood up to be counted? What would happen if people were in such serious need of work that they were not willing to live off their families or retire into the shadows? What would happen to Japan if these people were to become unemployed for real? What would happen if they went so far as to demand benefits and relief?

These are real problems which cannot be dismissed or glossed over. In fact, the sooner they are looked into before they reach a crisis point the better. A good start would be to change the definition of unemployment to make it a bit stricter and to more seriously study the evolving employment situation. It might then be discovered that further measures would have to be adopted for job security or job creation, this time not only for employees sponsored by major companies but the mass of individuals who want work and also the coming generations. Finally, more ingenious efforts will have to be made to tap the latent sources of labor which exist, among women, older workers, and elsewhere, instead of letting them go to waste.

People Or Robots?

Toyota Motor Company has always been proud of its staff. It is intelligent, hardworking, eager young people like this who are the real secret of our success, they say. And Nissan, coining a noble but not terribly original slogan, insists that "an enterprise is its people." These companies and many others have always claimed that Japan's progress as a modern manufacturing nation hinges on people . . .

And yet, slowly but surely, they are driving people out of their companies. In the automobile industry, there is a very sharp increase in automation once again, this in preparation for the long-awaited "small car war." But it is beginning to look more and more as if this war will be different from any past ones in which the enthusiasm and intelligence of the workers were aroused to overcome any difficulties and raise productivity. Instead, it will be like something out of science fiction where it is not the few remaining human beings who will be fighting it out but machines and robots.

Toyota is already using about 400 industrial robots in its factories and it keeps on ordering more. By 1983, it is expected to have a total of 900 robots. Nissan Motors, keeping in step, has also announced that it will be buying 300 units. Toyo Kogyo has decided to buy 50 and Isuzu will follow suit. These robots are being used especially in hard or unpleasant jobs, such as spot welding. But they can be used for many more tasks as new types are developed and production costs fall. Once they are cheap enough, Japan can expect a real invasion of the robots. (The Japan Industrial Robot Association boasts that production will keep increasing by 24% a year over the decade.)

The demand is certainly there. After all, robots are hardworking, diligent and polite. They are willing to work day and night and don't stop for a lunch break or to chat with colleagues. They don't complain about the personality of the foreman or go on strike against the managers. They do what they are programmed to do and otherwise keep quiet. When they are cheap in addition, they will be highly preferable to human beings in many ways. Of course, they don't wear white uniforms, sing the company song, or bow to superiors, but that can probably be programmed in with time.

It is not only in the automobile industry that such changes are taking place. When Nippon Kokan had to build a new steelworks in Ohgishima, it was not only ultramodern and integrated, it was also highly automated. Thus, NKK was able to reduce its labor force from 18,000 to about 8,000 in ten years. That means that about a thousand jobs were lost each year. Modernization of Japan's steel industry is continuing apace and it would not be surprising if it kept on eliminating several thousand jobs a year for a long time to come. There is increased automation or mechanization in most of the other industries, chemicals, electronics, textiles, plastics, anywhere it can be done.

These new factories are actually quite eery affairs. One gets a very strange feeling to walk along assembly lines with hardly any personnel. In Nissan's Zama plant, where 96% of the spot welding is done by robots, there are only 67 workers per shift for a production of 1,300 cars a day. One feels uncomfortable moving along the miles of passageway at the Ohgishima works and watching the molten steel turned into bars by massive machines with hardly a soul around. The employees, where there are any, often seem to be just observing the machines. To even call them "workers" seems a bit generous. More often they are operators, sitting in an antiseptic glass-enclosed room and looking out on the actual production work. They may have to pull a switch now and then, if it is not precontrolled. Otherwise they just kill time. If there is a failure, if the machines or robots don't work, the human element may have its chance. But increasingly even the trouble-shooting and corrections are done by computer.

Computers are having much the same effect, not only in the factories, but in the warehouses, stores and offices. They are more versatile, and thus more voracious in replacing human beings, because they can be used in many more sectors, including services like banking and insurance, standard administrative work throughout the economy, to handle ordering and invoicing in distribution, as well as to guide the machines and robots in industry. Japan doubtlessly finds comfort in the fact that its own computer production is growing and absorbing some workers. But hardly as many as are being replaced. And the good (or bad?) news is that computer production, which grew at a rate of 10% a year over the last decade, is expected to forge ahead at 16% a year during the next. Since computers are now smaller and cheaper, this means they should be able to make people redundant at twice the old rate.

It is hard to know the cumulative effect of such measures because automation has not become a major issue in Japan. But a look at the statistics will indicate that it must be substantial. The slimming activities of manufacturing and industry in general have resulted in an amazing situation where production has been boosted well above the pre-oil shock level but employment has never caught up. There would be no problem if those who lost a job in one industry, say steel, found another in, say, robotics or computers. Instead, there are fewer people employed in manufacturing today than ten years ago.

It is not really so easy to understand the purpose of this sudden spurt in automation. It is hardly as if Japanese industry were so backward and uncompetitive that it had to upgrade to survive. In fact, the competitive edge of Japanese automobile or steel plants over their counterparts abroad is still tremendous. Nissan and Toyota can turn out ten cars with the same staff in the time other companies only turn out three or four. Japan produces the best—and the cheapest—steel. True, there is some apprehension as to what General Motors or Krupp are doing. But it looks more as if inter-Japanese competition is at fault. Toyota is most worried about Nissan, and vice versa. The same thing applies right down the line in every branch of industry.

No complaints, no goofing off, no wage hikes, in fact, the ideal work force. Robots replace even Japan's renowned workers.

Photo credit: Kawasaki Heavy Industries

There is little reason to assume that this process will not continue. Japanese managers tend to think in linear terms. Once they get a good idea they plough straight ahead without worrying about any disadvantages, side-effects, or harm to others, until the situation becomes so absurd that they have to change direction. This is the season for upgrading productivity and trimming costs. Not much more can be done to improve upon man while labor gets costlier all the time. On the other hand, loans are available, new technologies have been introduced, and once paid for the machines and robots will do their work and leave the managers in peace to deal with other headaches like sales and paying back the loans.

It is not even certain the managers paid much attention to the cost aspect. After all, a robot still costs about ¥10 million and there are electricity, maintenance and other overhead involved in keeping it at work. That is four years' wages for a young worker. Despite his weaknesses, an eager young worker might make some good suggestions and engage in QC activities while the machine just learns a few tricks. Machinery is not cheap either. The Ohgishima works cost about ¥880 billion and allowed a reduction of 10,000 workers. These workers could have continued in service thirty years for the same money. Of course, there were other reasons, improvement in quality, better use of energy and raw materials, cutting down on pollution. But it is far from certain that the cost element was sufficiently considered. It is just possible that the decision-makers were blindly following the old rule of Sakichi Toyoda, founder of Toyota, "whenever there is money, invest it in machinery."

Elsewhere, this mad dash into automation would have been blocked by the unions. However, Japanese enterprise unions, which have so many advantages, are particularly weak—or disinterested—in this matter. There are very good arguments in favor of automation for all concerned . . . if the immediate hardship can be avoided. Higher productivity means the company will prosper, better wages can be paid, and admittedly the workers will have easier jobs (the worst going now to robots or machines). The only proviso demanded is that labor not be laid off. This is usually accepted by the company and automation proceeds with the backing of the company's union. Only the broader federations, especially Sohyo, raise the overall problem of rationalization, albeit in a rather abstract manner.

Those who are really hurt are not consulted. They are the part-time or casual workers who will no longer be needed. They are the outside subcontractors who will not have to be used. Especially, they are the young employees who will not be recruited at the bottom. The reduction of personnel takes places mainly through attrition with very few young people entering while older ones are retired out. Not ever being in the company, they have no say as to its fate. That also means that they have no say as to their own fate either. They are the thousands and ultimately millions of Japanese who will find that there are fewer jobs to go around.

If this is not the companies' concern, or the unions' concern, whose is it? One would assume that it will have to become the concern of those who did not participate in creating the problem, first of all the government, and eventually society as a whole. For, it is impossible to leave people without jobs, especially young people, and most particularly in a country like Japan that depends for its social and political stability on relatively full employment. Most seriously, it will be the problem of coming generations, which are being deprived of opportunities they might otherwise have had.

Will the human being survive in this atmosphere? This is far from certain, although there are a few hopeful signs. When certain companies went too far in automation, they found that the remaining workers were doing a less good job and that morale was falling. It actually got to the point where it was decided to scrap some of the machines and reintroduce a human-run factory. With this, productivity picked up again. Perhaps the human element, when stripped of its prerogatives and emasculated into the servant of machines and robots will revolt, and minor mistakes where humans should not be replaced will throw things out of kilter.

At any rate, the latest spate of rationalization and supposed efforts to make the worker's life easier are proceeding so rapidly that the first impact will be to make more workers redundant. If they are then transferred from manufacturing, where they at least had a valid job to do, to a tertiary sector which has already absorbed huge influxes of personnel, the new job they get will be only marginally useful and the increase in productivity at the factory will be lost in the rest of the economy. If they cannot find any job, that will be a personal and ultimately a national tragedy.

Age Of Job Suitability

It is one thing to be without a job because none is available. It is quite another to be without a job because one will not accept the kind of work available. Whereas, throughout most of Japan's history, people were willing to compromise with reality and accept whatever job was going, either because they felt it was unworthy to be unemployed, or because they needed the money desperately, things are changing now. It might be felt that the recession would force people to swallow their pride again. But this is not the case and some aspects of the recession actually enhance the trend toward a more fastidious choice of occupations.

Traditionally, junior high and senior high school graduates moved promptly into a job of a commercial, clerical or blue-collar type. They have always been a popular source of recruits and never found it hard to obtain a job. Even in the midst of the recession, there were three job openings for each person aged 19 or under. With this, they could readily pick and choose and many of them tried several employers before finally settling down. Increasingly, however, young people have opted for another, more appealing choice . . . namely not to seek work but rather stay in school a bit longer. Whereas in 1965, 27% of the junior high and 60% of the senior high school graduates sought employment, by 1979, only 4% and 43% respectively where doing so. As a matter of fact, these much sought after employees became so rare that they were referred to as "moonstones" or "golden eggs" by potential employers.

Once having graduated from college, obviously the members of the educational "elite" were not willing to accept the same sort of jobs that were offered to those with less education. No, they wanted good positions in good companies. To some, this represented the top thirty chosen each year by the students, to others the magic circle included several hundred or those listed in the stock exchange. But almost all were determined to enter a company which qualified as large, with over 500 employees, and which had as prestigious a name as possible. That all could not accomplish this was becoming increasingly clear during the recession. But they still tried, making the dash to get through this narrow gate a frantic one.

For example, in 1977, the Ministry of Labor found in a survey of eleven famous private colleges that fully 80% of the job seekers were intent on joining a "first-class" firm. Unfortunately, only about a quarter of them were likely to do so. The question arose as to what to do with the remainder. Evidently, they could go to second-rate companies and, if worst came to worst, third-rate ones. The universities were flooded with applications from lesser firms and there were far more openings than candidates. For example, Hosei University received offers from 7,000 firms but concentrated on 2,000 of them. Chuo University received job offers from 7,800 companies but not a single student bothered to take the recruitment tests of 5,500 of them.[6]

Thus, as of the recession, those students who were obliged to find a job eventually had to accept employment in less impressive companies. But not all were that hard pressed. Many students decided to flunk a few courses to stay on at college an extra year for employment reasons (*shushoku ryunen*). Others became *ronin* and kept an eye out for a job. The tendency to accept second best was constantly resisted due to the realization that, in a system of lifetime employment, such a decision could be fateful throughout a person's whole career. And it made students far more selective than if they felt it was quite natural to try a few jobs before settling down or that a big company would accept them later on even if they had first been with a smaller one.

Although there were few enough objective differences between many big and many smaller companies, the students were very hard to please. Small companies could be just as well run, sometimes they provided better wages and fringe benefits, they were usually more personal and less bureaucratized and, grateful for having obtained university graduates, they would treat them much better than elsewhere. But the students had been so thoroughly brainwashed that they disliked these companies because they did not have the solidity to guarantee a secure life to career's end nor the prestige most coveted.

Such an experience was obviously even more painful for the employers. They liked to hold on to their labor force, too. Yet, hiring college graduates increasingly came to look like a big risk. One small company owner admitted that he had recruited ten graduates from first-rate universities the year before but that half of them had left only six months after starting work. Another small company employer called the relationship with these students a "one-sided love affair."

The situation regarding female personnel was often more difficult. For, the women also had the alternative of taking up occasional work or simply retiring to their parents' or husband's home and not working at all. There was relatively little pressure on young women to take a job. The prestige associated with some types of work might have been a reward. But more often than not accepting such a job, other than one briefly before marriage and as a temporary experience, was not evaluated very highly. In fact, many a husband was upset that his wife should work and make him look like a poor provider and the mother-in-law was adamant that a wife should not forsake her family for a career. Only older women, usually from less affluent categories, were seriously in the labor market. And even then there were clear limits to what work would be accepted, recession or no recession.

Thus, the public employment offices received untold thousands of men and women seeking work. But rarely the kind of work that was available. The women came looking for light office jobs, whether they had clerical skills or not, and left if none were on tap. They were not interested in dozens of openings in other categories such as shop attendant, waitress, manual worker, switchboard operator, or nurse. Where one could ever find the old docile and painstaking assembly line workers of yore was far from certain. It was even less likely that new generations of women would enter trades such as laundry and dry cleaning, household domestic service, or the like. Among the men, there was a growing shortage of people willing to accept normal blue-collar jobs, let alone menial or heavy labor and work in unpleasant or dangerous environments. There was already a shortage of day laborers, road or house constructors, carpenters and similar crafts. And many sons would not become farmers or fishermen like their fathers.

The situation was toughest, and most paradoxical, in small and medium enterprises. Although unemployment was still high, they were constantly complaining of a labor shortage. Not only couldn't they find unskilled labor or assembly line workers, they had openings for technical workers, technicians and researchers. Many small distribution and service companies were in a similar bind. In order to attract new staff, some of them are making serious efforts despite their tighter financial straits. They are increasing wages, improving the retirement payment and pension schemes, and introducing the five-day work week. But one thing they cannot change, that is their size. This seems to be the main reason so many potential employees refuse to come. No matter what efforts they make to upgrade in such a climate, they will always have trouble recruiting. And the trouble will become increasingly acute since the smaller companies are already stuck with a rapidly aging work force.[7]

Japan, having caught up with the West in so many ways, is finally entering the strange employment trap other more "advanced" countries know so well. Although there is unemployment, and people are seeking work, there are plenty of jobs which they turn their nose up at and there are plenty of jobs which just go begging. Thus, in the midst of the recession, the Ministry of Labor's Employment Security Offices carried nearly a million active openings as compared to one-and-a-half million applications. Yet, they were unable to fill the vast majority of their job offers. Indeed, the number of "matches" between potential employer and employee shrank from 158,000 in 1970 to 117,000 in 1979 (at a time when there were over a million unemployed). The success ratio, if that is what it can be called, actually fell from 14.8% to 7.7% during that period.[8]

That this situation is more than a passing one is intimated by the fact that the older people are less picky than the younger ones. People in their forties and fifties, who encounter very few job openings, realize that those existing are usually pretty bad. Nevertheless, men accept jobs as janitors, night watchmen, handymen and other low status positions despite the fact that some of them were once senior salarymen or even managers. Married women are hired for menial jobs in factories or sales outlets. But young people who, throughout the recession, had more offers than could be filled, maintained a relatively high level of unemployment that could have disappeared overnight if not for their excessive expectations.

A whole generation of young workers now believes in "job suitability." It is not a question of just any job or even one that pays well. It is not a question of the candidate suiting the job. No, the job must suit him! Thus, a government counselling service in Tokyo receives hundreds of workers in their twenties and thirties who come to complain "I don't understand the significance of working" or "the present job does not suit me." Company personnel officers are repeatedly shocked to learn that an apparently successful employee has suddenly quit because the "job did not suit my nature" or he wanted "to find the true meaning of life." And university placement offices admit that many of the young people they are recommending will accept a job and then decide whether it suits them or not. If not, they do not hesitate to leave.[9]

There is bound to be another kind of difficulty in the future as well. For, some employers have begun to revolt against the kind of human material being sent them. These are especially people with good academic background who are forced to apply for jobs that would ordinarily be beneath them. Their qualifications, however, are not really needed for such low level jobs and many company placement officers will regard them as overqualified. That could be tolerated if only they had the qualifications that were needed. But usually they just have a diploma without any practical skills or directly applicable knowledge. This means that they are no more useful, and probably harder to get along with and more expensive, than less qualified persons. While the students' expectation gap grows, the employers are gradually finding that the labor available does not meet their expectations either.

This means that Japan is heading for a serious predicament. Previously, for all the lesser jobs and smaller companies, it drew on junior or senior high grads. There was also a steady stream of girls from the countryside who were less picky than those in the cities. Small-scale industries could usually find staff if they were willing to locate near smaller towns or in agricultural regions so that farmers could work out of season or even full-time if their wife tended the farm. And many of the most menial trades were traditionally held by the *burakumin*. By now this segment of the labor force has shrunk considerably and some of the sources have just about dried up.

Other countries have solved similar problems by accepting immigrants or bringing in "guest" workers. Given the density of population, cultural and linguistic differences, and the reluctance to accept foreigners, this possibility does not exist in Japan. The alternative so far has been for small and labor-intensive industries to "migrate," that is, to relocate in places like Korea or Taiwan where labor is cheaper and less demanding. But this also leads to a decrease in jobs and adds to unemployment. And it is obviously no solution to how one finds workers to do the unpleasant and degrading jobs that will always exist.

Of course, if the Japanese made an effort to discriminate less strictly between jobs which are "suitable" and the others, the problem could be overcome quite readily. But such snobbery is very deep-rooted and follows customs going back many centuries. The close alignment between education and employment has only reinforced the tendency. So, there is reason to fear that the situation would only become worse if, ignoring the cultural aspects of the unemployment problem, something were done to reduce the "hardship" of the unemployed. The choice between accepting an undesirable job and living a bit off unemployment benefits might actually breed a new generation of jobless who do not regard it as particularly shameful to be out of work and who would not think it beneath them to accept a dole . . . although they would find it unacceptable to take a second-rate job.

Lest anyone claim that such fears are pointless in Japan, renowned as it is for an exceptional work ethic, it might be mentioned that the first signs of such a trend have *already* appeared. Recently, the Ministry of Education was amazed to note that, rather than rush off to a job right after graduation, as many as 10% of the college grads chose not to seek employment. And the Ministry of Labor is aware of a growing number of young men and women who work for a while, then quit, and only look for another job when the money runs out. Others purposely misbehave at work so they can be fired and thus qualify for unemployment insurance. After the benefits cease, they look for another job and figure out how to get fired again.

The Unemployable

Throughout the world, government officials, economic planners, businessmen and workers keep their eyes on the unemployment statistics. There are solid reasons for wanting to know how many of those seeking work are out of a job. But, in order to have a really good idea of the basic health of the economy, one should also keep a close watch on just how many are in the job market at all. It is quite possible for a country to have negligible unemployment, like Japan, and yet find that its labor force is steadily shrinking so that those who do work have a growing burden to carry. Those who fail to enter the labor force sometimes have excellent reasons not to work, sometimes rather poor ones, but they are still not even potentially employed. To distinguish them from the true "unemployed," namely those seeking work, they might be called the "unemployable."

There is a figure collected by most labor authorities which shows the number of persons of working age who are either working or looking for work. It is the participation rate. Since it still includes those not working but only seeking work, it does not really show who actually is carrying the burden of the economy. But, with only 2% or so unemployment, the deviation is rather small in Japan. Although a country can change its definition of working age, that has not happened recently for Japan. Thus, the participation rate is a reasonable basis for following certain long-term trends.

These trends have been major. If anyone had bothered following them rather than the comparatively modest increase in unemployment, they would have been regarded as ominous. During the long period of growth and on into the recession, the share of working age people (i.e. 15 and over) in the labor force has kept on dwindling. It dropped from 70.8% in 1955 to 63.4% in 1979 or 7.4%. The decrease for men was somewhat smaller, just from 85.9% to 80.2% or 5.7%. That for women was more drastic, from 56.7% to 47.6% or 9.1%. Nor is there much hope that this drop has ceased as a whole, although there has been some improvement over the low point in 1975.[10]

To some extent, this is a perfectly normal phenomenon. There is a tendency in all advanced countries for the participation rate to decline and Japan has simply been falling into line. It now has a participation rate that is roughly similar to that of the United States, Great Britain or Australia. It is still somewhat higher than France, Germany or Italy. And it results, so far, basically from natural demographic and social changes. There are fewer young people, many going to school longer, and more old people, some of whom must retire.

Not so long ago, most students went to work about the age of 15, when they finished junior high school. Since then, the trend has been to carry on at least through senior high school, only entering the labor force at 18. In fact, if senior high school is made compulsory, the real minimum age for employment in practice will be 18 and not 15. At the same time, more and more students have been continuing on to the university, already a larger share than in most advanced countries. Thus, the participation rate among teenagers is unusually low, less than 25%.

At the other end, the changes have been even more striking. With the improvement in health services and greater affluence, the life expectancy has been increasing at a rapid pace, rising to 74 years for men and 79 for women. Much of this increase has only taken place in the past two decades and it is likely to continue a bit longer. Thus, gradually the percentage of older people has grown. However, since social security and welfare provisions have not improved as rapidly and some older people have to work, while others want to for personal or social reasons, the participation rate for those 65 and over is still unusually high, about 27%.

Nevertheless, both as assistance to the aged improves and the economy squeezes out the elderly, more and more of them will leave the work force. This means that, for all practical purposes 65 can be chosen as the statistical threshold to old age and those from 15 to 64 can be regarded as the productive-age population.

A look at the trends in these three age groups indicates that the decrease in the percentage of those actively engaged in the economy will continue. The juvenile population (0–14) has been falling since early in the century and is less than 24% now. Those of productive age (15–64) peaked at about 69% in the early 1970s and has dropped to some 67% since. The elderly population (65 and over), however, has not stopped growing. It was only about 5% in 1950 and has since grown to over 9%. But this is nothing compared to what is expected in the future. For, by the year 2020, the juvenile population should fall to about 20% while the number of aged hits nearly 20%.[11] This will leave only 60% of the Japanese in the working age category. And, with falling participation rates, perhaps only half of them will work.

All this is perfectly natural, if you will. There is no reason young people should not go to school longer. The need to increase skills for the knowledge-intensive industries of the future is a more than adequate justification (whether or not they actually learn something useful at school). It is equally natural that older people should rest after a hard working life. Reaching increasingly old ages, more and more of them will be in no condition to work anyway, due to ill health, infirmities, and so on. But it is obvious that these perfectly natural trends are being accelerated by the effects of relative affluence. A prerequisite for higher education for many is the ability to pay

Fewer people to work while the others play or rest. Fewer hands to feed more mouths.

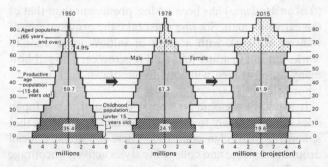

tuition and living expenses. A comfortable, and earlier retirement, demands the wherewithall. An increasing number of Japanese can afford this.

But less natural trends are also at work. Among the young people, there are a fair number who do not hesitate to spend an extra year or so taking examinations to get into the college of their choice or simply any college. Some students now prefer spending an extra year or so in college before looking for a job. A few bum around or travel abroad to "learn the meaning of life" before entering the grind of lifetime employment. Most female college graduates claim to seek work, but as many as 30% remain jobless. Male graduates wait for the right job and switch jobs if not satisfied. There is even a small minority that just works for a while and doesn't get another job until the money runs out. This has resulted, for the first time in recent history, in a growing class of youth without any fixed occupation.[12]

Among the women, various currents can be noted. Younger women often speak fondly of having a career and many of the married women find it impossible to get by in harder times without a job. At the same time, the more affluent husbands can offer their spouse a comfortable life without work. The phenomenon of the Lady of Leisure (*Yukan Madamu*) has been no less prominent than that of the career woman. So, one must take the protestations of wanting to work with a grain of salt. Women want to work; but not just any job. And it is too early to tell how many more women will actually be drawn back into the labor force.

It would be pleasant to stop at this point. Alas, Japan does not seem likely to escape the abuses of affluence that it laments in foreign countries. There are already social dropouts. Leisure and college life styles actively encourage this. There are also derelicts and bums. Anyone who doubts this should keep his eyes open when passing through Shinjuku station. If the present problems of juvenile delinquency, violence in the schools, and drug addiction were to worsen, as they have been doing from year to year, they would contribute to either an increase in those not working or a decrease in their value if they do work. Finally, any major boost in unemployment benefits or welfare would make it possible for some who now look for a job to live off the state instead.

Even without such unpleasantness, Japan has fallen into the same bind as most developed countries where fewer and fewer workers will have to carry the burden. This burden, it is already obvious, will keep on growing both as concerns the swelling of the non-working population and the expense of keeping it going. It is not merely a question of youth staying at school longer. The cost of keeping them at school grows the longer they stay and the higher the level. The cost of looking after the aged is growing even more sharply. The number of old age pension recipients is expected to increase three-fold by 2010 and the medical expenses may rise even faster.

This will be a serious enough problem for Japan as it is. But it can never forget that it is in a competitive situation and here, too, it is catching up with and even passing its Western rivals. Its participation rate has fallen as low as many of theirs while it is expected to have considerably more aged persons than any of them early in the next century. At the same time, its competitors in the developing world have a much younger population and scant welfare. Japan's handicap is aggravated by the fact that, thus far at least, it pays its older workers more than young ones due to seniority pay scales. This could make it lose its competitive edge pretty fast if it does not use its people more wisely and purposefully in the future!

Where Can The Unemployed Go?

If there are more unemployed or poorly employed than is generally admitted, if there are many people who could readily become unemployed with further rationalization or the next business slump, if there are yet more who claim they would like to work, the question naturally arises: where can the unemployed go?

This question is unfortunately seldom heard in Japan. One would expect the government to be particularly active in raising it. Yet, as explained, it does not concede that any unemployment problem exists so it does not ask the question. If anything, the government has only been making things worse. MITI has been encouraging investment abroad although in many cases this leads to a migration of industry and a loss of jobs. Not until last year did the Ministry of Labor notice this and begin a study on the employment impact. MITI has also been encouraging an increase in productivity through rationalization, while the Ministry of Labor promotes it as a means of keeping wages up. Despite the clear imbalance between supply and demand on the labor market, the Ministry of Education has done little to produce the kinds of workers needed for today, let alone tomorrow.

More seriously, the government does not seem to understand the basic threat. In the past, success was attained by, or perhaps despite, rationalization, investment abroad, and a poorly adapted labor force. Thus, for example, the Ministry of Labor insists that there is no reason to fear any induced unemployment now since earlier efforts at streamlining by major enterprises did not bring about any serious "confusion."[13] This ignores the fact that the situation has changed completely in between. During the period of rapid growth, other industries could expand to absorb any workers laid off. Now there are fewer new opportunities. With slow growth, it is even harder to absorb the annual increments in labor, let alone those who would like to work if the possibility arose. Yet, MITI's Industrial Structure Council optimistically predicts that the 1980s will be a period of full employment.[14]

In the private sector, there is frequently even less concern with the employment implications. Companies are eager to increase productivity to keep up profits and remain competitive. An alternative, as far as profits are concerned, is to go through "weight reduction" which includes dropping excess personnel. To the extent they do this by attrition, that is, by stopping the recruitment of new staff without dismissing the present employees, there is no objection. In fact, the regular employees expect to gain as well through higher wages. This is usually done with the approval of the unions, since they only represent the interests of the existing work force for whom security of employment is sought. Most of the potential unemployed are simply people who will find it difficult to enter the labor force and thus have little power.

Another reason the basic question is not asked is that many Japanese assume they have already found the answer. There is widespread optimism about Japan entering the postindustrial era with knowledge-intensive industries that will increase both wages and employment. There is talk of using its "highly-educated" work force to develop "frontier industries." Even assuming this optimism were well founded, that Japan did have such clever people and a headstart on new growth industries, it is uncertain that solutions could be found to the employment problem. Most of the futuristic industries are not only knowledge-intensive, they are also capital-intensive. They cost a lot of money to set up, will use sophisticated equipment including computers, but they have rather little need for manpower in large quantities. None of them offer the employment opportunities of Japan's old-fashioned industries that are now phasing out.

Even if the only hope resides in the tertiary sector, it is certainly not in those segments that have been taking in the most personnel in recent years. Distribution, both wholesale and retail, have expanded their share of labor rapidly. Services related to personal needs have done the same, through fast food outlets and the leisure boom. At the same time, by using more staff, they have made their own products yet more expensive and are discouraging buyers. They have provided a form of work-sharing and have managed to absorb millions who would otherwise be unemployed. But in so doing they have helped make Japan an even higher cost economy and been counterproductive.

This means that before getting better, the situation is likely to get worse. Due to the high cost of labor, any sector that is labor-intensive has trouble surviving in Japan. This applies double to industries which require manual or menial labor. More and more of the "backward" industries can be expected to migrate. But they are not the only ones. Due to the great concern with pollution, industries which are the worst polluters are being forced to move abroad and they contain many of the processing branches. Even relatively clean and modern factories sometimes are built abroad, instead of at home, because the developing, and increasingly developed, nations raise tariff barriers against Japanese imports. It would be necessary for the "frontier industries" to grow at an incredible, and very unlikely pace, to make up for this loss in jobs.

For the situation to get better, Japan would have to find, and develop, alternative industries. A few, such as electronics, mechatronics, and robotics, computers, and pharmaceuticals are well underway. But, for nuclear energy, aeronautics, ocean development, bioindustry, or space technology, Japan is not in the forefront. It will take huge R&D expenses, many years, and a lot of luck for them to develop. More rapid progress could be made with business-related services, such as leasing, computer software, and the like. Yet, no matter how much they may contribute to the growth of GNP, the employment effect will be secondary.

There is much greater scope for employment in other fields which are less frequently thought of in intelligent terms. It has already been some decades since the Japanese noticed that the quality of life was not quite what they hoped for and that the environment was decaying rapidly. This led to some expansion of the service sector and equipment to prevent pollution. But far-reaching positive measures were never attempted or even really thought of. Nor is enough being done to provide adequate social and welfare services. Many Japanese are dreaming of a much better life in the 21st century. But Japan will be no better—and probably worse—unless something concrete is done!

One group of activities which must be promoted for the future to offer real promise involves the creation of a physical framework more in keeping with people's aspirations and material possibilities. It is necessary to stop the urban sprawl and start constructing properly planned agglomerations. This entails an increase in viable housing units at accessible prices. It also means inserting them in genuine communities with decent amenities, sanitation and paved roads. There must be enough schools, hospitals, community centers and other public facilities. Something must be done to clean up the ecological mess created by earlier growth and to provide green belts and parks. These are all projects that have the advantage of employing considerable labor.

Even more can be expected of activities to create a

proper social framework for Japan. If it is to become a truly knowledge-oriented country there must be an expansion and improvement in the teaching staff. While its men and women work, there must be suitable day-care and recreation possibilities. Like every society, there will be the handicapped, backward and delinquents who need more serious attention. But the bigget challenge is bound to be how the greying of the population is met. Slogans about being kind to the aged are not enough. Only trained personnel can look after their needs correctly. With as much as 20% of the population in such categories, it will take tremendous numbers of welfare staff, psychologists, social workers as well as administrators and attendants to care for them. Maintaining health, for young and especially old, will require an even larger army of doctors and nurses than today. Here, if anywhere, are sectors in which the need for increased manpower will be strong.

Of course, nothing will be done unless the government can come up with valid proposals that are appealing enough for the taxpayers to accept greater sacrifices. The sources of this funding will have to be fed by some growth of the economy, if the companies manage to overcome their problems. And it will take a bit of old-style discipline in the work force to remain efficient and among youth to learn the trades and professions required. All this would be possible if Japan, Inc. which has been a fading myth in recent years, were to become a palpable and positive reality.

NOTES

1. *Labor Force Survey*, Prime Minister's Office.
2. *Survey on Employment Situation of Older Workers*, Ministry of Labor.

3. *Report on National Life*, Economic Planning Agency, 1979, p. 104.
4. Even the authoritative Nikkeiren put the figure at about 2.5 million, *Conditions of Labor Economy in Japan*, Japanese Federation of Employers' Associations, September 1978, p. 15.
5. *Labor Force Survey*, Prime Minister's Office.
6. *Mainichi Shimbun*, December 3, 1977, and *Japan Times*, October 2, 1977.
7. *White Paper on Small and Medium Business*, Small and Medium Enterprise Agency, 1979.
8. *Statistics on Employment Security*, Ministry of Labor.
9. *Nihon Keizai Shimbun*, October 10, 1980, p. 22.
10. *Labor Force Survey*, Prime Minister's Office.
11. *Population Estimates*, Statistics Bureau, Prime Minister's Office, March 1980.
12. *Report on National Life*, Economic Planning Agency, 1979, p. 123.
13. *1980 White Paper on Labor*, Ministry of Labor.
14. *Japan's Industrial Structure*, MITI, 1980.

8
Japan's Only Resource

Time Of Trial

As we have seen, the situation in Japan looks quite different when, rather than concentrating on the most dynamic sector of manufacturing, one takes a look at the rest of the economy. In the other sectors, only wholesale and some branches like banking have shown much sign of rationalization or improvement in productivity. The rest are still having considerable difficulty in advancing and some have actually slipped back.

The whole distribution sector has grown larger without becoming much more efficient in the sense of using less people to accomplish the same work. Wholesaling, which attained some results, could not get away from its excessive use of personnel. And retailing still has an extraordinary number of staff working in tiny, barely viable establishments. In agriculture, there are too many farmers growing more rice than is needed or producing other crops that could be imported more cheaply. The bureaucrats are more numerous than before although a fair portion could probably be done without. Services, the supposed hope of the future, are shared between a small number of modern, business-related branches that show promise and a much larger number involved in meeting personal needs or providing leisure activities that contribute little to the economy although somewhat enhancing the "quality of life." Once again, there are simply too many people concentrated there.

There is a tremendous waste of women. Those who are eager to enter a career after school are often relegated to minor tasks and wind up quite happy to leave the work world. Older women, obliged to return for various reasons, are only integrated in relatively low-level, second-rate jobs. They are rarely made regulars, the younger women retiring to raise a family, the older ones just hanging on as part-timers. Even their wages have sunk recently despite the already modest level. This treatment will hardly increase their eagerness to show ability or initiative.

The use of younger men is somewhat better, if not quite as good as might be hoped. One problem is that attitudes are changing rapidly. There is less willingness to show extreme devotion to the company and a growing tendency to put in less time, less effort, and certainly less of one's soul. Individualism has grown and with it an incipient distrust of the company. Yet, nothing much is done to take advantage of more positive aspects of the change like a willingness to work rationally or show initiative if given a chance. Meanwhile, the young salarymen and their seniors engage in office work according to old customs and methods that are frequently continued even if proven to be less than efficient.

Finally, there is a bit of unemployment which refuses to go away. Despite all efforts, the 2% level, which was regarded as exceptionally high after the oil crisis, has come to be a basic residual which is hard to eradicate. Those most stricken by this phenomenon are the hardest to help, namely the older workers. Equally important, due to a lack of jobs, or more exactly, a lack of suitable jobs at suitable pay, there are large numbers of people outside of the labor force who claim that they would like to work.

For the very first time, there are also expanding categories which do not really care to work, most of them young women, some highly educated, and even some men.

These are serious problems individually, cumulatively they assume an alarming dimension. If one takes the number of salarymen just killing time, superfluous bureaucrats, farmers growing unnecessary crops, extra hands in the distribution network, and those who add little concrete to the services, one gets a figure in the millions. If one takes the number of women and young people who are poorly employed because they could be doing more if given a chance, one again gets a figure in the millions. If one then takes the number of people who could be hired if wages were lower or who would work if they were higher, a third figure in the millions is obtained. Putting them all together one gets a figure of such a magnitude that it represents a goodly portion of the total labor force and population.

Cumulatively, these problems also have a qualitative dimension no less worrisome than the quantitative one. For, Japan is spawning a whole series of dual economies. The first dual economy was between the modern manufacturing and less productive agricultural sector. This has not really changed except that, with farm subsidies, side jobs, and the sale of land, most farmers are earning good money. The next dual economy arose between the more advanced, capital-intensive industries and the "backward," labor-intensive ones. This was paralleled to some extent by distinctions between large and small companies. The gaps have not really been closed here either, with employees in the smaller companies earning less and productivity lower there as well as in some ailing sectors.

Adding to this, we have new dual economies, sometimes based on wages, sometimes on status. Those working in the service industries earn a bit more and those in distribution a bit less than in manufacturing. But their proportionate contribution to national product is much lower due to low productivity. Only a few branches, like leasing, advertising, banking and finance, have done better. The more traditional branches have not really improved. Moreover, they are still looked down upon as regards prestige. Women are paid considerably less than men and also downgraded. The situation of part-timers, temporary personnel, and outside workers has only gotten worse as compared to the regulars, who are fewer than before. The unemployed, a category that can no longer be ignored, is in the lowliest position.

There would be less ground for concern if one felt the situation could readily be improved. Admittedly, Japan has shown an extraordinary ability at renovating anything related to hardware, to production techniques, to new technologies, to science or research. It has no trouble adopting new machinery, introducing new processes, or rearranging the physical layout of its factories. But it has found it hard to deal with the "soft" aspects, with anything related to people. Here, change must be more gradual and subtle. People must be convinced that change is good and, with a strong streak of conservatism, there is not even an attitude of "let's try and see if it works." The tendency is rather to cling to what one has become accustomed to as long as possible.

Many of these problems could be solved quite simply if a rational approach were adopted. As long as the basic reaction is likely to be emotional, concerned with things like mutual relations, status, traditional virtues, and so on, it is hard to admit problems or come to grips with them. Thus, as so often happens, today's problems actually turn out to have roots going far back into Japan's history. Some of them had even been "solved" at one point, only to have the solution unravel with time. This means it will take an exceptional effort to bring about reforms.

Meritocracy is a virtue of the modern age which ran strong in early Meiji days and just after the war. But it was quickly swallowed up in the seniority system which once again reduced the role of youth and heightened the authority of older people, whether capable or not. This has proven strong enough to block or vitiate any more recent attempts at payment by merit, by performance, by ability or the like. The relatively poor treatment of women, despite anything in the constitution or labor laws, can be traced back to stronger traditional patterns. The prestige of manufacturing, or banking, or foreign trade, as opposed to services or distribution, goes back to Meiji days. The preference for large units to small goes even further back. Yet, both prompt a continued elitism and distaste for work in small companies or the tertiary sector even today.

That these attitudes and traditions are incompatible with the present needs is not sufficient to modify them. It will take a strong and prolonged effort to overcome these vestiges. Perhaps this has already begun since some young people now seek work in smaller companies or less privileged branches, either because they prefer this or just have no other choice. Change may also be encouraged by the constant lip service being paid the postindustrial society which will be based on services rather than industry. But it will obviously take a long time to create new traditions and virtues to replace the old. The failure of even such crucial goals as meritocracy and equality show how hard this will be.

Time Of Challenge

No matter how great the obstacles, it is obvious that change must come . . . if Japan is to succeed in the future.

The reason it must come is that the very foundations of Japan's past success have been largely undermined. It has little choice but to admit the new situation and to seek another path.

During the period of rapid growth, many things could be done that are no longer possible now and minor mistakes or waste could be ignored since the main goal was expansion. It was in that period that the "typical" management system got established. The workers' desire to hold on to their jobs just after the war was reinforced by management's need to hold on to its work force as more opportunities opened up. When it constantly sought more and more staff, obviously it was in favor of lifetime employment and rarely thought of dismissing anyone. It was also willing to offer greater benefits to reward loyalty as long as the organization was growing, with more young workers at the bottom to carry the burden of those on the top.

In the present period of low growth, things have begun to change for the company. It finds that it has enough staff, in some cases too much, and thus it is more selective about who it hires and in some cases actually takes to firing (or imposing "voluntary" retirement). It finds itself with far too many old people, more expensive, but not always more useful, than the young employees. Once it ceases expanding, a company cannot set up new divisions or subsidiaries as readily and thus has fewer attractive titular posts to which salarymen can aspire. All this is quite enough to shake the management system and to weaken its appeal or legitimacy, both in the eyes of management and labor.

In more difficult economic times, market share has to take a backseat to profit. It is no longer possible to hope that a larger share of the market will eventually pay off with bigger profits when major commitments have to be met immediately. Since labor, more of a fixed cost than a variable one where it is so hard to dismiss staff, represents a big chunk of overhead, it is necessary to use each person carefully. Thus, the merit schemes which were toyed with during the rapid growth period begin to have more validity. It is necessary to get the most out of each individual employee even if this weakens the group somewhat. At the same time, the younger workers show a greater interest in being rewarded for what they do and think of work more as a "contractual" than a personal commitment. Even if they do not like incentives, there must be some means of coaxing out that extra bit of energy the workers once supplied in return for appeals to company patriotism.

The crucial element, however, is the simple fact that labor has grown so expensive in Japan. No matter what the sector may be, whether related to the domestic economy or exports, whether in industry or services, each employee costs so much that he or she must be used well. Companies think twice before hiring nowadays and they want to get their money's worth. The branches which use proportionately more personnel thus come under the greatest pressure to rationalize. Although the progress in distribution, services, even small industry, has been slow, they are in a tighter squeeze than ever and must either use people better or use fewer of them if they are to survive.

This points to the need to keep on improving productivity. It is uncertain how long present trends can continue in the already well advanced manufacturing sector. There will always be new inventions, new technologies, new processes, making it possible to replace people with machinery or have them accomplish more. But the increments gained in productivity for a given investment in machinery are likely to be smaller and also, now that Japan has caught up, it will be harder to find new opportunities. Moreover, as the manufacturing sector reduces its labor force, during a period when other sectors may find it harder to absorb more staff, there is likely to be pressure to stop rationalization. The unions are pushing harder than ever for job security and the government would come under pressure if unemployment increased.

On the other hand, there are many branches where so much can be done to increase the present low level of productivity. It makes more sense to introduce investments there because the pay-off in savings on labor will be larger and faster. From now on, the front must move toward the tertiary sector. It will have to overcome the mental hang-ups about service implying a more ample use of human beings. And, as the consumers' income ceases growing as rapidly, the general public may realize that goods can only be obtained more cheaply by doing away with some of these frills.

Obviously, here, too, unemployment will come as a threat. It was in order to protect the small shopkeepers that the government introduced limitations on the chain stores. But the smaller units will keep on disappearing anyway through attrition or bankruptcy. It is far better to seize the promise of shifting labor into the branches of the tertiary sector that have not been developed sufficiently and can play a much more active role. This includes some of the business-related services and especially those connected with information. More personnel will have to enter the social and welfare projects the government will have little choice but to launch to care for the aged, the ill, or the children of working women. Finally, there will be a need for teachers to train the future staff of whatever knowledge-intensive industries Japan may develop.

Although change must come, and the promises are as impressive as the threats, so far any progress has been painfully slow and hesitant. In business, one reads about a new system to reward merit in company A and another attempt at integrating women in company B. One discovers that company C is thinking of new ways to use older personnel, while company D offers greater initiative to the young. Elsewhere, company E is "revolutionizing" retail distribution and company F has launched a new fashion in service establishments. Meanwhile, the government has adopted some more legislation and is talking of actually implementing a few old plans. These attempts are all encouraging. They are also sporadic and diffuse. There is no impression that they are part of an organized whole, that even piecing them together one could come up with a new management system to replace the old or an updating of the primary and tertiary sectors to compare with what has been done in industry.

In addition, the attempts at reform are still too timid and too few. They are only undertaken by a number of companies known for their innovative spirit and the fact that they are already ahead of the others. Thus, one does not really know if the movement will be followed by the more conservative or backward companies. And one does not know, nor could one even hope to know for some years, whether the experiments will succeed and spread or bog down and then be discarded. It is about time that a more conscious effort were made under a broader direction. This should involve not only the companies but also specialized bodies like Japan Productivity Center and Japan Management Association, business associations like Keidanren, Nikkeiren, Keizai Doyukai, the trade unions, and of course the government.

If no action is taken, there is reason to fear that the outcome will be more negative than positive, namely that the old system will start—or rather continue—disintegrating before something else is found to replace it. It is amazing how rapidly the sacrosanct management system has shown its weaknesses in this new era. Its decline has already sapped the company as an institution and created serious problems for older employees, temporary workers, female personnel, and even regular employees and managerial staff.

Change can come by default, as the basis for the old order collapses, or it can come by positive action, efforts to build a new foundation. Much of the change so far has been dictated by events while even the supposed leaders have floated with the tide. But it is not too late to make a concentrated effort to overcome the present difficulties and create something better for tomorrow. There is a growing consensus as to where Japan's weaknesses lie and what its future strengths might be. They all revolve, one way or the other, about making a better use of the only true resource the country possesses . . . its people. If greater efforts are not made to use people well as of now the Japanese will be condemning themselves to failure.

9
Epilogue: "Learning From Japan"

We are presently living in the age of the "Japan boom," a time when the earlier neglect of Japan has been overcompensated for by a frantic effort to find out what makes this apparently unique and exceptional country tick. One of the major features of this movement has been an attempt to borrow from Japan, as it supposedly did from the West (and Korea or China earlier on), namely in such a way as to blend the best of both cultures. Admonitions to "learn from Japan" have been offered for crime prevention, education, social and political harmony, and now especially business management.

If the Japanese companies can accomplish so much, then there are certainly worthwhile lessons to be learned! Yes, there is no doubt about it, many lessons can be derived, positive, negative and superfluous. But, what will probably count most is not what Japan has to offer but what the West decides to borrow. Judging by the track record so far, it may succeed no better than Japan in the past by borrowing as much good as bad and tons of frills with no intrinsic value that simply look good. There is also reason to fear that, just like Japan, many of these lessons will be hastily learned and poorly digested. Western management experts have apparently run out of fresh ideas and managers are frantic for some way to compete which leads them to clutch at the flimsiest of straws.

Whereas once upon a time information on Japan was

transmitted by people with some reasonable knowledge of the country and who made a decent effort at being objective, since the boom any number of instant experts have gotten into the act. Others who tired of writing for restricted academic circles have gone popular, watering down and distorting the material as they went. We now have whole books coming from people who boast almost no direct contact with Japanese business and who build their theories by cribbing from earlier writers. The latest fashionable theory is not even about Japanese management in Japan but Japanese-*type* management in America while the prime example for learning the art of Japanese management is a company generally regarded as one of the most un-Japanese. Yet, the worse the quality of the product, the more it sells.[1]

When deciding to borrow from Japanese management, it is essential to remember certain things. The first is obviously that Japan's society is very different from that of the West, or Africa, Latin America and most of Asia. Even if it is not quite as unique as some claim, it is certainly different enough to wonder whether what succeeds there will succeed elsewhere. Among the characteristics that make Japanese management work are relatively strong hierarchical relations (not egalitarianism!) whereby superiors normally receive some of the respect that usually has to be imposed more crudely. There is a lively tradition of group action and cooperation, but only within rather small groups. And loyalty, discipline, diligence, and so on are still much admired although gradually fading virtues. Methods evolved to deal with such people will necessarily be different from methods adapted to dealing with more individualistic, indisciplined, but perhaps imaginative and self-directed employees.

That Japanese management cannot be transplanted so readily has been admitted by those most directly concerned, namely the Japanese companies which have opened offices and factories abroad. No matter what untutored journalists may claim, there is no such thing as a Japanese factory working exactly the same way in Cardiff or San Diego as it does in Tokyo or Osaka. Wherever they go, the Japanese managers have had to adapt to local circumstances for legal, economic and especially cultural reasons. None of their overseas ventures implement lifetime employment, recruitment from school, or promotion by seniority. At most, they introduce improved methods to the factories and add a bit more friendliness to relations by mixing with the workers or providing more fringe benefits. Yet, in most cases, the process has not even gotten as far as Western multinationals because the Japanese don't like to appoint foreigners to top posts.

The next thing to worry about is whether what the experts claim to be Japanese management really is. Some of them do not know the system well enough to describe it. Others just pick out likely aspects (those not yet "discovered" by their rivals) to present as the *key* to success. And a few try to dress the Japanese system up as an ideal model making Japan little more than a foil to the West, what Westerners do wrong, Japanese do right. This has led to a tremendous amount of mythologization. Thus, in the massive flow of supposed information about Japan an alarming share is deliberately or unintentionally mistaken and any attempt to use it could have unwanted consequences. Even what is right will not provide the promised cure-all.

If managers feel that their primary problem is a lack of diligence, discipline, and loyalty, they will look to Japan. If workers want more understanding, decency, or fulfillment, they will look to Japan. But they will look in vain unless they realize that Japanese managers are so worried about losing their workers that they have constructed a vast machinery to tie them down, one that could hardly be replicated abroad. And, as every poll shows, the Japanese workers are not really very happy. Many are angry, frustrated, or depressed. Indeed, comparative studies have sometimes shown them to lead a less satisfying life than Americans or Europeans. Japan is just another country, not utopia, and although specific techniques can be borrowed it would be hard to instill the overall mood (which most foreigners would find stifling anyway!).

So, trying to create the best of all possible worlds, which seems to be the goal of many writers, is not really feasible. But, at least, let's try not to make an even worse world by borrowing exactly those things that burden down Japanese society and are generally disapproved of there. Only an academic like Ezra Vogel could swallow the line that Japanese education is a model for anyone. As has been shown here and elsewhere, although the educational system may be fine at lower levels, "examination hell" destroys the personality while relaxing at college fails to impart much knowhow. This explains why Japanese companies engage in so much in-house training, for the incoming staff rarely offers any usable skills. More seriously, it would be folly to go so far in reversing adversary relations as to install an age of cooperation between business and government or the rule of "fair share." Only the naive are unaware that this results in unacceptable and harmful collusion against the general public.

Another point that most experts miss is that the big Japanese companies, those so often praised like Matsushita, Sony, Toyota, Nissan, and many others, owe their "success" very largely to subcontracting. By creating subsidiaries (not divisions!) and using suppliers, all of which are dependent on them, it is very easy to manipulate financial returns and also to increase efficiency. The most labor-intensive, unpleasant or unprofitable tasks are simply hived off to the subordinate companies which assume the primary responsibility for quality control, carrying inventory, and keeping costs down. The parent company becomes little more than an assembly and marketing operation. No wonder it shows exceptionally high productivity and good profits! As for the lesser members of the "company family," they can do reasonably well in the upturns, but they will be badly squeezed in the downturns, while the parent company always gets through in fine form. There are obviously moral and legal reasons for not proposing this to their Western clients. Still, the fact that it is never mentioned as a key to the art of Japanese management, which it most definitely is, makes one wonder if the management consultants are just stupid or purposely avoid anything that could clash with the overall picture of cooperation and harmony.

Thus, the first two rules are not to borrow what does not exist and not to borrow what is actually worse than you already have. When it comes to business management, a third rule is necessary: not to assume that all management techniques are equally valid explanations of Japan's success. As this book shows, Japan has managed to raise productivity and create an efficient and reasonably harmonious approach to production *in the factory*. It has failed miserably in modernizing any other sector including the administration of industrial enterprises and the art of management itself is very backward and inefficient. Indeed, it is undergoing serious review and has been deemed by many top managers, and their subordinates, to be long due for an overhaul.

Unfortunately, what is being purveyed by the experts is largely a mishmash of factory productivity, quality control, etc. and traditional management with lifetime employment, job rotation, seniority system, and so on. With time there has been a tendency to thin out the former and add bigger chunks of the latter. This makes a very tasty stew, but one many Western managers may choke on later. For, it is the former that is really at the root of Japan's industrial strength and export prowess while the latter has been a drag. If the sorcerer's apprentices think that things like trust, subtlety, or a company philosophy will make them more competitive they are seriously mistaken.

What can be learned? Two things. First of all, it is possible to borrow a number of specific techniques that have proven effective in Japan and could well apply to other countries. The other aspect is to take Japanese management not as an alternative, replacing Western methods with Japanese ones, but rather as a corrective. What is wrong with Western management is not so much the essence as that over the years it has gone too far, it has bloated and distorted certain characteristics, and lost its effectiveness in so doing. Japan's management system, in the meanwhile, has gone in the opposite direction. By considering one another, even without borrowing anything, it should be easier to see where such exaggerations have occurred and to move back toward a middle position.

There is no doubt that the rest of the world can learn much from Japan when it comes to productivity *in the factory*. For the past three decades, manufacturing productivity in Japan has risen more rapidly than anywhere else in the world and almost reached the American level, not exceeded it as some "experts" claim. In such a situation, its products naturally become relatively cheaper and easier to sell. But the prime achievement has been to wed concern for quality to rising productivity. This has been Japan's greatest contribution to a technique it borrowed from the United States. Since this particular technique travelled well, and was even improved in Japan, there is no reason to doubt that it can be transplanted again.

However, when we try to discover just what caused the rise in productivity, things become a bit confusing since there are both "hard" and "soft" explanations. One is that the Japanese increased productivity rapidly by introducing new machinery and technologies from abroad and thus caught up quicker. The machinery and technologies, by the way, also help improve quality. The experts on business management deny that this is the main reason, largely because they don't know much about such things and can't make money selling it to their clients. But there is no one in Japan who doubts that the primary explanation is machinery and not people. Moreover, during the coming years it will become increasingly difficult to claim that people play a decisive role in boosting productivity since the present phase consists of driving people out of the factories and replacing them with more efficient—and cheaper—numerically controlled machine tools, automated assembly lines and robots.

So, if your company wants to learn from Japan, don't only send the personnel manager, send your top engineers and plant layout specialists. That is where they can really learn something about improving productivity and efficiency. However, you would be wise not to let the Japanese know who they are or what they are trying to do. With a strong tradition of industrial espionage, their hosts will naturally be concerned that the visitors may play the same tricks on them.

Do send the personnel manager anyway. For, the other side of the process is still quite important and, although it may be relatively easy to acquire new machinery, it will not be so easy to overcome the objections of the unions or get the workers to use whatever machinery there is to the best effect. One method that can be borrowed, and actually is being tried at present, is the quality control movement. QC circles are established among small groups of workers who get together to discuss, among themselves and without the presence of superiors, the various troubles they may encounter or improvements they could make. To this can be added the older system of suggestion boxes.

However, it should not be forgotten that the social context is quite different. Japanese workers, unlike their counterparts in the West, often have a severely limited social life and find it hard to know their colleagues informally. They therefore find such meetings a rewarding human experience. Elsewhere, most workers would prefer mixing with friends, relatives, or people with similar interests rather than their colleagues once again. To hold them, it may be necessary to have the QC meetings on company time and also to offer more than a token reward for good ideas. This is no reason to feel that one has betrayed the Japanese system. Recent studies show that the Japanese companies with the best QC activities and the highest levels of suggestions *also* subsidize their groups and pay more for useful suggestions.

The crucial problem is how to treat the labor force. It may dislike productivity drives that result in more work for the same pay or lead to layoffs. And the approach applied so far of lecturing workers on how they must perform better to defeat the apparently model Japanese employees does not go down too well. As a matter of fact, the "learn from Japan" campaign increasingly looks like another trick by management to make the personnel a tool of company policy. It might therefore be wiser for managers to stress that any improvement in the situation will require efforts, and probably also sacrifices, by both sides and then to take the first step toward a more cooperative, but not necessarily condescending or servile, relationship.

This takes us further toward the "soft" side of management. There is no doubt that the workers must be won for the cause of revitalizing Western industry (or developing Third World economies). Given the strength of the trade unions, it can hardly be through coercion and must arise from some form of common interest. This is solved in Japan simply by long-term, if not lifetime employment, which means that gains will be enjoyed later by those who stay on. But it is definitely reinforced by dominating the union, a process that is quite far advanced in Japan.

This obviously cannot be done in the West where unions are so strong and commitment to the company so weak. People will not work harder just because they are told to do so. But, if they are brought into a team, treated properly, and shown the advantages of cooperation, they can become quite amenable. The advantages, in a materialistic society, had better be concrete most of the time. Much can be done through incentives, attaching part of wage hikes to rises in productivity or, if the company really is weak, letting the staff know that failure to make serious efforts could result in its collapse. There is no need here to go into the sweeter methods, the attempts to play up to, or talk down to the workers, to make them allies rather than adversaries, to put them in the right mood or matrix, and all the other drivel fashionable among management experts, for there is an ample literature on that.

In the office, it would be rather unwise to go too far in copying the Japanese since their methods are interesting but hardly efficient. Job rotation, if suitably adapted, has some value. Massive job rotation for the whole white-collar population, as in Japan, does create some broad knowledge of the organization for everyone. But it is terribly disruptive to have so many people changing functions so often. For a small core of managers, however, those who show promise and may become the top management of the future, it is another matter. If they are quick learners and dynamic, or else hopefully they would not be chosen, they could benefit tremendously and make up for any tendency toward overspecialization. But to discard professionalism in a day and age when technologies and specializations are more complex than ever would deprive Western companies of one of their prime assets. Applying the interminable Japanese decision-making methods might give an impression of doing something while actually sapping the vitality of companies which got where they are by devoting more effort to implementation than consultation.

What about the basic features of the Japanese management system? One could hardly propose them except in very exceptional circumstances and that may explain why they have rarely caught on abroad. Lifetime employment, seniority promotion, and the rest, are best in times of rapid growth and would be most unappropriate during a period of stagnation or outright recession. That is why the system is even being questioned in Japan. Moreover, lifetime employment would not take in an open society with strong individualistic traditions. Even if a company wished to offer lifetime employment, it could not do so where people just work for money. No one would willingly accept seniority payment if he hoped to earn more elsewhere, so remuneration on this basis would probably keep the deadwood and lose the most capable and dynamic elements. Recruitment directly from school assumes a loss of freedom that few would accept.

If lifetime employment is out of the question, this does not mean that attempts to come closer to it rather than moving yet further away would not be welcome. Things have come to a pass where insistence on showing ability immediately or the risk of being fired for minor mistakes are grotesque. On the other side, employees who constantly hope to better their lot by moving from company to company every few years, and now every few months for some, are almost a national shame. It is perfectly obvious that excessive rates of turnover provide not greater flexibility and mobility but near chaos and insecurity in organizations which can only succeed with a fair degree of continuity. It does not take a very talented management consultant to notify a company to offer more rewards for staying longer, to give due attention to those who have worked their way up through the ranks, and not to change people at the top too often since that shakes the whole hierarchy.

Thus, there is no reason some share of the wage, even if modest, should not be geared to seniority and there might be at least an informal understanding that capable employees will get the first crack at higher positions that fall vacant. In addition to this, there are any number of things which can be done in the way of fringe benefits. Long-time employees might enjoy housing, education or family allowances. This would combine with existing methods such as stock options. After all, Japanese companies hold on to their workers not purely for reasons of affection or loyalty but because such virtues are palpably rewarded.

But putting as much stress on a company philosophy as Professor Ouchi does is patently absurd. Due to Confucian strictures against making money and later demands that business serve the nation, most Japanese companies have developed some sort of woolly philosophy. Often it stems directly from the "great man" who was their founder, although nowadays there is a strong overlay of professional PR fluff. Few Japanese employees are imbued with a strong sense of acting to fulfill the philosophy, many do not even know what it signifies. They dislike, but patiently listen to, the periodic ramblings of their superiors as to what the company's goals should be. But there is absolutely no correlation to be found between companies with a particularly noble or appealing philosophy and those which succeed in any concrete manner.

Urging their clients to conceive new philosophies would thus seem to be the last refuge of the management consultant . . . or almost. Messrs. Pascale and Athos have gone one step further by suggesting an assimilation of Zen, a religious trend that is considerably more popular among Western hippies than Japanese salarymen. It is hard to see how the present confusion in corporate circles could be cleared up by introducing such "tools" as vagueness, indirection and implicit communication. And the seven basic elements of business management do not seem much more promising, although it is most impressive that they all begin with the letter S. Yet, even by adopting Zen precedent and repeating the seven Ss a thousand times a day while seated in the lotus position, it is unlikely that any Western manager will ever attain enlightenment.

However, the reference to Zen at least offers some insight as to why so many foreigners go wrong. They take words at face value while Japanese clearly distinguish between *tatemae* or appearances and *honne* or reality. So, what the great "experts" present as the ultimate wisdom of the Orient is nothing more than the empty rhetoric of aging executives and devious bureaucrats that no Japanese in his right mind would pay the slightest attention to.

In conclusion, one could still suggest that foreigners "learn from Japan." Indeed, one could exhort them to do so and promise very worthwhile returns if they succeed. But they will have to be very careful in determining what actually is Japanese management and what it is purported to be by the assorted Japanologists, Japan-mythologists, and Japan-apologists. Then they will have to decide which characteristics are really beneficial and which should be scrupulously avoided. Finally, they will have to see which ones can be adapted to their own social environment and how the transplanting should be done.

NOTES

1. Most of the references are to proposals or concepts propounded in *Theory Z* by William Ouchi, *The Art of Japanese Management* by Richard Tanner Pascale and Anthony G. Athos and *Japan as Number One* by Ezra Vogel and more diffusely by such authorities as Peter Drucker or the Harvard Business School *gakubatsu* (university clique).

Glossary

amaé: dependence (often self-sought) on superiors

amakudari: "descent from heaven," system where retiring bureaucrats obtain cushy jobs in subordinate companies or bodies

arubaito: part-time or casual jobs

bucho: department head

kacho: section chief

kaigi: meeting or conference

kessai: approval or sanction

kobun: "child" or inferior in an *oyabun-kobun* relationship

kohai: junior(s)

koin: blue-collar worker

kondankai: informal meeting

kun: term applied to a male inferior

meishi: business card

mikoshi: portable shrine carried in Shinto festivals while leader directs bearers on which way to move

moretsu shain: dynamic company-men now known as "workaholics"

nemawashi: "root binding" or behind-the-scenes efforts to gain consensus on proposals

nenko: seniority system (also called *nenko joretsu*)

oyabun: "parent" or superior in protector-protégé type relationship

ringi-seido: consensus type decision-making system

ringisho: document circulated upward with proposals from junior staff for approval by senior staff

ronin: person waiting an extra year or more to enter a better university or company

samurai: member of former warrior class

san: term applied to a superior or equal

sempai: senior(s)

senmon-shoku: specialist or professional post
shikaku-seido: job classification system
shokuin: white-collar worker
shussé: success, moving up the career ladder
tenshoku: switching jobs
zaibatsu: prewar conglomerates, since reconstituted as "groups"
zaikai: top business leaders, influential business circles

INDEX

Bibliography

Azumi, Koya, *Higher Education and Business Recruitment in Japan*, New York, Teacher's College Press-Columbia University, 1969.

Ballon, Robert J., editor, *The Japanese Employee*, Tokyo, Sophia University/Tuttle, 1969.

Clark, Rodney, *The Japanese Company*, New Haven, Yale University Press, 1979.

Cole, Robert, E., *Japanese Blue Collar: The Changing Tradition*, Berkeley, University of California Press, 1971.

———, *Work, Mobility, and Participation*, Berkeley, University of California Press, 1979.

Cook, Alice, and Hayashi, Hiroko, *Working Women in Japan: Discrimination, Resistance, and Reform*. Ithaca, Cornell University, 1980.

Doi, Takeo, *The Anatomy of Dependence*, Tokyo, Kodansha International, 1973.

Dore, Ronald P., *British Factory, Japanese Factory*, Berkeley, University of California Press, 1973.

Economic Planning Agency, *While Paper on National Life*, Tokyo.

Hanami, Tadashi, *Labor Relations in Japan Today*, Tokyo, Kodansha International, 1979.

Hirschmeier, Johannes, and Yui, Tsunehiko, *The Development of Japanese Business*, Cambridge, Harvard University Press, 1975.

International Technical Information Institute, *Foreign Managers Office Handbook*, Tokyo, ITII, 1981.

Iwata, Ryushi, *Gendai Nihon No Keiei Fudo* [Management Climate of Contemporary Japan], Tokyo, Nihon Keizai Shimbunsha, 1978.

Japan Institute of Labour, *The Problems of Working Women*, Tokyo, 1981.

Japan Productivity Center, *Rodo Seisansei no Kokusai Hikaku ni Kansuru Chosa Kenkyu* [International Comparison of Labor Productivity], Tokyo, Industrial Research Institute, 1981.

Lyons, Nick, *The Sony Vision*, New York, Crown Publishers, 1976.

Mannari, Hiroshi, *The Japanese Business Leaders*, Tokyo, University of Tokyo Press, 1974.

Marsh, Robert M., and Mannari, Hiroshi, *Modernization and the Japanese Factory*, Princeton, Princeton University Press, 1976.

Marshall, Byron K., *Capitalism and Nationalism in Prewar Japan*, Stanford, Standford University Press, 1967.

Ministry of Education, *Attitude of Youth Toward Work*, Youth Policy Headquarters, Tokyo, 1980.

————, *Handbook of Statistics*, Tokyo.

————, *Survey of National Characteristics*, Tokyo.

Ministry of International Trade and Industry, *Japan's Industrial Structure—A Long Range Vision*, Tokyo, 1978.

————, *Outlook and Issues of Industrial Structure in the 1980s*, Tokyo, 1980.

————, *White Paper on International Trade*, Tokyo, various.

Ministry of Labor, *Survey of Japanese Employees' Life After Retirement*, Tokyo, various.

————, *White Paper on Labor*, Tokyo, various.

————, *White Paper on Women's Labor*, Tokyo, various.

Nagai, Michio, *Higher Education in Japan: Its Take-off and Crash*, Tokyo, University of Tokyo Press, 1971.

NHK Public Poll Office, *Nihonjin No Shokugyokan* [Occupational Awareness of the Japanese], Tokyo, Nihon Hoso Kyokai, 1979.

Nippon Recruit Center, *Employment motivation of female university* students, 1980.

————, *Employment motivation of (male) university students*, 1980.

————, *What do (male) freshman employees think?*, 1980.

————, *What do OLs think?*, 1980.

Nishida, Kozo, *Koreika Shakai No Kigyo Senryaku* [Corporate Strategy in an Aging Society], Tokyo, Yuhikaku, 1979.

Okochi, Kazuo, Karsh, Bernard, and Levine, Solomon, editors, *Workers and Employers in Japan: The Japanese Employment Relations System*, Tokyo, University of Tokyo Press, 1974.

Ouchi, William, *Theory Z*, Reading, Addison-Wesley, 1981.

Pascale, Richard Tanner, and Athos, Anthony G., *The Art of Japanese Management*, New York, Simon and Schuster, 1981.

Prime Minister's Office, *Labor Force Survey*, Tokyo, various.

————, *Survey on How Japanese Women Feel About Marriage, The Family, Their Role, etc.*, Tokyo, various.

————, *White Paper on Youth*, Tokyo, various.

Rohlen, Thomas P., *For Harmony and Strength*, Berkeley, University of California Press, 1974.

Small and Medium Enterprise Agency, *White Paper on Small and Medium Enterprises in Japan*, Tokyo, various.

Taira, Koji, *Economic Development and the Labor Market in Japan*, New York, Columbia University Press, 1970.

Uchida, Yukio, *Nihon No Kaisha Wa Amachuarizumu* [Amateurism of Japanese Companies], Tokyo, Management Inc., 1980.

Urabe, Kuniyoshi, *Nihonteki Keiei Wo Kangaeru* [Study of Japanese Management], Tokyo, Chuo Keizaisha, 1978.

Vogel, Ezra F., editor, *Modern Japanese Organization and Decision-Making*, Berkeley, University of California Press, 1975.

Whitehall, Arthur M., and Takezawa, Shin-Ichi, *The Other Worker*, Honolulu, East-West Center Press, 1968.

Yoshino, M. Y., *Japan's Managerial System*, Cambridge, MIT Press, 1968.

————, *The Japanese Marketing System*, Cambridge, MIT Press, 1971.

Woronoff, Jon, *Japan: The Coming Economic Crisis*, Tokyo, Lotus Press, 1979.

————, *Japan: The Coming Social Crisis*, Tokyo, Lotus Press, 1980.

high school graduates, 208–10, 220–23, 243–4.
home workers, 122–3.
Honda, Soichiro, 57.
housing, 160.
human relations, 19; changes in value standards, 20–1; cost, 49–51; in business, 61; in companies, 44–51, 53–4, 68, 106, 273; in service industry, 88–9.

import restrictions, *see* protectionism.
individualism, 21, 69, 73, 75, 263, 281.
internationality, lack of, 56.
Isuzu Motors, Ltd., 64, 237.
Ito, Masatoshi, 167, 174.
Ito-Yokado Co., 167.

Japan Air Lines, 130.
Japan Housing Corporation, 160.
Japan Management Association, 270.
Japan National Railways (JNR), 160, 163.
Japan Productivity Center, 18, 270.
Japanese management, as model for foreigners, 5, 7, 272–84; reforms, 6, 20, 22.
job classification system, 80.
job description, lack of, 27–8, 53.
job evaluation, *see* evaluation system.
job hopping (*tenshoku*), 5, 69, 77–8, 96, 100, 215, 218.
job hunting, *see* recruitment.
job market, 149, 219–20, 222–3, 230–2, 243–4, 247, 257; *see also* recruitment, unemployment.
job rotation, 28, 53, 105, 158, 206, 277, 280–1.
job security, 68, 268; *see also* lifetime employment.
job suitability, 248, 249–50.

kacho, 46, 62, 73–4, 90–7, 106.
kacho-byo, 94–7.
Keidanren, 270.
Keizai Doyukai, 270.
knowledge-intensive industries, 12, 21, 175, 192, 253, 257.
Kokusai Denshin Kenwa (KDD), 161, 163.
Kurosawa, Kazukiyo, 17–8.

labor, breakdown by sector, 149–50, 163, 172–3, 179–80; breakdown by

Books by Jon Woronoff

WEST AFRICAN WAGER

ORGANIZING AFRICAN UNITY

HONG KONG: CAPITALIST PARADISE

JAPAN: THE COMING SOCIAL CRISIS

THE COMING ECONOMIC CRISIS

INSIDE JAPAN, INC.

WORLD TRADE WAR

Books by L

$Y 1,200,-$